An Adam Andava collection

Putty In Your Hand

DISCLAIMER. This is a book primarily of personal letters from the author to his [now] wife. Information contained herein is provided "as is" without warranty of any kind, either expressed or implied, as nothing herein shall be construed as professional relationship or health advice. All information in this publication is based on the author's experience, education, personal observations, interviews with others, and opinions, which may differ from those of other professionals and from other men and women in relationships.

All information herein is meant for information and entertainment purposes only. Your individual path to learning and relationships is not guaranteed, as each person may not use this information in the same way; each person is different in many pertinent ways, and each relationship is unique. In no event shall anyone be held liable for any losses or claims of any kind whatsoever alleged to be arising out of or in connection with the contents of this book, directly or indirectly.

All photos, separate articles, and quotations used in this book are either our original product, are in the public domain, have been licensed for public use, or are otherwise used with express permission of the owner, or have no known copyright restrictions. Please contact us if you believe any of your copyrighted material and/or photos are being used without your permission.

For information info@adam.andava1@gmail.com

Cover design by Adam Andava. Font design by Tanya Schupp. Book design and composition by Adam Andava, *a nom de plume* for reasons of his family's privacy. The letters contained in this book are published at the request of the author's wife to help women have more successful marriages. Editing, publishing, cover and book marketing assistance by Margaret Hampton. Foreword by Aria Demetri.

ISBN-13: 978-0692765500 (A Better Marriage, LLC)
Printed in the U.S.A. For Worldwide Distribution.

If you enjoy this book, please leave a Review on www.Amazon.com
*PuttyInYourHand.net * ABetterMarriage.com*

This book of select love letters is dedicated to my precious wife, Mixie, my treasure on earth. In these letters (written to her during our internet courtship) I included 'the good stuff,' the real deal women are seldom told about men, so she could use it on me once we married.

Now, because she knows about these man-charming essentials (and how to use them on me every day), we can live a vibrant love affair... *every day*.

Ohhh, he got me good!

Goodness, it's rich! *Putty in Your Hand* speaks to me in ways that resonate every fiber of my being, both physically and spiritually. Like the *Song of Solomon*, its pages boil over with intimate thoughts of love — sensuous yet tastefully expressed — reflecting the rich purity of an undefiled marriage bed.

The letters are deliciously written by Adam Andava to woo a woman he met on the Internet and later married. Some of them enlighten, some seduce, and some tantalize. Some letters are powerful. Some are even more powerful. Some can excite a woman on many levels, rushing the circulation and igniting the nerves.

How did his letters affect me? They left me coming undone at my seams, touching a chord in me no man had reached before. Words like none other has spoken, he speaks, nurturing and satisfying the lonely places within. Seldom do I feel the touch of a man's spirit as I have felt his.

As nectar calls to the hummingbird, his letters draw me hither. I read them over and over, even when they are not before my eyes. In stimulating anticipation my heart is unable to stop racing; I am left breathless as my mind rushes across the pages. Such is the power of his words, delighting the senses and fascinating the imagination.

His thoughts (so alive you can almost feel them) sweep into the very heart of a woman's soul. He seems to know, even without being told, what I have endured and secretly still fear. He somehow understands my depth and complexities and accepts me. And although I understand my role as a woman, he has defined it even more comfortably and safely, making all things look brighter.

His 'love-thoughts' honor women. They also show how we could be cherished even more, very much more, were it not for the things we do that turn a man cold — things revealed in *Putty in Your Hand.* If only we women would stop and think about the harm we cause ourselves, we would finally end the madness of the self-destruction of our own happiness.

Most of us believe we can hold a man's heart willingly captive. But for how long? If we do it *Putty's* way, it will be for a lifetime — and I don't need to tell you what that means. Now women everywhere can have a new hope, a lifetime of passionate intimacy with a devoted husband who cherishes you and is dedicated to *your* happiness.

What makes this really amazing is, just about every woman can begin experiencing these rewards *immediate*ly if she simply begins flowing with her natural role (as *Putty* so convincingly proves), instead of against it (as we women are so apt to do).

Now that you know Adam's letters speak of a precious kind of love, a new and exciting depth of love, did you know that this *lovestyle* is explained in the Bible as the only way for the co-equal man and woman to have a truly successful '*4-P Marriage*' — Permanent, Passionate, Peaceful and (near) Perfect? But unfortunately most never hear of it; they miss out on the 'real' thing, a truly fulfilling and happy marriage.

Now the plot thickens. As Adam unwraps this lovestyle, he insists he will consider nothing less, and that the woman he marries must adopt it, too. She agrees. . . but then starts shilly-shallying (vacillating). She struggles within herself, because she needs to see for herself that every one of these promises he is making is real, that he will be what he promises to be. From there on, it seems every letter increases my appetite for the next as even more excitement prevails.

Does Adam finally weaken on his insistence of living this oh-so-romantic lovestyle? Or does his consistency in being an honorable and godly husband-prospect show her that she will be the heiress of its splendor, and yield to his noble manner?

Don't worry, I won't ruin the ending. But listen, nothing has improved my life as easily and in such abundance as has my learning and living the truth in *Putty's* precious pages. Now I'm applying 'putty' to all the cracks, and with each new 'application' my heart flutters and passion soars.

Never did I expect love and happiness to have such security and depth and height — no one prepared me for such luxury!

—Aria Demetrius

~~~~~~~~~~~~~~~~~~~~~~

The revelations about men that await you inside this book are not fiction but reality, to carry you on a safe and pleasant journey to your place of solace and joy. There, your passionate lover is expecting you, in anticipation of giving you experiences that will take your breath away.

~~~~~~~~~~~~~~~~~~~~~~

T A B L E   O F   C O N T E N T S

ENTR'ACTE : FAMOUS QUOTATIONS

[That Every Woman Should Want To Know By Heart]

WHAT'S INSIDE THIS BOOK?

All the good men are gone.

You've heard that said, haven't you? That's because mostly it's true. Many of the good men *are* gone; they've gone to the women who know how to attract them. Still, there are just as many good men out there looking for good women as there are good women looking for good men.

But there's more to it than that, isn't there? Sure, there always is, because after a woman *attracts* a man, she has to *be able to keep him.* And while she's at it, she might as well *change him into something amazing*, right? Like into the kind of man women have always wanted but seldom gotten? . . . Until now.

Why now? Because now women have an expert source from which they can learn about a unique power that *attracts, keeps* and *changes* a man. That expert source is *Putty in Your Hand*, and as every reader will quickly appreciate, that power lies easily within each woman. Unfortunately, most women will never discover they have it. Even then, they have to learn how to use it. Here's where *Putty* comes in; it even makes learning how fun.

Funny, though (and not in a comical way, either), how women are born with a power they'll never know about. What's *really* amazing is, a woman needs a good man to help her find and learn how to activate it. (And a man needs the fire that power gives her to make his love for her complete.)

Very soon, one fortunate reader of *Putty in Your Hand* is going to personally experience this man attracting, passion flavored, ultra-feminine power. Once she does, her husband will find it impossible to stay away!

And wouldn't you just know it? Her perceived femininity is going to soar to extraordinary levels! She's going to become more *naturally* exciting, more alluring, more beguiling than other women, and far more potent and tantalizing than sex.

So just who is this extraordinary woman? *You are!*

Yes, you!

Yet I wonder . . . Once I teach you how to find and unleash this powerful captivation, once it inflames your desirable man's heart to want and need you like never before — far beyond all you've ever imagined or hoped for — are you going to take unfair advantage of him?

No, I'm not talking about sex, and no, you didn't just wake up on another planet. *This is reality*, not fiction. Once you trigger his heart, be ready; the change will be stunning! There will be no gradual transition. Very quickly his now-awakened heart will throb, hungry and thirsty for you, and if you will work with me by doing what I ask of you, then *Putty in Your Hand* can help make this happen for you! Not just once, but again and again.

How will you feel, able to influence and stimulate a man's affections like that? Go ahead. Think about it. It's okay to fantasize, to plan on having your willing captive — a man set permanently aflame by your unquenchable, intoxicating power — captivated with such fervent desire for you that he can *never* tire of the familiarity of your relationship.

Smart women know! . . .

Sex alone won't keep a man. Whether you're sexy and pretty or not, sex just isn't enough to melt his heart or to make him your romantic putty for life. Women who rely only on sex usually wake up one morning to find themselves abandoned, trapped inside a lonely revolving door with yet another empty dream and broken relationship.

But if you want to *keep* your man tuned-in for life (and what woman doesn't?), then you must keep him occupied with your 'captivating power' (more on this later). Furthermore, the more you use this power, the more he'll want to please you, *and*... the more your limits and your joy in being born a woman will expand.

I've already said it's amazing, and it is, how every woman is born with this captivating power, doesn't know it's there, and needs a man to help her find it (and he needs her to make his life complete).

Because of its particularly beguiling nature, this captivating power is very real, very tangible — and *very* tantalizing to the man it's used on. It's perceptible both by the physical and emotional senses. It is a felt affectionate connectedness in the form of a tangible presence of delightful intimacy, and its force is powerfully felt both by the man and the woman who use it! There's scarcely a man out there who won't succumb to it. It is *provocative.* It is *irresistible.* It is *addictive.* (But it only works if 'applied as directed.')

Provocative? — Yes, it arouses, excites and seduces his psyche!

Irresistible? — No man can withstand its soft, ultra-feminine and compelling effect!

Addictive? — He can never leave the woman who unleashes it on him!

You need only to know its source and how to release it, and I'm going to teach you both. You can then produce it, over and over again, and become powerfully captivating, just like the woman in this book did after I shared it with her. Furthermore, after she began developing her captivating power and set it loose on me, I married her. (How could I not?)

All her life Mixie (an affectionate nickname I gave her) unknowingly had the same qualities and potential power as you (you are a woman, after all). Yet like most other women, she was unaware of exactly what captivates a man, what *really* causes him to lose his composure over a woman and succumb to her spell.

So, through the letters I wrote to her — many are in *Putty in Your Hand* —Mixie learned how to expand and enhance her qualities through captivating power, just as you will. Then, once she began using this new power, she became all that any man could hope a woman could be . . . The woman I needed her to be . . . The extraordinary woman that others only dream of being . . . the Woman she has now become, just as you can, too.

Understanding Men . . .

Now let's move on from captivating power to something else . . . to understanding men. To introduce this, however, I need to tell you briefly about my experiences in trying to learn to understand women.

I hate to admit it, but I used to be a mix of dumb and dumber. I liked women; I just never understood how to connect on a woman's feelings level, how to hear your silent cries to be appreciated. Then, twenty years ago, I somehow found myself as the only man in a group of divorced and unhappily married women. Each week, as the group's facilitator, I became ever more deeply touched and involved as I felt each woman's pain.

Week after week, I became immersed in their tears as they revealed stories of anguish about insensitive men who had crushed their hearts. Each session I empathized with these women's experiences and hardships, while a basic thought continued to run through my mind. *I wish there was some way those sorry, no-good, insensitive men could realize just how much harm they've caused these women.*

Yes, there I was, a smug and self-righteous judge of these men. After several weeks, however, I came to a shocking realization: *I am just like the men these women have been describing* . . . And so I began to change.

Today, however, even after years of learning and listening and changing — of continuing to major in *"How to Understand Women"* — it seems I'm no closer to graduating than when I first began. Will I ever graduate? No, simply because you ladies are too wonderfully complex. Still, I'm beginning to see some light (if only a glimmer).

At least, through whatever understanding I've gained over the years, I can help you not to have to endure an aching loneliness (like those women in the groups I facilitated), or to suffer through a gradual drifting apart, or to painfully agonize over a former lover who has abandoned you for the arms of another. *Instead, you're going to learn how to always know what turns him on to turn you on. And especially, how to avoid turning him off.*

Why did I tell you about my learning experience with women, and my harsh awakening to my own failures and insensitivities of years gone by? I've told you these things because, just like me, you're going to have to make some internal adjustments. You're going to have to start thinking differently about the opposite sex, and go to work learning all you can about us, just as I have been spending all these years learning about you.

It won't take you years to learn, however, as it did me. With *Putty in Your Hand*, you'll be 'inside' the mind of a man almost from the get go; you'll eavesdrop on what he's thinking. You'll learn what triggers his passion, and what *really* keeps it ignited. (If you think it's sex, think again.) You'll discover how to keep his heart occupied with you, and his mind filled with intimate thoughts of you, and you alone. You'll know how to make him live and breathe you ... and you'll become expert on how to keep him addicted to you, to the point where you can write your permanent signature on his heart.

Can't you just imagine the peace, confidence and power this will give you, along with all the positive changes you're going to be making in the relationship?

Picture his gentle and loving responses to you as his face lights up when you walk in, and when you feel his heart melting in your arms. And can't you just hear the sound of his voice praising you to others as he says, *"She's my special treasure, the very air I breathe?"*

To be desired and cherished and adored . . .

To be desired and cherished and adored, to have a tender and lasting connectedness with the man of your dreams — these are the things you want, aren't they? If your answer is *yes*, then you must take the time to understand him — not his traits, habits or preferences, but his very thoughts and the values he places on each of them.

You may think you already know as much about men as you need to know. You may incorrectly believe (as do most) that all a woman has to do to attract and keep a man is to create some sexual atmosphere from time to time. But the problem with this thinking is that the woman who does this sort of thing is putting herself in direct competition with thousands of other women doing the same thing. No matter how beautiful she may be, what do you think the odds of her continued success will be against so many other women?

Isn't it time to stop using outdated thinking that never worked for long to begin with? For example, did you know that a man's *actual* preferences concerning women are often far different from the articles in women's magazines? This usually means that what a woman might pass along to another woman — something she has somewhere read or heard concerning how a man thinks — can often be doomed from the start, because it may only be just so much baloney, thought up by an unrealistic writer for some magazine.

If this is the case, and the erroneous information keeps getting passed from woman to woman, then there are going to be a lot of misconceived notions circulating out there about men. This is one reason why so many women get frustrated when men don't react to something the way women thought they would (or should).

Unfortunately, those women who rely on the 'grapevine' approach to learn about men, instead of making a genuine effort on their own to understand them, are why some men will leave one woman for another. "She didn't understand me," he will say of the previous woman. Sound familiar?

Don't let this happen to you. Instead, learn what works! *Putty in Your Hand* includes things men hide from women (for fear of being shamed) that are so essential for a woman to know about and understand.

But *Putty's* love letters go beyond that. They tell the rest, too! They tell it all . . . from a man's perspective, for a woman's benefit. The letters throw off the covers to reveal a man's *unspeakably intimate* desires, so that (this is a very important point) you will learn exactly what those desires are and how to fill them. As you do, he's going to see you as forever blossoming in his presence . . . and what an adored and cherished flower you will be!

ACKNOWLEDGMENT

Behind most books are a half-dozen or so contributors, but not here. Behind this book there are hundreds — each giving generously of her time to teach me things men don't know about women. I wish I could individually thank each of you, but I can't. I owe too many too much.

You've deepened my admiration of the fairer sex. You've enhanced my understanding of your needs. You've opened my eyes to things I just assumed women know about men, but don't — including one thing especially, and that is what every woman absolutely must know to keep a man tuned in and turned on, and especially what she must know to avoid turning him off.

There's no way I can thank you enough for everything, including your flattering compliments concerning my freely distributed *"for women only"* writings and the *"indispensables."* That applies also to your suggestions and encouragement concerning *Putty in Your Hand*, that I make its letters available to every woman. Had you not persisted in your nudging, I never would have gotten around to publishing it.

Also, to all women everywhere, my respect for, admiration of, and awe stricken fascination with you is immeasurable. It is for you this book is published, and it is for you that I make this promise: If you will act on the simple yet essential things you learn from this book, your 'magnetic attraction score' will soar.

Then, if you're single, you'll attract even more of the desirable types to choose from. Or, if you're already married, your husband is going to see your change, and he's going to change, too . . . for the better.

It may be quickly, or over time. But either way, married or single, you're going to get the man you deserve. Even more than that, he's going to become *putty in your hand* (and you're going to love squeezing him through your fingers).

It took just one email and the right profile to light my fire for the girl who sent it. Fifteen months (and 300 letters) later, we were married. And oh! It's been glorious ever since!

Of the letters, 100 have been selected and arranged in a mostly non-sequential order for this book, but begin with the first email I sent to her. Titles have been added for ease of reference.

In the letters I tell Mixie what really turns a man on — deep inside and for all time — things few women know because even fewer men talk about them. This turn on is not what you might expect. Essentially, it gives power to the wife to become ultra-feminine and cause her husband to be manly and enamored with her. This balancing of power between a man and a woman encourages an ever-increasing love affair and ever decreasing conflict.

We would both love your comments. We want to help you experience the fullness of joyful relationship in marriage that we have.

~ Adam and my princess, Mixie

The Love Letters

1 The first letter

Thank you for writing to me, and for the compliment. Now let me pay you one.

Of all the match sites I've frequented, and of all the women who've written, you're the *only* woman who apparently understands the need for 'that certain balance' between spouses. Frankly, you took me by surprise, because I've visited a bunch of date sites, but no one has even so much as hinted that they knew about this perfect way to a great marriage . . . until you.

You've overwhelmed me, which isn't easy to do given my background. I've devoted the past 20 years in the study and teaching of this subject about the husband's diligent and loving care of his wife, and the proper response of the wife to her husband. Yet during those years, few women (and even fewer men) were willing to be wholly vulnerable to each other and true to this nature-ordained concept that you identified. Isn't it sad that couples are making themselves miserable because of their apparent unawareness of this perfect pathway to happiness? Yet it's always been nature's way to assure jubilant marriages.

You can imagine then how refreshing it was to read your unique profile, since it clearly showed that you understand the how and why of creating and then maintaining the most intimate of relationships, nature's way. So, I would especially enjoy hearing more from you about your views on this and any other subjects you would like to discuss.

Meanwhile, my subscription on this date site expires today, so please use the email address below when you write back.

Till then . . .

2 To love and be loved in return

I'm told a man can experience a wonderful life by being with the right woman, the woman he can join alongside who desires to back-stop him, and can. Although I've never experienced it, I believe with such a woman there's no telling what a man could accomplish, with her and for her.

Women can be so incredible! What would we men do without you? When a woman writes the music, a man's life sings! Can't you just imagine the notes they could play together and the love they would share?

Do you remember the lyrics to one of Celine Dion's favorites, "Nature Boy?" – *The greatest thing you'll ever learn is just to love, and to be loved in return?* Imagine, if a person never learned anything more than that, they would have learned about the greatest thing of all . . . *love.* Now imagine being able to say to another person, "*The greatest thing in all the world is loving you"* (and mean it from the heart).

I think that's a lot of what being married is all about – for a couple to *love* one another, passionately, and to do so with every fiber of their being! Don't you?

3 I know you need . . .

Since your purpose for signing onto the dating site is the same as mine — to find an eligible spouse — I think it's a good idea for you to know up front what my attitude is concerning what a wife can expect from her husband, and I would like to hear back from you concerning the same. So here are a few of the things I am convinced you need from a husband, things he should be responsible and accountable for on your behalf:

The first thing that comes to mind is that I know you need a man with the right attitude and who uses balanced thinking. Well now, see, you can stop me right there, because my thinking is biased not balanced. I will take a woman's side on just about everything.

I know you need a husband who considers his wife an equal lifetime partner; equal in every way while different in function and purpose.

I know you need a husband who listens carefully and with respect to what you say, takes it to heart, and honors you for saying it.

I know you need a man who will value his wife's built-in intuition when it comes to advice, warnings, and making choices about things.

I know you need a man who is worthy of your trust — a promise keeper who is faithful, kind, fair, seeking godly wisdom to know and to do the right thing, and who holds your trust as sacrosanct.

I know he needs to be a man of integrity, so you can honor, respect and depend on him, and who puts your needs above his.

I know you need a husband who will trust, honor and respect you, one who will truly value your heart and intents, your perspectives, knowledge, accomplishments, efforts, intuition and dreams.

I know you need his recognition, admiration and appreciation for your devotion.

I know he must be richly in love with you and completely devoted to you, for you to receive the best of nourishment from him.

I know you need a husband who will seek to please you in more ways than you can count, large and small, who makes you delight in pleasing him in all the ways you have been gifted to do.

I know you need more attention than an ordinary woman... and more understanding... from a loving, gentle, kind and considerate husband who knows you are worth that extra TLC and will lavish it on you.

I know you need him to be his best for you; how else can you be your best for him?

I know you need a supportive man who encourages and helps you to achieve your dreams, to be the "you" that you want to be in life, one who seeks to learn from your strengths while helping shore up your weaknesses.

I know you need a "servant-leader" husband (who comes to serve and not to be served, even as he leads). Such a husband will stimulate in you a desire to serve, in return... but in the holiest, safest, most honorable and secure of relationships.

I know as a team, teammates need to have individual and joint guidelines so they know where each stands, and that well-articulated and fair guidelines for each husband and wife should be agreed upon, to avoid conflict or insecurity, and to improve communication, peace and harmony in the relationship.

I know your husband must see, cherish and respect you as the competent, mature woman you are, even when overcome with his instinctive man's heart to protect you from all manner of harm, and taking delight in images of you romping, carefree as a child.

I know you need a husband who does not believe in double standards – one who is even-handed and believes "what's good for the goose is good for the gander," whose eyes and desires are only for you, and who is a good "accountability partner."

I know your husband must be committed to learning about you, continuously, to be perceptive of your emotions, needs, and the things that will make you happy.

I know the man you marry must demonstrate that he has mastered himself and has self-control, so he has no need to abuse his position, to seek to control you or make personal gains at your expense; but instead, through tender love and sound *leadership*, he will create a desire in you to follow his lead.

I know your husband should provide you with trustworthy guidance in times of uncertainty or confusion, and also respect and appreciate the insights and loving guidance you give him in your own areas of strength.

I know you need your sexuality and sensuality to be fully appreciated, nourished and explored often, for the mutual pleasure and fulfillment of you and your husband.

I know your sexuality needs to feel deeply aroused, in your mind, soul and body, and that you can never be all that you can be unless your husband knows how to cause you to burn inside for him... and how to take care of you.

I know an unappreciative husband will soon become a lonely husband.

I just wanted you to know that I know, and understand, that marriage is more about giving than it is about receiving.

Mixie's Reply

Thank you for such a thoughtful and comprehensive list of what a woman needs in a husband. You are right on all accounts! You have perfectly and correctly listed what I need and want in my husband, and I won't settle for less.

I confess a little surprise that you know so much about women. Your words suggest you are unlike any other man I have ever known, and that intrigues me. You have obviously given a lot of thought and consideration to women, to their conscious and subconscious wants and needs on multiple planes. It's a rare man who makes the conscious effort to prepare himself to be not just good, but great, and for life. Can you really be that good? [smiley face was inserted here.]

Clearly, physical love and emotional desires form just one component of a good marriage. Without the rest at the core, those can even wither and die, often faster than youthful bodies begin to sag with age. There are so many ways in which we must be compatible if we are to truly experience the depth of bonding, intimacy and commitment we both desire. As ***Antoine de Saint-Exupéry said,***

"Love consists not in gazing in each other's eyes,
but in looking outward in the same direction."

Do we, or will we, look outward in the same direction, with shared core values, hopes and dreams, and with a shared vision? Let's explore that thoughtfully as we get more deeply acquainted; much more besides, because people must be in total agreement on so many things affecting their relationship if they are to have a superior marriage. That's the only kind I want.

So help me understand where you stand on all the things important to you, and tell me more about your vision for a great marriage. You showed your understanding of what I need in a husband, but I now want to understand more about the man's view. What (other than sex) really attracts a man, and what will captivate him for the long term.

I know what's written in women's journals and what we women presume and assume. But I certainly wouldn't trust "Vogue" or

"Cosmopolitan" to discern the truth about what a real man, a good man, wants in a real woman. So please help me out here. What will keep him devoted to her, and her alone, for life?

As for me, I feel I have a lot to offer as a wife. My heart is interested in being the "right wing" for my husband, by his side in all things, wherever possible. I will provide a watchful eye, knowledge, intuition and insights to support and protect him, as his right hand, even as he supports, guides and protects me. I know a wise husband heeds the wisdom and intuition of his wife when he has a good one, just as a good leader heeds the advice of the sage in his midst. A woman's intuition can be her husband's best friend.

My husband and I will compliment and balance each other, so the whole is greater than the sum of the parts. God made both man and woman in His likeness, giving each one certain of His attributes and character. Only together, then, is there completeness, and one is of no less value than the other.

I will wholeheartedly love, honor and serve a husband I know I can respect and trust completely, one who honors, respects and truly values me for who and what I am. He will be a husband who seeks godly wisdom, one who is kind and tender, and who seeks to please me on multiple planes, as I will seek to please him. Then I will feel that I cannot do enough for him, because by his own attitudes and actions, he will stoke that desire in me.

Consider that when we give great pleasure to the object of our affection, then we receive ever more joy for ourselves (if they are loving and appreciative). It is the law of giving and receiving. And you're right, marriage is more about giving. The reward of selfless giving is multiplied back many times over. So if both mates freely give, it can create a positive snowball of joy!

Back to your list. When and if I can have a husband who is the embodiment of all that's there (combined with romantic attraction), *then* I know I will have a deep desire to yield to him. I will desire to yield to his leadership as well as to his body, secure in his love and protection of me, and in his commitment to help me be the best I can be. I will be able to trust his judgment, and I will feel confident he also values and trusts mine. He will have my back, and I will have his. We can make a powerful team together.

Then I will finally feel free to let down my guard, those invisible walls of protection all people construct. I will be able to risk being vulnerable, to open myself to him completely, and to love him in the utmost depths of my body and soul. That is what I want.

As you must know, husband and wife are to meld as one spirit and one flesh, to love and to cherish each other 'till death do they part. Only then can a marriage be truly fulfilling. My husband will be body of my body, flesh of my flesh, and I will be his in every way — including the spiritual melding that occurs in marital intercourse. *True oneness.*

That's an awesome yet sobering thought. It makes this get-acquainted time, our mutual inquiry and sharing so vitally important. It calls for deep personal soul-searching and heightened awareness. It calls for careful, honest appraisal of the other person and our potential match in all the important things, long before physical contact and what I refer to as hormonal complications. (Those cloud judgment.)

It's also important to understand that melding of body and spirit does not mean relinquishing individual thought, judgment or standing. It does not mean losing your identity. But it's the strength and power of two well-matched, committed individuals coming together as one that can create a union no man can put asunder. That's what I want.

With all of that said, I hope you now have a better understanding of me, and where I'm coming from. I must confess to a slight nervousness as I dare to look more deeply, realizing you just might be the answer to my prayer. I must be totally honest with myself, with a critical appraisal of us both.

Do we both want God as the head of our marriage?

Do we really share expectations and vision?

Will I meet your expectations?

Will you meet mine?

4 The role of a husband

Thank you for sharing your ideas on what the role of a wife is. You've shared some good stuff, too, about the kind of husband who generates the necessary confidence and trust. And I agree with you completely about it being the husband's role to stimulate the desire in you to fulfill your roles lovingly and joyfully.

Since you've asked me to reciprocate, I'll mention some characteristics I feel a husband should have. Notice I said *some*; the full list of a husband's necessary attributes could easily fill a book. But then again, so could a wife's, and neither list is ending. It's continuous, something to work on every day. Also, since we're limiting this to the role of a husband, I won't add the role of a father to it.

I believe every man should be a real gentleman, and also appreciate and try to understand women as best he can. In the role of a husband, especially, he should be particularly needs conscious of one woman. This is the one woman he wants to love, serve, and faithfully lead for life, the woman whose needs he places ahead of his own whenever possible.

He is her champion and guardian protector, her confidant and best friend. He is tuned in to, and ever mindful of her emotional changes, attitudes, and current feelings. This means he is ever learning about his wife, ever growing in his ability to 'read' and fulfill and complete her. This requires that often he lovingly ask her if he can get her something, even something as little as bringing her a cup of coffee. Or what if there is something big that seems to be troubling her. Then with sensitivity and sincere caring, and in a gentle loving *tone,* he can ask her if there is something she would like to talk about.

This more or less goes with the above, in being able to read his wife. A good husband is a good communicator and an even better listener and observer of his wife's needs. This means he is a one woman man with an attitude and desires that seek to be aware of and serve her needs, whether she verbalizes those needs or not.

Another characteristic of a good husband is that always he is careful to maintain for his wife an environment in which she can feel secure. This includes financial security and, if possible, financial independence.

A good husband is like a wife's private gigolo, self-trained in the art of being knowledgeable about, sensitive to, and skilled in exploring and satisfying his wife's specific and distinct needs, and capable of going the distance. In this regard, a good husband is considerate, not selfish, and knows when to postpone his self-oriented desires. But unlike a gigolo, he is totally bound to her alone, to her body, completely, and she to his.

These characteristics alone are not sufficient to fully express the role of a husband; nevertheless, they should give you a running start in knowing not only where I'm coming from, but also what I am striving to become.

5 Mixie the pixie

Hi Li'l Pixie,

Yes, I called you *pixie*, because lately I've been thinking of you as a mischievous little pixie who likes to "mix me up." So, I've come up with the nickname, "Mixie the pixie," because of those times you get me emotionally mixed up with things that initially frustrate me. But then later you do something that turns me all warm inside.

Here's an example of a time you mixed me up: It's when at first you didn't get back to me about the five love language types when I asked you about yours, so that we could tell where we stood, compatibility-wise. I had to ask you about it again, as if you weren't interested.

That's the frustrating part.

But then, instead of just looking at the simple list of only five lines that I sent to you, you go right out and buy the book. Then you get into it in a big, big way for me, which makes me feel all warm inside and turned on to you — not to mention that according to the book, our five love languages align almost perfectly.

Maybe it's just that you and I go about the couple's discovery process differently. Everyone has their own best way of doing things; that's to be expected. I dive into something I'm interested in (that's you) in a big way, and then begin digging for facts with a big shovel. When I feel I have the facts necessary to make the right decision, I make it, either to proceed forward or to simply walk away.

Here, however, I'm still somewhat in the dark and don't know what you're thinking. Since your insightful initial response to my list of what a woman wants in a husband, you've shared very little, really. You've seldom asked more about me, or made voluntary comments about yourself, your preferences, etc., as I have mine. I need to know these things about you!

I feel like I've been full time with you, and yet you've been only part time with me. And that's okay; I don't mind moving back to the level you want to be on. That is, if you want to continue writing.

Yet there were a couple of times when you said you would write. You didn't. There have been other times when you said you would be home for a phone call from me. You weren't. This is all beginning to seem like the lines of a song:

> You say it's yes, and then it's no;
> You say you'll stay, and then you go.
> You're undecided now, so what are you gonna do?
>
> First you say you do, and then you don't.
> Then you say you will, and then you won't.
> You're undecided now, so what are you gonna do?
>
> Now you want to play, and then it's no.
> And when you say you'll stay, that's when you go.
> You're undecided now, so what are you gonna do?

What's going on here? Maybe we're not on the same interest level. (Mine is now beginning to dwindle.) Perhaps you're playing with me. Am I just entertainment to you?

But then again, when we talk, you seem very much into the relationship. Are you playing hard to get? Or is it that you're so busy with your many activities and commitments that you're forgetting to keep some of them?

Your life is yours to live, of course. I just want to know at what point it intersects with mine.

Do I seem harsh? I don't intend to be. I'm starting to have feelings I've never experienced before. So I'm just trying to be careful that I don't fall in love with someone who doesn't feel the same for me.

Actually, if I were with you at this very moment, you would already have my arms around you while you rest on my lap (such a sweet place), hearing me say good things about you.

Let's think about that for a minute . . . What would it be like if we were together? Right now. What would it be like for you to be on my lap, right now, with my arms around you? Would you be testing my soft and vulnerable eyes as you hear me speak in the voice you have come to know as kind and gentle?

I would begin by saying . . .

Mixie, you sweet girl, you're God's very own. And already you're becoming a blessing to me in only a short time. Now, with you sitting here on my lap and snuggled tenderly in my arms, please hear the warmth in my voice as I share my thoughts. And if I seem to have gotten uptight about such a little thing as an innocent oversight or forgotten promise on your part, it's only because I need you to understand my perspective.

You've said you're looking for a trustworthy leader in a husband. But what kind of trust would there be in a leader who didn't keep his word? Every leader I know has his own style of leading, and you may decide that you don't care for mine — in which case I would certainly understand. Yet despite style, every leader has to hold both himself and those he leads accountable, always, and for the same actions. There cannot be a double standard; he cannot tell you to do one thing while he gets to do the other.

Let me shift gears a little bit here, to the time I said you reminded me of a filly, a thoroughbred filly, and how every filly needs her groom.

Now a filly is a filly, and she will always act like a filly. (Thank God for femininity and "little girls" of all ages who know how to use it on men!). Meanwhile, the groom is totally responsible for the care of the filly, because she's busy doing what she does best: being a filly.

Now a filly likes to run and play and kick up her heels. So what fun would it be if she had to always keep an eye out for possible harm looming on the horizon? After all, the groom watches for oncoming harm, because that's what good grooms are supposed to do. But the filly's superior "hearing" and instincts help protect the groom too. A good groom knows that if a filly is acting up and refusing to respond to the rider's direction, there's a good reason for it. But normally, if he needs to guide her to the left or to the right, then it should be a soothing correction, not forceful. It's a beautiful relationship.

A good groom enjoys protecting his filly from getting into danger, because it gives him a chance to indulge in his favorite pastime: filly watching. Especially when he gets to watch this one filly.

In fact, only this filly if he has the rare privilege of her belonging to him. He has resolved to commit the rest of his life, his energy and his love solely to her good, forever.

And so a good groom very much enjoys taking care of his filly, brushing her, washing her, watching over her when daily he walks her to the green pasture to run and play.

He protects her by building a white picket fence to establish boundaries around the pasture. Of course, if speaking about a husband and wife instead of a groom and filly (as in this analogy), the married couple would design and construct this together. At any rate, this fence declares to the outside world that all within this fence is under the protection of the groom; that this is his filly and her pasture, and no one may encroach on it. The white fence also declares to the filly that beyond that fence, the groom is unable to watch over and protect her.

Nevertheless, there are times when the groom sees that his filly needs to feel more room, to explore and to grow, and so he enlarges her pasture and he goes with her out beyond its borders. He doesn't leave her alone; it is together that they regularly enjoy new adventures.

There are also times that his filly becomes afraid. This is no time for harshness, as harshness will make her kick . . . and fillies can kick hard! And so the groom needs to adapt and apply at this time a bit of know-how, and that is to be gentle with his filly. Otherwise, if the groom is forceful with the filly, she will fight back with everything she has, and never give him what he desires from her.

So instead, the groom comes up beside her, often bringing one of her favorite things to divert her mind from the fear and get her back into a calmer state. He talks to her, soothes her, stroking her neck and shoulders reassuringly, and walks her away from what might be causing her fear. In the meantime, he seeks to understand the source, and faces the fear with her. In a sense, he surrounds his filly with assurances and love, so she feels protected and safe, and if need be, more closely watched over and cared for.

Despite what kind of filly-trouble she may or may not get herself into, the groom will always bring the filly in each evening and brush her, pet her, and talk kindly to her, knowing that she is his responsibility, his pride and joy. Moreover, good grooms brush their fillies at least twice a day, and thoroughly, and never ask anything of them work wise without brushing them first, ever! Umm . . . what this suggests for married couples . . .

And so, Mixie the pixie girl, with you still on my lap, you see that I'm not scolding you because of an innocent oversight or forgotten promise on your part. It's just a concern I wanted to clear up between us. Anyway, my Li'l Pixie, I've carried on long enough about my filly example. But I love the image. Anyway, it's time to go run and play now if you like, and kick up your heels in your own flirtatious way while I so enjoy watching you. (Big Happy Grin here.)

6 Why I pulled the plug

The profile you read is much different from the one I posted on the various other dating sites. On those I confessed that I used to be a pretty poor catch. I talked about how little I used to know and appreciate about women. I wrote about how long and hard since then that I worked on my personal growth in preparation of being worthy of the right woman. I also said that women in general deserved a lot better than they were settling for.

Having written those things, an unexpected, large volume of mail began coming in. (But keep in mind that I was on a large number of dating sites.) What was especially surprising was that mostly women would write, *"You're just what I'm looking for,"* or, *"Are you for real?"*

At first I was sure it must be insincere flattery. Yet as more of it continued to come in, I got to thinking that all of it couldn't be insincere — there were too many women saying the same things. Either way, my ego went through the roof. But after I came down from Cloud Nine and my ego deflated back to normal, I still wondered if I was growing into what women apparently wanted in a man.

Maybe this is being petty, but with all the work I've done on myself to try to become more like the kind of man a woman would want, I've always felt that I ought to be worthy of an equally good woman — a woman who has worked on herself to try to become more like the kind of woman a man would want.

But how many of these women writing to me were taking the effort to grow into what a man would want? Honestly, I have to say not many. It seemed as if they had been wasting their years pursuing mostly self-oriented interests. Like little children who never grow up, whose worlds still revolve around themselves, these women were all about what *they* wanted. It didn't matter that most of what they wanted wasn't reasonable, instead of, at the least, occasionally thinking about what a man would want and need in a wife. It's no wonder some women keep finding themselves getting in and out of relationships on a regular basis.

So why did these women think that all they had to do was simply say they were interested, and then I would just roll over for them? Didn't it matter that my profile included the kind of woman I was looking for, and to please not write me unless they fit the description I was looking for?

Yet they didn't seem to care about what I wanted or what I felt; they disregarded what I had said and chose to write to me anyway. I wondered if perhaps they hadn't even taken the time to read the profile. (It seems there are women who just blindly throw hooks into every pond to see what fish they might catch.)

What I wanted didn't matter to most of these women. And for many, it was all *(and I do mean 100%)* about what *they* wanted. Finally, I gave up and pulled the plug on all the sites on which my profile appeared. All except one, that is. Since I hadn't been on that particular site for years, I couldn't remember its name or web address. And as you know (fortunately for me), that's the site where you found me.

7 My education in Women 101

Their stories were heartbreaking. Any lesser word could not describe what I've seen and heard in the various women's seminars and small group workshops I've either attended or facilitated over the years.

You might think it strange for a man to attend women's events, so I'll explain. My purpose in attending those seminars, and then later to facilitate group codependency sessions for women was to learn all I could about women while also encouraging them. But then, my education took a turn I never expected; I learned about me, too.

As women shared their hearts, mine began empathizing and agonizing over their pain. Occasionally in a session the weight of their anguish would overwhelm me. More than once, unexpected floodgates of compassion would suddenly burst open within me. At these times I found myself totally out of my depth, submersed in disturbing emotions and trying my best to hide what was happening inside me. *This isn't right*, I thought. *Men aren't supposed to show their feelings.*

Looking back, I think my (over) reactions were due to guilt. I hadn't realized that I'd been just like the no-good men who had hurt those ladies. Week after week more women came, and with them more painful memories, many of which distressed my heart. Although I would try to be 'the man,' I remember particular occasions when it was through my tears (carefully hidden behind two hands supporting a bowed head) that I more clearly understood the pain behind their tears.

I listened. I learned. Not from just a few women, but from

many, and for years. Numerous other women since then (those I've communicated with on the Internet) taught me still more.

Do I know a lot about women? I wish I could say I do, but that would be untrue. I only know enough to know that a man should not allow himself to become frustrated when trying to understand a woman's logic. The mental exercise might drive him insane. LOL. Yet as confusing as women are to men, we can't get around the fact that you are fascinating beyond measure, and . . . we need you.

Wouldn't it be ridiculous for a man to presume he completely understands women? Yet as I wrote to you earlier, there have been brief moments filled with egomania when I have been tempted to think just that.

For instance, do you remember how my profile was written from a woman's point of view? So when women contacted me, some wrote that I knew more about women than they knew about themselves. (Yes, some actually said that.) I was sure it was just cheap flattery, but as more women continued to volunteer the same opinion, I began to wonder if they really meant what they were saying. That's not exactly a cure for egomania, is it?

So with my head already inflated beyond two hat sizes larger than normal, I began to think that *yes*, I really had been taught a lot about women, by women. At least I remember thinking that I wouldn't be getting all that mail and all those compliments if my profile wasn't hitting somewhere close to what they wanted. Finally, it seemed, I had begun to think in terms of women's needs and desires.

Unfortunately, with all the rush of attention I was getting, I was fast becoming . . . well, just imagine that if you had poked me with a sharp pin, you might have seen something like a balloon rapidly expelling a prolonged blast of air as it jetted its way around the room, before dropping to the floor in an utterly deflated state. LOL

In the moments (although admittedly few) that I was humble, however, I still dared to wonder if perhaps what these women were saying concerning my knowledge about them was true. Had I actually learned that much about women? Was I finally beginning to understand and get in step with their feelings? Was I starting to align myself and empathize with their needs?

As a woman, you know the answer to that far better than I. But at least, because of my experiences in the women's seminars, group sessions, and elsewhere, I can appreciate a woman's perspective on things a lot more than before. So maybe that rapport was showing through in my profile.

Why did I bring all of this up — the women's seminars, the group sessions, the effect those women's stories had on me? It was so you can understand why I said, generally speaking, that I felt like I know you after only a short while. And now I'm hoping you will teach me about yourself and allow me to get to know you even better, beginning at the center of your heart and working my way out.

I'm (hopefully) not scaring you, am I? I'm not talking about learning all your secrets and private thoughts. Not all at once, anyway, and not ever, unless you want to begin sharing them with me as you continue to trust me and know you can be at least a little more vulnerable to me than you were at the beginning.

At least, with the aid of our enneagram and Meyers-Briggs™

personality test results, and the other tests that we now have returned to us, plus what you've already shared with me, already I'm understanding (at least partially) what's going on inside you. Remember, testing is one of my professional fields of expertise, so these things enable me to know the upside of you, and the downside, so that when I tell you I know you but want to know more of you, you can know that I truly do care about the real you, warts and all.

8 I let you down

I let you down. I'm sorry. When you called this morning to tell me you were reading some of my emails again, you were crying. When you said they made you feel very special, and that one in particular had touched you deeply, I didn't know what to do or say.

I could use the excuse that you're shy when speaking outright about your needs. But still, I should have been more sensitive, especially when the one that had touched you so deeply was about my knowing what you need. It was as if, here I am being put to the test about the things a husband should know to do in various situations. But my mind was just plain stuck, and because I was caught 'off guard,' I failed the test.

Though I'm continually learning more about you, I let you down. I need much more time with you so my heart will always instinctively know what you need. I want to learn more about you so I can be more sensitive. Even when you yourself don't know what you're craving to fill your yearnings, I want to be there to help.

I let you down . . . this time. Yet I don't want this to become a pattern that I excuse. I need visual; I need to see your facial expressions, your body language, before I can even hope to come close to caring for your needs.

Already, you have become an extension of my mind and my heart. Now I, most intimately placed in you, want to become an extension of yours.

9 You really hit me hard

Okay, well, you hit me hard. You really got my attention. You showed me an ugly side of me I thought I had gotten rid of. You showed me that at times I can be petty. That was your word, "petty," so I wrote it down in my *"Ouch, Things To Work On"* book.

But you also showed me something else, and it was oh so marvelous. You showed me that you could diffuse me. And you did.

Right before my eyes, I melted. I felt all the built-up tension I had been creating in myself since the night before, just whoosh right out of me. Just like opening a hot Dr. Pepper bottle, all the pressure suddenly vanished, and I felt all soft and warm and glowing, inside and out. And you did that to me, for me, for us — and in a very special and meaningful way, a non-threatening way that damaged none of my male ego.

You are just incredible. You are teaching me even more of the benefits concerning how and why a man needs a woman, a soft creature with a warm and understanding heart, to change and mellow the hearts of men. Because of you, I am so very excited about that concept, since now I am actually experiencing it with you. And I love it!

I love getting changed by you. You make it so easy and rewarding to be all the man I can be for you. And you caused me to realize what I thought I was trying to be for you was not only possible, it would be inevitable. And when you pointed out to me that I unknowingly was acting exactly like a person I did *not* want to be, it made it easy for me to get myself back on track. So . . . thank you.

10 You asked what types of women I've known

You asked me about the types of women I've known. With few exceptions, they came out of problem marriages, where either they or their ex-husbands wanted to leave.

No one plans on a marriage going bad, and these women were no different. Yet there's always a reason any of us has marital problems in the first place. It might be because of the way we grew up, having less than a desirable marriage modeled to us by our parents. Or perhaps it's because we lost one or both of our parents (and the security that goes with it) when we were young. Or we suffered the agony of child abuse, or a host of other reasons.

For whatever reason, most of us grow up bringing relational problems with us into our marriages. And then the conflict begins. But it's only until some of us realize that it is we, not others, who have a particular relational problem that we begin doing something about it. And even then, it seems, it's only because life has motivated us by beginning to force one of its lessons upon us harshly that we earlier in life decided to skip over. But only when we choose to fully acknowledge our problems and start addressing them can growth and healing begin to take place. Otherwise, they can fester and cause an unwanted divorce, which means the problems we did not address will follow us into the next marriage.

As you would expect, of the women I've met, some were unhappy, some needy, and some were truly wonderful. Also, some were open-minded and teachable, and some were not. Those that were teachable I could reach and encourage in their understanding of nature's plan for the woman's glory via the husband, and the husband's fulfillment via the wife. Those who were not yet teachable were unable to hold up their part in a relationship, primarily because they were refusing help by hiding a painful self-image behind a protective attitude of arrogance.

There were also women who were just too immature and thus not ready for marriage, although they had already been married (some at least twice.) One was a woman who told me she had been married five times, with two of those marriages lasting under six months. Whatever problems these women suffered were not totally caused by them, however. I'm sure they also had a gripe or two, and justifiably so, about the men they wish they had never married.

I mentioned that I've known needy women. Surprisingly, it was that group I used to be drawn to—probably because of my built-in desire as a man to feel needed. And so, through encouragement and acceptance, I hoped I could turn things around for them. And I also thought I might find one woman that I could be interested in, while she, at the same time, would be learning and growing, too. But then I realized I wanted to help women who weren't interested in the kind of help I was offering, because it would require a change in their habits, hearts and attitudes.

The truly wonderful women I mentioned that I've known had unfortunately been planted in sun-parched soil and left un-nurtured. The men they had known had not appreciated them. Furthermore, the women's magazines they read were telling them their clothes were out of date; their skin was bad, and their bodies too fat or too skinny. Meanwhile, TV was telling them their looks were aging, their sex lives were lacking, and most everything else in their lives was falling apart.

There seems to be no end to the lengths some advertisers and their clients will go to sell things (including their own souls) to get rich off a woman's weakness. Instead of building women up as they could be doing, they tear them down, just by keeping them feeling insecure and unhappy with themselves. I'm speaking in general terms; of course, certainly not all advertisers and not all women fit this list.

Nevertheless, these were the women I spent the most time with to know them better. Although their former "gardeners" had failed to tend and care for them by giving them moisture and nutrients, I hoped to do better, to bring new life back into these women. My experience has been that neglected women blossom beautifully once the right gardener finds and cares for them — a man who would give them ample attention and understanding. And maybe . . . for the first time in their lives . . . they would begin to feel pretty and desirable.

As I said, these were truly wonderful women. As I spent time with them and watched them bloom, we would begin to share our respective philosophies. Unfortunately, it became evident that with some, we did not (and probably never would) share the same values. And so, with such a wide gap separating us, we decided to part friends.

Then there were women who just weren't willing to grow, regardless of the care and attention they were given. They chose to continue to see themselves as victims whose lives were stagnating, and they didn't seem to care.

Finally, having failed to find the right woman after numerous attempts, I decided to drop out of the dating scene altogether. I removed my profile from all the sites that I could remember having been on, and soon forgot about the idea of looking for a wife. That was more than a year ago. But now I've met you and am looking forward with great expectations that we just might make a really fantastic couple.

11 Integrity: True to my profile?

Last night you were troubled by your friend's concern about "trusting men on the Internet." I think it's good to have a friend like that, one who will watch your back. So let me give you something tangible you can take back to her, something that will show that I've been truly consistent to my word. To do this I would like you to review all the promises that I made in my dating site profile. Then, you and your friend can be the judges.

Have I kept my promises? Have I been true to my word? Or did I just write down a lot of stuff with no intention or ability to make it happen for the woman I decide I want? Will I cherish her as I said I would? Am I going to put my all into her daily as I said I would?

So please read my profile again, and then judge my integrity as to whether I've been doing all along what I promised I would do for the right woman. That should give your friend assurance that all is on the up and up concerning your "Internet man."

12 The woman I want

I like you, Mixie girl. A lot! We've got a good thing going. And BTW, I'm still continuing to work on my pettiness. LOL

Last night you were making an observation about my being a very thorough and careful type guy. Yes, that's true, especially when it comes to knowing what I want in something. I've made very few mistakes by being this way, but the truth be known, the few I did make were whoppers!

It can take a lot of time and care to find exactly what a person needs and wants. So once I find it — whatever it is — I go hard after it. Then I take care of it. Exceptional care, because it has to last. I'm never going to throw it away, that's how much I wanted it. Maybe that's why I'm so meticulous when it comes to what I'm looking for.

You see what I'm getting at, don't you? I'm being just as cautious (even more so, actually) in seeking a woman, because the woman I want/need will be able to stimulate my mind, body and spirit.

That's the broad stroke of the brush; so now let me fill in the blanks. As you read along, you'll want to choose which of these you can imagine yourself in.

I want a woman with whom I can feel spiritually connected. And I want her to feel so spiritually connected with me, and so confident of my love and acceptance of her, that she will know from the very depth of her soul how valued she is to me.

I want to develop for her a bond of total trust that will enrich her heart, more every day if it were possible. She will know her voice will always be heard, her suggestions never mocked, her ideas never laughed at, and never will she be taken for granted.

I want to be an enamored suitor to that woman for life. I want to be madly, crazily in love with her. To do that will require my love, respect and admiration for her to grow stronger and never level off. And every day I want to try to think of a brand new creative way to please her.

I want her devotion, trust, love, respect, and the encouragement to see me become all that I'm capable. Therefore, I want a woman who doesn't want to compete for control by taking a man's role. Instead, since she would want me to be the man and lead, I would be stimulated and inspired to be her lover, nest and safe haven; her gentle man, counselor and watchman; her supporter, partner and comforter.

If you were a composite of that woman, then I would want to be your defender, protector and safeguard. I would be your compass, coach and best friend. I would be your go-to person and confidant. And if you wanted me to, I would want to be your problem solver.

I would want to be your pilot and ship's captain, your navigator through troubled waters, and your lighthouse that guides you to peaceful harbors.

If you were that woman, then I would want to have an ongoing torrid love affair with you, and I would teach you how to make me crave you, lust for you, and only you, with a fervent fire that can never be quenched.

I could add lots more: you would be affectionate, considerate, sensitive (in the positive sense), a great communicator, work with me to keep peace and harmony, share in the responsibility for our relationship, seek mutual welfare and growth, and etc.

As I have said from the beginning, with the woman I want, I can extend her pleasures into the realm of nirvana. But the only way I can do that is if she has a willing spirit.

So, have you been able to see yourself in these smaller strokes of my brush?

13 Glue for couples

Last night I said I would love to have a good woman who was my best friend. A woman I could count on. A woman I could be proud of, love and trust, respect and pamper, adore and cuddle. But what I didn't get to tell you is that I get cautious when I read that fifty percent (50%) of first marriages in this country end in divorce. Then when I read that 67% of second and 74% of third marriages end in divorce, I have to tell you, this really gives me pause for concern.

Meanwhile, according to divorcerate.org, Japan's divorce rate is a much lower 27%. I wonder if a review of the customs and mannerisms of Japanese husbands and wives in traditional marriages would provide the reason why?

There is a proverb that says he who finds a wife finds a good thing. However, I've never understood how that statement could be true of every single wife, any more than saying she who finds a husband finds a good thing. There's good'uns and there's bad'uns. But maybe that statement about finding a wife is actually saying that it's up to the husband to cause a woman to want to be a good wife because of the way he treats her, and vice versa.

However, if it had said that he who finds a *good* wife finds a good thing, I could most easily understand. Still, most proverbs are intended for generalized application only, such as that one, of course.

Nevertheless, if there's a woman out there of whom it can truly be said she will be a genuine helpmate, then let me be granted an invitation to the tryouts to see if I can woo her. As with training for the Olympics, I believe I have been in serious preparation and am ready.

So I'm wondering, do you and I know ourselves well enough to have really examined and thought through the process of just how difficult at times a second marriage could be? Can you, a faithful lifetime partner in one marriage, and I, with a past marriage that failed, come together as one and produce peace and intimacy?

Work? It would be tremendous work on both our parts — perhaps more on your side because of all the patience you would need to live with me. We would need all sorts of glue to hold the thing together, too, and for my part, I just want to be sure I get it right this time around.

You know, there's a funny thing about most types of glue. They can hold two pieces together, but the pieces must be kept in perfect alignment under pressure while the glue is doing its job. Once dry, the bonding is complete and the two pieces cleave together. So much so that if one were to be pulled away from the other, both would be damaged, because they would have become a part of each other.

It's the same with marriages. Each spouse must stay the course while their "glue" is setting up to perfect the couple's bonding process, instead of trying to escape the "heat."

I don't blame anyone for wanting his or her life to be easier, but I'm not talking about that. I'm talking about a person allowing life's hard knocks to smooth out their rough edges, such as obtuse personality characteristics and behavior. Otherwise, that person could remain emotionally immature instead of growing up to behave as an adult partner. Whenever that happens, the "marriage glue" isn't being allowed to do its job, and the marriage will fall apart if the couple fails to achieve true intimacy first.

I believe the variations in people's personalities also create certain patterns that a student of such things can use, that constitute yet another type of glue, the glue of compatibility. There are many ways a couple can determine their compatibility (or lack thereof). One such way is to take a battery of tests, as we have, that produce the ideal compatibility combinations of personality paths.

Another is to know that the best marriages occur when the oldest child (me) of one family marries the youngest child (you) of another. This is according to "*The Birth Order Connection*" by Dr. Kevin Leman. Dr. Leman has concluded that aside from sharing the same spiritual beliefs, this is the most critical factor in a happily compatible marriage.

Another is that a "daddy's little girl" (which I'm picking up you might inwardly be?) fits well with a man who needs to stroke and touch a lot; she won't normally feel suffocated or overly caressed.

Another is the five love languages. Still another glue is the combination of the couple's primary and secondary personality traits — choleric, sanguine, melancholic and phlegmatic temperaments — since certain combinations attract and others repel. But there are quick, simple and accurate multiple-choice tests that we use to determine that.

Another (and this is just my perspective), less weight sitting on a man's lap is better managed than more.

So, taking all the above "glues" under consideration, what is some of your thinking — or is that a sticky question?

14 Successful relationships require work

I'm not willing to be a glutton for punishment. That's why I don't always play by the world's so-called rules — some can doom marriages to failure. Now that I'm further along in my understanding of nature's (not society's) rules for *How to Keep the Right Spouse Deliriously Happy,* I've learned better. I'm thinking that maybe you have, too.

I want my lifetime teammate and myself to be big winners. I'll settle for nothing less than a teammate who will allow me to show her how to dwell inside me and become a part of me. I want her to show me the same about her. And I want both of us to grow to make that intimacy happen.

For better or worse, I've worked very hard on myself to become who I am today. Yet I readily admit I'm a work in progress that will never be finished. Nevertheless, I'm further along today than I was yesterday, and I intend to continue striving, to become better tomorrow than I am today.

I want the woman I marry to have that same attitude about her personal development as I do about mine. If she's not yet as far along as she could be, or wants to be, at least she's working on it and making progress. And if she is — or maybe she's even further along than he — then she's expecting her future life partner to be doing the same.

15 What does a man want in a woman?

You asked me to tell you about men, what we look for in a wife. I've already told you some about my personal preferences for obvious reasons, but those cannot be generalized to apply to all men any more than a woman's personal preferences can be generalized to apply to all women. Every man is different. Yet if the men I know who are extravagantly happy with their wives weren't already married, they would surely want a woman just like the wife they already have; that is, a woman who has femininity (and lots of it!).

A better man expects to have a better or classier woman, which means she will have respectable traits, such as being ladylike, moral, honest, modest and polite. All these would count high with the man who holds himself to high standards. Also, a woman should be interesting to talk with, able to share the events of the day, be sociable, and share a common interest.

Although the list could go on, I'll finish here with three of the more important ones, especially to women seeking marriage:

1. She should be a woman of excellence and integrity. (If she lacks integrity, the rest of the package doesn't matter; forget her!)

2. She should not be argumentative or controlling with her husband. (It's impossible to have a fight if the other person won't argue.)

3. She should be developing her natural femininity-related

> gifts. She should be learning about them, improving, growing and exerting herself — as opposed to letting them waste away. Many of those gifts will keep her husband coming back for more . . . and still more.

In life, as in nature, every living thing must continue growing to live. When it stops growing, it begins dying. The person who wastes away their life in a rut is living in an open-ended coffin.

I know you're going to test me on what I think are natural femininity-related gifts. Well, one we are all especially familiar with is the innocent "Shirley Temple" coquetry exhibited in girls beginning at a young age, and developed all the way into adulthood. While it's encouraged in most little girls, in others, unfortunately, this playful behavior is shamed.

The real shame is that society (this includes family members and significant others in children's lives) manages to squelch this most feminine of attributes, leaving its victims with fear and shame and insecurities as adults. Is it any wonder that these emotionally and sexually suppressed women are confused as to who they are and what their role as a woman is supposed to be?

After these victimized women marry, they continue to carry a "parent voice" in their minds from their childhood. Since this voice is disguised as if it were their own thoughts, they accept those thoughts as truths, instead of what they actually are: a conglomerate of false condemnations from their childhood such as: "good girls don't behave that way."

These girls go through life as self-condemning and shamed women. Not wanting to feel "dirty" inside, they suppress their sense of sexual freedom by withholding permission to be sexually intimate with their husbands. (You mentioned a friend who has been going through this.)

Other women are more fortunate. They're the ones who survive "society" by reaching adulthood with their feminine gifts and "sexy" traits still intact. These are strongly demanded by men who appreciate those qualities in a woman. That includes me.

Yet a woman shouldn't expect an undeveloped gift or talent, even sex, to do much good for her in attracting a good man. It can't just sit there undeveloped and be expected to work very well. Any undeveloped gift or talent is just that, undeveloped.

Which means that by itself, sex isn't going to do the job of getting the better man; the woman is going to have to work on developing her femininity, too. Even the older aunt you spoke of can get her husband's attention focused back on her with a good dose of this, and a woman is (almost) never too old to begin producing it.

Successful people aren't paid the big bucks simply because they're lucky, and certainly not because they allowed their gifts to remain undeveloped. They're paid well because they developed their talents. They can do their roles with excellence because they studied and practiced and continue to do so.

Likewise, a woman's gift of flirtatiousness requires just as much attention, practice and skill as does any other major gift. And flirtation can come with so many different faces, and be applied in so many different ways. It's during these practice sessions that a floor length mirror cannot be overused. The same applies to making video recordings for a later playback to mark progress. (Women who think this is overkill should forget about the whole plan, and just go back to their dull and ordinary marriages.)

Since I've never seen you face to face, I've not yet had opportunity to observe how well you have developed your flirtatious attributes. However, this is the one gift that a girl should never stop developing.

How many women would you guesstimate have wasted one or more of their female-related gifts they could otherwise be applying in a wife's role? Even if a woman happens to be a beautiful woman, if she otherwise has a lazy, self-centered or unpleasant disposition, then her gifts are wasted on her. Like the proverb says,

"As is a beautiful woman with a sour disposition,
so is a pig with a nose ring of gold."

Beauty that lasts is the inner woman, and this includes her attitude as well as other areas. Beauty is also the way she handles herself, in public but also in private. Both are especially important to most men.

As you would expect, the woman who gets the most attention from a man in either area is the woman who has never stopped improving on her femininity; i.e., she's dripping wet in it. Such is the level to which a girl can elevate herself. And although she is neither born at this level, nor do her attributes rise to this level automatically, still, I would love to see you at this stage.

Here are some of the earmarks of the woman who has developed her womanly characteristics. At least these are some of the things I look for. Nevertheless, there are lots of good unmarried men of there who prefer a not-so-feminine woman, but I'm not one of them. Anyway, some of the things are:

- She steps aside and waits for men to open doors for her;
- She walks a certain way, she stands a certain way, she sits a certain way;
- Her wrists and hands are turned a certain way, and
- She tilts her head a certain way.

I'm not saying she should be robotic or feel unnatural while she does these things. Of course she should be natural. I'm only saying she should smooth out her movements to make them graceful, and this will come with practice. I've noticed in your photos certain of these feminine postures or positions, and I don't mind telling you, they give me some really great romantic thoughts.

Anyway, getting back to the list, a good woman is not vulgar. She dresses in a certain way (feminine and kind of sexy, yet ladylike way) that attracts the right men, yet never gives them cause to disrespect her.

She never attempts to take the lead. As an example, let's say a restaurant host or hostess breaks a rule of etiquette by erroneously asking *her*, *"How many in your party?"* But instead of answering the person, she deflects the question by looking at the man whom the host or hostess should properly have addressed.

She doesn't cut corners, but instead chooses to make the effort to develop her feminine attributes. As she does, she will become all the more confident and assured, not to mention attract favorable attention to herself.

Women who are not interested in self-improvement will never bother with the above stuff. Instead, they assume they should be treated with respect just because they're females. What I think they're really asking for, however, is courtesy, which every person deserves. But I think respect is something that must be earned, by man and woman alike.

Now then, if you've heard that men think about sex all the time, it's fairly true, at least much of the time. I heard a psychologist tell his radio listening audience that a man thinks about something related to sex on an average of every seventeen seconds. That's amazing if true. If it is, we men have it worse than I thought. Perhaps he meant to say every seventeen minutes.

That's why femininity can hardly be mentioned without including a major ingredient: sexuality. There is *nothing* sexier than the woman who *knows* she's sexy; she doesn't have to dress the part, she *is* the part (and men notice this). She knows and applies what Hollywood makeover artists used to teach new and upcoming starlets, when grooming them in preparation of putting them into films — before society's standards for women started slipping.

Some women have asked me where flirtatiousness and other "tricks of the trade" (to round out a woman's attributes) are best learned. This poses a real problem for them, not having been taught by their mothers and/or grandmothers. But if that information wasn't available to a girl as she was growing up, as it was to you, then I tell them they can observe the demeanor of those women who have it and use it.

Or sometimes it's the husband who must teach the new bride about such things, to help her further develop her femininity. Besides, every wife should learn what her husband likes, and satisfy those "itches," just as he must explore what she likes to satisfy her wants and desires.

Which reminds me . . . women have hands; they should use them. This goes for husbands, too, in lovingly, tenderly and gently exploring and completing their wives.

Especially important, though, is for a wife to win the Recognition Award. She does this by showing honor to her husband. The wife with this attitude is probably thinking, *What are some ways I can better serve my husband's needs that I'm not fulfilling now? S*he will want to see that he receives from her all the blessing she's capable of giving him.

Here's an example of something that dishonors her husband: If she's capable of practicing and improving her gifts for his benefit, but doesn't, then it's not honor she's showing her husband, it's dishonor; it's saying in effect that he's not worth her extra effort. Her pride is saying: *I'm good enough as I am. Besides, my husband doesn't deserve anything better anyway, so I don't need to improve* . . . Or . . . *I'm so great that there's not a woman out there who can distract my husband and take him from me.*

However, a woman should remember this: She doesn't have to be beautiful to keep her husband seduced, but she *does* have to be seductive and stay ahead of her competition. That requires skill, and skill requires practice. Lots of it! And floor length mirrors. Because one thing that attracts a husband even more than his wife's respect is sexy movement. (Especially if he's thinking sexual thoughts every seventeen seconds. LOL)

Wives who want to learn exotic dancing should first realize that a learning curve is going to be involved; it may not be as easy as it looks. It's going to take some time in working out every detail, every movement and every gesture. Becoming graceful in motion to increase her seductive powers over her husband cannot be overstated, though. This is because her "competition" is the pornography on TV and billboards, in magazines and movies, and on the Internet. And let me assure you, the people in those industries are *very* practiced at their skill!

So whenever a wife thinks exotic dancing is going to too much trouble, she should first decide where she wants her husband's mind to be, on them or on her? I could tell her this: the wife who goes to the effort to become a skilled exotic dancer (for his eyes only in private, of course) because she thinks he's worth it, is going to have a *very* appreciative and stimulated husband!

Incidentally — and this idea just popped into my mind — those women are mistaken who think men talk to other men about what they do with their wives in the bedroom. Men don't do that, at least none I've been around. Those women may be making this mistaken assumption about men making loose talk because they themselves are talking among the other women, or because they don't have a good man to begin with.

There seems to be no end to the number of women who enjoy wearing seductive clothing in public, but these are not the women who gain a man's respect. A woman should never degrade herself in public as some women do. But neither should she be naive by thinking that the sex-related messages from these women aren't getting through to her husband. At least some are, consciously and/or subconsciously.

The best way she can fight this and win is to beat these women at their own game; i.e., to become, *at the very least*, as seductive as they are. This means she must observe what they do (that seems to work on her husband) and how they do it. Then, assuming she feels comfortable, she needs to practice it, and finally, apply it (in private, of course). There are "clean" videos available that teach these various arts and skills; from Amazon, Barnes & Noble and other places; they're listed under "exotic dancing." An extra benefit to be gained from the exercises is getting flabby areas firmed back up again.

I've talked to women about their need to compete for their man's attention; unfortunately, most feel defeated before they even start. Not realizing that everyone starts learning new things at the same place: the beginning, they won't make the effort to do the work required. So why are they surprised when they discover their husbands are looking elsewhere? They shouldn't be. After all, a husband has to be all the more committed to remain faithful to a wife who has allowed herself to become unattractive to her husband. A wife who is too lazy to practice developing femininity, or to keep her figure, or whatever, is apt to experience negative results.

If she wants him to be faithful, she has to seduce him, if not with exotic movements or body language, at least with feminine gestures and touching him. But for a woman, being seductive is not all that difficult. I mean, come on! What woman isn't born with the DNA to turn every man into a melting candy bar?

If a wife feels she is losing her husband's interest, then just as one fights fire with a hotter fire, a spouse should fight sex with hotter sex. It's far better than the alternative of losing your spouse simply because you have chosen to waste your gifts. And neither husband nor wife has any excuse, since there are numerous, legitimate books out there on the art of making love.

I realize I'm being pretty blunt about all this, but somebody needs to be! The wife is only half right who thinks it's her husband's responsibility to choose not to react to all her competitors' sexual bombardments for attention. The other half is, as his wife, she needs to give him something as an even hotter substitute for the other.

What about the times she is not feeling well, but her husband wants to make love? Then by all means, she must not let him feel rejected by her. (A man's ego protection mechanism is incredibly brittle and thin.) She simply has to tell her husband the truth; that she understands he wants to make love, but she is feeling ill and can he wait for a better time? That's easy enough, isn't it? And any reasonable husband will not only understand, but will seek to help his wife feel better by going downstairs and getting whatever home remedy he can find in the kitchen cabinet to help her feel better by morning.

Okay, so hopefully I've been able to touch the tip of the iceberg in answering your question. Or at least to give you a general idea of some of what men want in women, although I admit much of it reflects my own personal taste.

16 God's natural laws

Isn't it odd that the most obvious truths are those we often fail to consider? Either we ignore them, or else we trip over them.

One truth in particular that I'm thinking about — one so many of us fail to recognize and thus we hurt ourselves and others — is that every science, every field, every activity, every *thing*, whether microscopic or macroscopic, whether initiated by humans, animals, plant life, planets, solar systems, whatever, anything and everything, is governed by specific natural laws, each of which must work in harmony with the others. It's mind-boggling. Every natural thing created, everything brought into being. Everything. All complies and works in harmony with its corresponding laws.

Yes, everything is in harmony, everything . . . except humans (much to their regret). And that boggles the mind even more.

Why do you think other living things, by instinct, comply with natural laws applicable to them, whereas we humans tend to think we can just pick and choose the laws with which we want to comply? Oh, sure, we have free will and can choose to abide by those laws which fit our purposes, with which we are happy to live in harmony to get what we want — the benefits from electricity, gravity and the like. But with that same free will, why do we ignore those laws that are closer to home, those that fall into a "personal" category? Ignoring a natural law that applies to personal relationships, for instance, is hardly different from a person ignoring the law of gravity by stepping off the edge of a cliff. Except, however, that person won't be around to violate another law.

When we ignore laws, problems occur: spiritual, emotional, health, financial, relational — many kinds of problems. And if you and I want to be honest with ourselves, we would have to say that most of the major difficulties we have encountered in our past have been caused by our own failure to acknowledge and obey those certain laws.

And that's regretful, because if we had heeded those laws, we most likely would have avoided those problems — especially those we bring upon ourselves, and others, too, that pertain to human relationships. But we don't like to be honest about our own mistakes, do we? It makes us look bad, so we blame our problems on some thing or some one, but never on ourselves.

It's madness! Can it be that we humans are actually that dumb? No, but I do think we are too proud and too stubborn to give in. We become arrogant toward cooperating, and yes, stupid enough to think we can get away with it. Yet no one really does get away with going against natural laws, do they? There is no "beating the odds" with this one, is there? We all pay for our bad choices; some sooner, some later.

Everyone knows some problems can grow quite serious — not only for those who cause them, but also for those whose lives are involuntarily and inextricably connected to the problems caused by others. What makes it even sadder is that most of these problems can be avoided simply by choosing to comply with the laws (and staying away from people who don't).

The Bible's wisdom books, such as *Proverbs, Ecclesiastes*, and *James* tell us everything we need to know about all the laws concerning relationships and how to live in harmony with them. Yet knowing how to do that is only half of it; the "doing" part is the other half. But once we learn to live well (honorably), live wisely, and live humbly, we begin to get the idea. Because it's the way we live, not the way we talk, that reveals what's in our hearts.

Those people I know whose lives reflect harmony are enjoying a level of success in many areas of their lives, while other people are only experiencing frustration in theirs. They cannot begin to imagine how much of the abundant life they are missing. But as we begin to live in harmony with nature's laws, things start going well for us. We can learn to use them for our benefit, to prosper even, by taking "free rides" on them. We can piggyback on the power they produce, too, like the law of electricity.

Eventually we recognize we don't have power over these natural laws, any more than we can relocate the sun or the moon (I exaggerate). We aren't even in absolute control of what might happen to us in the next five minutes; we could be struck by lightning. So once we face the fact that something greater than ourselves is in charge, we begin to see we are only along for the ride. We also begin to realize that the control we thought we had has been only an illusion, and that all along we have been using erroneous thinking. And, it seems, that kind of thinking does us harm in just about everything — including relationships between men and women.

I know we've already talked about this, that ever since Adam failed to protect Eve from the serpent's guile, most women have been unable to relax with their husbands at the controls. As a result, some women seek to run things themselves. But are they happy doing it, or are they instead living on the ragged edge? Isn't the contented wife the one who can leave the controls to her husband when he is in harmony with nature's law? Then she is in harmony, too. And because she and he both are, they can be at ease.

If someone should doubt that such a law exists, they should do a before-and-after comparison of the same couple. First, when she leads, then after, when her husband serves as the leader. Compare her complexion, her blood pressure, her general feeling of well-being (relaxed or uptight?), her overall attitude, and so forth. There's always a difference between working against the flow and working with it.

Thus, the wife who allows or insists that her husband be responsible for many family decisions is rightly and properly relieving herself of those everyday matters that ordinarily would place stress on her. She leans on one of God's natural laws and flows with the power and protection of that law instead of against it.

When you get to thinking about it, there doesn't seem to be much difference between this concept and that of citizens who vote a particular person into a government office of leadership, does it? The way it is supposed to work is for the elected person to work for the voters' good, not his or her own at the voters' expense.

It should be the same way in a marriage. The husband, as the appointed leader, should be working in the wife's best interest, all the while respecting and valuing her opinions and advice. He may be the captain, but she is often the navigator, and the navigator is the one who keeps tabs on the direction.

The way I see it, a wife is a gift from heaven — the living, breathing, exciting creature called "woman." Furthermore, God has designed her to be able to do numerous and marvelous things with and for her husband, the recipient of the gift. But God did not design her to lead in addition to all her other responsibilities, because her responsibilities are many and are equally important as his. Instead of her taking the lead, God appointed the husband to be the protective cover over his gift while he listens to her advice, leads, provides, loves and serves her.

Of course, the more adept the husband is at leading, and the more sensitivity he shows concerning his wife's needs and positions, then the more secure she'll likely feel, the more freedom she'll have, and the more graceful and eager she'll be to respond to him.

When a wife encourages her husband to take the lead, it liberates her from the pressure that can prevent her from living as freely and thinking as clearly as possible. In a relaxed state of mind, she is more apt to come up with good ideas and advice to help her husband steer the right course. And when she does, that husband can do a better job at the "wheel," responsibly and lovingly steering the family down successful paths, knowing his wife is standing beside him watching his right wing.

A husband who has a helpmate like her is almost always going to have more sensitivity about her needs. I know I would bless the day such a woman was born if she was married to me. And since a woman's sense of well-being and her emotional environment are so profoundly influenced by the treatment her husband gives her, she can only be expected to respond according to the quality and consistency of the leadership, edification and affection she receives and accepts from him.

You can see where I'm trying to go with this. There is nothing more beautiful, more compelling, than to look at one of God's loveliest creations doing what she truly wants to do. This is because she has been relieved of the burdensome activities (that are normally husband-related in healthy families) that would otherwise prevent her from enjoying the fun and freedom of extra time of her own.

On the other hand, there is nothing more disgraceful, more smudging, than to see husband or wife sink into a bog of useless conflict with the natural law that governs their growth, success, and the fruitfulness of their marriage . . . even their happiness! (But even when one sees this behavior, it may be the other spouse's actions and attitudes that actually caused it, so one shouldn't be hasty to judge.) There's also nothing more distressing to see than husbands and wives injuring themselves emotionally and in other ways by bickering; this accomplishes nothing but discord.

Marriage is not a "look-good" thing in public; it requires the care of a 'rose' daily at home and abroad. If treated right, it will bloom. By virtue of what each spouse does at their respective ends of the see-saw, they affect or touch what will happen at the other end.

Therefore, you and I must work in perfect harmony with God's laws at all times. Because, although our individual happiness is not wholly dependent on the other person, nevertheless, just knowing that the one we love is happy, and that our marriage is sound, contributes to our individual happiness.

This is why I will give the woman I marry the best and most loving care and support I know how to give, and as she asks me to improve in any area, I will strive to do so. As I do, she will be enabled to freely do those things she was gifted to do. And as those things increase, so will her need increase for still more support. To provide it, I'll keep myself in a continual state of 'going back to school' by further educating myself on the arts and skills of caring for and helping a 'flower' bloom and flourish. And since through my eyes I will see her as the exceptional, one-of-a-kind woman, I'll see to it that she finds herself in the winner's circle time and again.

I believe the woman is the glory of man. As my woman, she will be the glory of this man, and I intend to glorify her beyond her imagining. Just as I mentioned on the phone, in-laws judge husbands by how well their wives blossom and flourish. I intend to do everything in my power for my wife to be able to do what she was created to do while I steer our ship. I may be the captain, but she will be my first mate. And I am going to love her and protect her and do what's right by her with *all* that is within me.

17 This is becoming like déjà vu

You like to think of yourself as a filly. And you are. The "most-est" and " wonderful-est" kind of filly there ever could be! And that's how I like to think of you, too.

I also think of you as a pixie, although not necessarily Mixie the pixie (except when you're confusing). Instead, I think of you more like a special pixie, a pixie extraordinaire. You're youthful in mind, exciting in charm, and full of mischievous energy. You're just like a wee little fairy sprinkling pixie dust everywhere – even though at times you're filled with much impishness blended with unmatchable sweetness.

And how do I see you at other times? Well, at other times you're filled with the kindling that lights my fire. You fill me with wonderment, fascination and the best kinds of anticipation of what life with you could be like.

But there are also times when you fill me with confusion. Like now.

It's not like I'm a total stranger. We've been talking on the phone almost every night now for months, sometimes for up to three or four hours (time flies when you're having fun). During most of those calls, we've covered a lot more than most couples would on an average date. Come to think of it, four or five phone-call 'dates' each week for just three months would be the equivalent of a year of regular week-end dates, at least in exchanging views about things.

But only you know the real you, the person inside, the unspoken buried treasure and hidden secrets, your innermost thoughts and motives. These are things that don't reveal themselves over the phone. They are usually only seen when one is observed around their family or under the stress of being late to a meeting because of a pileup on the freeway. So these things require our spending time together in person, not over a phone, although conversations and emails do help.

In looking back, I see that I've written an average of four times a week to you. So, along with the phone calls, you ought to be getting to know me at least a little bit by now. (I jest affectionately.) Plus, you've read my profile; you know specifically (almost to the smallest detail) what I'm looking for in a wife. Yet you've not commented as to whether you fit those 'details.'

You're just not giving me enough information about you, the real you I mentioned above. And have you not also read in that same profile how frustrated I've been over the past few years? How I've been looking but not finding all the necessary ingredients in the same woman? I need that woman if I am to be completed, so I'm able to complete her, too. You seem to have the right stuff, most of it anyway. But how can I be sure?

You alone know how well you fit those things I wrote about in my profile. Yet if you realize how very important those things must be to me, why haven't you said something by now?

This is becoming like *déjà vu*, when I first nicknamed you Mixie the pixie because of my confusion over your "undefined" level of interest. Surely by now you could have commented, couldn't you? By saying something to the effect of . . .

(A) Okay Adam, from reading your profile I know exactly what you need in a woman, and I'm not she. Furthermore, I can see that you know where you're going and how to get there, that you're your own man, that you're not a waffler, and so you know your own mind and aren't going to accept someone too much different from what is described in your profile. So, although it has been fun, I think we should just part friends and go look for someone else.

Or, you might say . . .

(B) Okay Adam, I know exactly what you've written that you need in a woman, and I honestly know that I have most of those ingredients. I also know I like what I've learned about you so far. Sooo, Adam the man, what are you going to do about it now that you've found me?

I've been patient about the confusion that the Mixie side of you creates, because I seem to have become infected with you, and with that pixie personality of yours, too! I'm beginning to wonder, are you a virus? You must be!

But for me to take two pixie aspirin and go to bed just won't resolve the confusion. It's time to lay some cards on the table. So my question, dear Mixie the pixie, is this: "Which one of these two women better describes you, A or B?"

18 Yes! . . . I love you!

Okay, baby girl, I'll admit it, but only this once. LOL. *Yes! . . . I love you!*

For better or for worse, I'm probably stuck with you anyway; now that you've finally figured out I'm good for you, and that you want me and need me. And oh, let's not forget you have even admitted now that you . . . *uh huh* . . . love me. Anyway, now that all those things have finally settled out in your mind, there's probably no way you would let me leave, even if I wanted to. (At least I hope not!)

Is this blowing my own trumpet? Of course not; I can't play the trumpet. But somebody's got to blow it, because the little emails you "manage" to send in between our phone calls aren't what I'd call taking care of your man. (Maybe they might take care of a little boy, but not a man.)

So there! Ignore my needs; go have your frivolous day in the pasture, while, BTW, not even having to concern yourself with your own needs (since you now have a groom for that). Oh, and don't worry about me, or my heart, or emotions, or need for you, or for my need for emotional support. I'll get by, dried up as I am, suffering as I am, gasping for the last breath of air as I am, hoping that you may have a second or even two seconds to throw a bone my way in the form of longer emails.

And yes, I finally figured out what you meant about my not forgetting that I love you. But next time be bluntly direct, won't you? I'm only a man. I was just lucky that I caught the jab, the secret cod- ed meaning you threw at me at the end of our last phone visit when you said you were "only kidding." Women are never "only kidding" or "just wondering" about anything. There's always something going on in their devious minds they're not willing to share. LOL.

Women scheme, plot and connive. Women are vicious and vindictive and hold grudges against one another. Women are dangerous as scorpions and lethal as snakes. There's a really old C&W song warning cowboys about bar women. The chorus goes something like this:

Cigarettes and whiskey and wild, wild women;
they'll drive you crazy, they'll drive you insane.

But the problem is, no one has ever told me how to break the habit of being held captive by a person of the "weaker" sex. (Weaker? Ha! Now that's a laugh.)

Then I met you, and oh boy, am I ever in trouble now. You've already poured your love potion into me to make me helpless against your wiles. (O.K., so I didn't put up much resistance. LOL)

So go ahead and laugh at me. Just remember, even an old dog has his day every now and then. But don't think you're getting away with all this; as your victimized lover, I'll make you pay . . . some day.

19 Some things to consider before marriage

Here's the beginning of the list we talked about starting. I suppose we could call it "*The List of Things Couples Should Consider Before Getting Too Far Into Plans for Marriage.*" I'll start by mentioning what comes to mind now, and add to it later if more things come to mind. Hopefully you'll have plenty of ideas to stimulate even more thoughts.

To begin, I'm thinking about "those" questions that should always be discussed ahead of time: Where to spend Thanksgiving and Christmas: his relatives or hers? How many children wanted: two or an even dozen? Whether to adopt? Messy or neat? Toothpaste tube: rolled or squeezed? A house in the country or two in the city? Go to the theater or watch TV at home? Save money or spend it liberally? Pet peeves? And so forth.

There are also the former environments of the two individuals that can either mesh or clash. You apparently grew up in a family that was loving and close, and I'm very happy you did. It means you're much more stable as marriage material, because a child that grows up in an environment where the parents' love for one another is obvious and liberally expressed in words, hugs and kisses, is much better off.

This is especially true since you were fortunate enough to be a "daddy's girl." Growing up with a father who spent quality time with you, who made you feel safe, valued and loved, who sat you on his lap and even rocked you while you were enjoying his hugs was indeed fortunate. A girl who grows up with a daddy like that also makes a wonderfully affectionate and cuddly wife. But even not-so-fortunate women can have a "break through," and if you ever want to talk about that for your friend's sake, just let me know.

Since you were faithful in your prior marriage to your late husband, you've already proven you know how to live with (or through) various kinds of conflicts. Besides, we know that each marriage has its own particular kinds of obstacles, and no two personalities ever lived together in perfect harmony anyway — certainly not every minute of every day.

So personalities need to be considered, too, and numerous other things that couples need to be aware of just to hold a marriage together. One example I'm thinking about would be the way each of us goes about things. You've had a lifetime in which you've established habits of doing things in certain ways, as have I. Neither of us is likely to change much regarding these habits, so we can reasonably expect some of them to clash. Thus we would need to work out in advance how we would handle this.

No doubt you and I have accumulated vast amounts of experience in different areas; we should share these. Also, each of us has different windows of perception regarding numerous things; we should share these with one another, too. Meanwhile, we should remember that each of us has a different family background with different mannerisms and customs, so lots of patience will be called for.

On the other hand, there are many positive things I already know about you. (See there? I *was* paying attention.) These things indicate my life with you could be very pleasant. And life for you, too, could be very pleasant with me according to our test results, if everything else continues to fit together. A major consideration, of course, is the chemistry, and neither of us knows how that will play out until we've spent some face-to-face time with each other.

But the most important thing of all is to love one's mate despite the little things that tend to aggravate, and the numerous inconveniences that require one to give when he or she would rather be on the receiving side, and all the other things that can cause tempers to flair and feelings to be hurt. Through all these things, love is always the most important ingredient.

20 Why would a woman want to yield?

When you asked me to teach you how to become an uncommonly feminine girl, I wasn't surprised. Actually, I've been waiting for you to ask, because once you are enjoying that stage of femininity, it's going to produce all sorts of wonderful benefits. Not the least of which will be a vastly pleasurable excitement in both of us, plus ultra-confidence in you, and an (almost) uncontrollable desire in me for you.

Around about now you may be asking how all of this works, why it works, where to begin, and lots of other questions. I can't teach it to you all at once, of course. But when we're finished, you'll be able to produce this mental, emotional, spiritual and physical phenomenon of chemistry between man and woman, almost as often as you please, and it will become as natural a part of you as breathing.

To begin, since we're talking about a natural phenomenon, we're talking about a state or process known through the senses rather than by intuition or reasoning. And this brings us to a concept of nature which includes people and other living things that we need to talk about, because these have a lot to do with how and why an ordinary woman can produce this chemistry to become an extraordinarily feminine girl with an awesome captivating power over a man.

To begin, a person sitting is not a threat to a person standing, and a person kneeling is not a threat to a person sitting. This is the result of a principle of nature operating within humans and animals. Thus, the same principle is in effect whenever two male animals are fighting over the herd of females and one backs down. One yields to and acknowledges the other as the leader, at which time the fight ends and peace resumes between the two.

The principle also applies to plant life. For a seed to grow into a beautiful flower, it must first give in to the process of decay and die. That's the only way it can become a flower. But the very idea of something springing to life and becoming its most beautiful and best *after* it yields to the decay process is just the opposite of what most would think who were not familiar with the process.

Now let's take a look at married couples and especially the wife for now, because I used the flower seed to represent her. It's the wife who is being asked to give in. But unlike the seed, she is not asked to decay and die before she can bloom. However, she *is* asked to surrender, to trust, and to hand over to her husband much authority and accountability. And that's scary when it's a new bride who is being asked to stop making many of the decisions in her life. It's easy to understand why. To trust him with this much say-so and responsibility that includes choices that affect her life can be not only difficult, but frightening to her as well. After all, her husband has no track record of making decisions that include both of them.

Therefore, she needs to know that although his judgment can never be perfect, nor his love, he will always listen to her and try to put her needs first. Let me say that in another way. He will invest himself into his wife in such a way that his love will never stop growing for her, because she is his #1 treasure. This means that she will always be the first thought that comes to his mind if a change of some sort might need to be made; meaning, her importance and needs will always be placed ahead of that change, whatever it might be.

Still, I can appreciate why most wives are afraid to relax their grip on wanting to control things, even though to bloom as that flower requires them to soften to their husbands' wishes. Yet this will elevate them to their most beautiful and best if they will allow it. But how can a wife be sure? She can't, although when she does begin to yield, it's usually not long before a husband worthy of her notices the bloom on his wife's face and begins wanting to give her the desires of her heart.

So, yielding often brings just the opposite although positive result from what one might imagine. For example, compare a very large tree to a reed. Which one is going to break when a 120-mile an hour wind blows? At first thought some people would say the reed. After all, the tree's trunk is solid and mostly inflexible — it's not going to yield to the wind. But its inflexibility is the very reason the tree *is* likely to snap, whereas the reed is flexible and thus will simply yield to the fierce wind and survive unharmed.

Masculinity

Opposite thinking also applies when men and women are asked to describe masculinity. Most men think of masculinity as rough and tumble tough because they think that's what women expect of them. And some women do. So, to impress them, that's what men flaunt.

Then there are other women who think a man should be like a James Bond 007, able to handle every problem, manage every situation, resolve every danger, and come away from it all still looking debonair, clean and tidy with white shirt unwrinkled and black tie on straight. (Oh, if only a man *could* do all that, wouldn't it be great? Or would it? Because then he wouldn't need a wife.) But, fortunately for me, none of this is what most women deep down inside want a man to be.

I'm glad you and I agree that masculinity is neither all macho-ism nor 007 perfection. Instead, my idea of masculinity is *power under control* — from which the fruit of gentleness grows. It's the strength of character combined with the powerful essence of a strong protector, the knight in shining armor, even a Zoro or Walker, Texas Ranger. This means that the more power a man has, the more gentle he can be. Therefore, when you see a self-controlled man, a powerful man, he will be a gentle man. He has no need to flaunt or prove that he's tough.

Femininity

What about *femininity*, Mixie? How would you as a woman describe it? Would you say it's like the flower seed that yields to the soil and water, with patience and inner strength growing through the dark and into the light so it can be beautified? Or like the reed that yields to the storm, then rebounds to its upright position? Many men associate femininity with concepts very similar to these.

For example, when men want to describe a desirable (that is, feminine) woman, they might think of words that imply soft, yielding, amenable, accommodating, and other words to that effect that would come under the category of being easy to get along with. Therefore, to a man, the more surrendered and soft a woman is, the more feminine (and desirable) that man will consider her to be.

Yet I'm not talking about a woman who agrees with everything her husband says. **That woman is not being true to herself or her husband** – on the things that really matter for a good marriage, husband and wife must agree wholeheartedly. Otherwise, it cannot be a strong marriage of equals if the wife feels constrained from expressing her opinions and extraordinary insights, with reasonable expectation that her husband will respect them and acknowledge when she's right.

Therefore, the husband that listens and pays close attention to what his wife tells him is a wise man. A lot of calamitous things can be prevented when he does, because a woman can often sense bad things coming. And for the wife who doesn't want to threaten her husband's position if he refuses to listen . . . it's okay to get angry and 'kick.'

That reminds me of the story about a man riding a donkey. Suddenly the animal becomes skittish and refuses to respond to the rider. Unknown to the man a cougar is just ahead on a rocky ledge, waiting to leap. Thus no amount of coercing will cause the animal to move. Why? . . . because the donkey knows more than the jackass that's riding him.

Recently a female friend I know was giving me her definition of a feminine woman. She said that a date palm is much like an ultra-feminine woman. The tree can weather even the most terrible desert storms and stand on its own. Yet at any time it will give you the best tasting, most nourishing, life-giving fruit one can imagine. Essentially, it is a very strong tree that in her words, "will, upon a gentle request, willingly and gracefully lower its branches to yield its sweet fruit." The point being, she said, is that "a woman of femininity is *more* willing, *more* giving."

I am not overlooking the role of the husband here, either, when I speak of an ultra-feminine, willing wife. As we spoke last night, you agreed that it's easy for a woman to yield when the tone of her husband's actions cause her to want to — by his serving her, by the little things he does unbidden, by his tenderness and affection, his gentleness, and by the way he asks for things. Yet a woman, by yielding, will stimulate that response in her husband if he's a good 'un.

The Yielded Wife

I mentioned Laura Doyle and how she wrote a lot about surrendering, so let's define the difference between two actions: (a) *following* and (b) *surrendering or yielding,* in the sense of how the words would be applied in the context of marriage.

a. **To follow** is to accept the leadership of another. To follow is to be attached.

b. **To yield** is to acquiesce to the wishes of another. To yield is to accommodate, to stop fighting, to cease opposition

Of course, to be attached to something or someone is not the same as being yielded — Many married (and supposed to be attached *and* yielded) women prove this every day when they resist or refuse to accommodate their husbands' reasonable wishes. Although they are attached in marriage, they are miles apart from being the wife their husband needs. Unfortunately, many husbands violate this relationship, too, by not always being reasonable, balanced and fair; i.e., by just being plain selfish ("I want it and I want it now").

So at this point I'm asking only that you "attach" to my leadership by following me. If you do this, then later I will be asking you also to yield to me. But that would be as my wife if we were to marry, so that by your softness and willingness, you will keep me forever captivated and passionate.

The yielding I'm talking about isn't about becoming someone's doormat, and it's certainly not about being subservient or inferior to another. I was given the opportunity to read a blog written by a top female executive that runs a major U.S. Corporation. (If I told you the name of the corporation, you would recognize her immediately.) But when she goes home at night, she makes sure her husband is the one in charge.

I have spent time in the offices of professional women who very much run the show. One is a university professor, another is a psychiatrist, still another is a senior partner at a law firm. Each of these women have told me that at home, each readily yields to her husband, and two said they enjoy far-out sex, but you would never know it by seeing them at work.

Since I've mentioned women who enjoy kinky sex, let me also say that the God of the Bible is all for sex, even the kinky variety, but between husband and wife. Hebrews 13:4 is proof of that. Then there is TheMarriageBed.com. It's a good resource for married couples looking for articles and blogs about sex and intimacy.

Many women are surprised to learn that the very idea of being a yielded wife would have been repulsive to Laura Doyle when her marriage began at age 22. Of course, that was before she even tried it. And she never would have, except for some real problems that were ruining her life and marriage — problems she later said she herself was causing — because even though her intentions were good, she was (to put it in her own words), *"clearly on the road to marital hell."*

One of the things that brought this on was her attempt to correct her husband (and the domineering manner in which she did that) thinking this would help him "improve." Well, it didn't. Instead, she said he resisted her controlling manner and resisted change (as do we all).

It would be better, I think, for the wife who believes she needs to correct her husband, to do it tactfully, and in private. But she also needs to *really* listen to him, to his perspective. In the same way he should gently address her in private when he thinks she's wrong. It's all about the way it's done, certainly not by nagging, harping, criticizing, demeaning or speaking harshly, angrily or demandingly.

Anyway, the more Laura's husband resisted, the more she tried to control him. The more she continued, the more argumentative they became. Clearly, her attempts to control his life and hers weren't producing the results she was after. Neither were the anger and frustration she uncorked on her husband.

When we talked you said a lot of women won't read a book about giving up control to their husbands; they would rather leave their marriages the way they are. They reason that although their relationships aren't all that good, they'll choose to stay with the same routine because it's the one they've adjusted to, the one they think they can control, and they can't see things ever getting better. Moreover, they won't go to work on their marriages because they cannot be assured that their husbands and their marriages will change.

Yes, I can see where that could be true of anybody, man or woman, stuck in a rut and not seeing a way out. However, you and I know that control is not the issue, don't we? In fact, their whole situation was out of control. Regrettably, most couples simply don't know how to influence or ignite the change that's needed; they don't even know it's possible. So instead, most fall into reacting with nagging and criticizing, which won't work from either side and will actually backfire.

Unfortunately, too many wives and husbands are unaware of the lovestyle they could be living. And so they remain stuck in their ruts and continue to use various forms of manipulative sex to get their way . . . And when they do have sex, that's all it is. Call it what you will: a raw, physical act, or whatever; it's not making love. Sexual intimacy should be a gift from one spouse to the other; a glorious melding into one that should be treated with the highest respect and tenderness.

Then these wives wonder why their husbands aren't responding favorably to them, longer term, as they would like them to. Still, just like you said, scoffers will be scoffers, regardless of whether they're male or female. And it seems scoffers always are the last ones to admit they're missing out on the good things, doesn't it?

Yet I think I can promise you won't miss out on what so many other women are. So begin *applying* my coaching in your life. You will be embarking on a voyage of discovery that will enable you to better understand the yielded state of being and the power it gives you.

This state of being is so profound, and so paramount in priority and importance to a healthy and happy marriage, that I cannot begin to convey what this will mean to you, and ultimately to your husband, too. He can become as one with you, and you can become one in him. He can expand your capacity and release your flow to be fully who you are, the refreshing youthful girl you have always been inside. Whatever that persona may have been while inwardly suppressed for a lifetime will finally be set free.

Within a woman's yielded state flows a unique sexuality. This rises from extraordinary depths, and with it comes a greater capacity for intimacy and appreciation for life's passion. By the time you have completed this process, you already will have become an uncommonly feminine woman.

21 Exquisite inner femininity

I've been learning so many wonderful things about you! Especially recently, since you're letting more of the real you show through. And since this has moved us up to the next level in our relationship (where things are more serious), I think the previous talks we've had about the sexuality of men and women should be elevated as well to the subject of sexual fulfillment.

So please give this email your utmost attention, because it's a foretaste of what should be waiting in the wings for you. And instead of it requiring you to get a new lifestyle, it's nature's gift to you of a new *lovestyle!*

Some women seem to have a natural sexuality. Yet even these women experienced a learning process from early childhood, because they observed from the adults around them what worked and what didn't. Then other women, not so feminine, put on sexuality like they do make up, but it's better than nothing. And finally, with some women, sexuality is just not there, period. So the old adage, *some got it, some don't,* applies. But the new sexuality I'm going to tell you about works for all three types of women.

When most people are asked to define the word sexuality, they usually think of someone like Marilyn Monroe. There are reasons for that, obviously, but the sexuality I'm going to introduce to you is as far beyond the MM level as the moon is above the earth. (Well, maybe not *that* far.) Nevertheless, the sexuality I want to bring to you (as I have to other women I have coached) opens up experiences that are sweeter, and with a far richer and deeper intimacy with their mates. And like the moon, this sexuality is alluring and romantic, breathtaking and exciting . . . and beautiful.

Some might think of physical desire, or the act itself, as bonding with another person. But I'm not talking about a temporary rush or sudden upsurge of desire in an elevator scene shown in a movie. Physical desire and the act are just two of the many on-going benefits of the lovestyle I want to show you, which itself can only begin *after* the *real* bonding is set in motion. So the focus is on the oneness, the connectivity, the harmony, and the passion shared by two lovers as a day-to-day bonding which grows richer and deeper throughout the years.

Moreover, what I'm referring to is much more rewarding and longer lasting than just the physical act. It's a whole new experience for two connecting souls, a bonding of rare depth and beauty and awe-inspiring dimension. Unfortunately, not many couples know about it, and I suspect fewer still ever experience it.

I had to pause yesterday in writing this. I've been trying to reach for deeper words, vast enough to describe the above experience, but I just don't think I can get there. How does one describe splendor when it catches one totally unprepared and beyond anything ever imagined? The nearest I can come to it for now is that it is two minds and hearts making love, night and day.

I don't know, maybe I can get closer if I keep on going here. So let's try this: Picture a wellspring: it's yours, and it's filled with a never-ending flow of fervent passion, superheated from deep within your mind and emotions, and it has been desiring someone who has been desiring you. And like you, he also has a wellspring of passion . . . just as unrelenting and just as intense as yours. And until now, these two pulsating wellsprings have had no outlet, no place to go. But now you see that your outlet is to be his heart, and his outlet is to be your heart.

Can you see it? Like two vibrant springs of water; rushing together to find one another, flowing together to become one. Like two aroused hearts, once they knit together, accompanied by feelings of harmony and a compelling desire for the intercourse between two bonding souls.

It is not a raging, uncontrolled passion like fiery physical desire. (That can come next.) Nevertheless, the desire is composed of tangible feelings and passion; but it is a soft and tender passion, oh so romantic and gently pulsing . . . through you into him, and through him into you.

This is an intimacy most would never have thought possible, not even in their wildest imaginings. Yet, this is the very lovestyle I want to introduce to you if we should marry. Then, once we go through the experience together, you will understand for yourself.

I'm not trying to make this mysterious, quite the opposite in fact. As I said earlier, I had to pause in writing this email because I was unable to reach the words that would describe the above experience. After allowing time for things to settle in my mind, I have 'found' some ideas that might help us further along.

This level and magnitude of oneness can last a lifetime, to be repeated again and again. Each time the memory is stirred, recalling the events that kindled the first time when true bonding struck. And each time the memory is stirred thereafter, a desire that arouses the senses will rush in, demanding to be satisfied as the mind is quickened and the energy re-enforced, as if it were the first time . . . all over again.

This is considerably more than captivating power, even more than exoticism. This is soul-*deep*, heart-*satisfying* intimacy, a bonding every woman should experience with her husband . . . and can, if she will.

But *she* must be the one to initiate this intimacy. To create it, she must exercise a matchless and mutually enticing seduction of her man that is without equal. This sounds difficult, but it is not. Still, there is one way and one way only that this can be accomplished, and that way is through her ultimate act of femininity. (I will teach this to you if we should marry.)

Although the power of this ultimate act of femininity is beyond compare with any other act of seduction, nevertheless I will try.

Just imagine that the 'drawing' power of the seduction is on par with the force of electromagnetic energy pulling two objects together; then you will have an idea of its power to draw him to her, invulnerable to outside manipulation, such as another woman who may be trying to wedge herself in.

Are you beginning to see its highly persuasive influence? And it is entirely under the wife's control to use, as she will.

So it is *first* her femininity, not her sexuality that turns me on . . . and which will keep me turned on, year after year. Her sexuality will follow, but it will be her enhanced femininity that will first captivate me as it begins to naturally express itself in an ever-increasing voluptuous manner. This, then, will develop into a particularly unique expression beyond her normal reach to produce that very enticing seduction I mention.

What I am saying is that this particular sexuality is by no means ordinary. What electromagnetic force is? It will flow only out of her captivating power, which in turn flows only out of her bountiful femininity.

Where this bountiful femininity will come from should be the topic of another email. But anyway, does this sound like 99% of the world's women have just been eliminated? Not so. Little girls are born with all the seed-bearing characteristics of femininity that they will ever need, seeds that will produce more than enough fruit for any man's appetite that hungers for this particularly exquisite form of joining.

And what healthy man does not hunger for this? Or woman? So it is this characteristic that I want you to develop in full, and I'm going to help you do it, every stage of the way.

After all, what is a little girl learning throughout her earlier years while she's practicing and experimenting in her mother's clothes and shoe closet? Isn't a part of it the various ways she can develop her femininity, and through that, her sexuality? Consider how little girls will naturally pose for photographs. Look how naturally inclined they are to primp. Notice their natural inclination to behave in seductive and amusing ways, to entertain or gain favorable responses from the adults present. There's more, of course, that you could add to this list.

You can call me spoiled or hard to get or whatever you like. Nevertheless, that won't change what I cannot help. I am a man whose inherent need makes it necessary for the woman I marry to have given birth to that which lies within every woman — a particularly extraordinary inner femininity just waiting to be awakened.

This new and unequaled, elegant and refreshing attribute will flow from her as naturally as revitalizing water from an underground spring. It will produce in her a soft-like mannerism that mesmerizes a man and holds him spellbound, helplessly and permanently drawn to her. It will be so tantalizingly provocative to a man that he will be unable to stay away. And if her 'old' femininity rated a 5 on a 1-to-10 scale, this will rate her an 11.

Although this may sound involved or a bit confusing or even exaggerated, it isn't. Still, it's one of those things that cannot be understood until it's experienced. Until then, the maximum effect a woman could be having on a man will remain beyond her imagining (and grasp).

One would think having this power would be incentive enough for a woman to want to release her inner femininity. Unfortunately, not every woman is willing to listen and learn how to do this. But you're not every woman, so I'm hoping you will want to learn how to produce it for us. Are you? Are you ready now to get yourself really involved and more serious about developing the level I'm speaking of?

Earlier I said girls are born with seed-bearing characteristics. Still, those characteristics must be watered and fed to grow. They don't just develop on their own. You must grow and practice your feminine characteristics to produce the seeds that will turn each one into beautiful, sweet-smelling blossoms that make a man want to stop to enjoy their fragrance and get pleasure from touching their soft petals while he feeds them further.

All you need remember at this point, though, is that this power is a lot simpler and quicker for a woman to give birth to than it is for me to explain in one email. It's just one of nature's secrets. You've got to experience it to understand how deep it can go. But oh, how marvelous it can be for a couple! And so I'm hoping, insisting actually, that you focus and practice more so you'll be ready when the time comes for this.

Why am I so insistent that my wife needs to have this kind of overwhelming power over me? For the answer, just think of a man who carries within him an imperative passion that never goes away, never gets filled, never stops asserting its demands, and never stops torturing him with unending, unrequited desires. Then you'll know. Only a woman in possession of this power can release and then receive my passion. Moreover, with this power she will be able to strike her match anytime she wants to start my fire all over again.

My very essence aches to be satisfied by this power, but no ordinary (that is to say: underdeveloped) woman can deliver it. Believe me, I've tried . . . it just isn't there. So there remains a burning inside of me, tormenting me, continuously reminding me of the void within me that can only be filled by the woman who has the unique power to drive men crazy. With this power, she will most assuredly awaken the sleeping lion within me.

When I have more time I'll go into more detail to explain how such a luxuriously soft and pliable woman can make all this happen to a man. It's very similar — almost an analogy really — to the soft and fragrant blossoms that lure a man into enticement.

Meanwhile, you already know about enough things to keep you busy for now. And as I said, I want to help you with them.

22 Your input is important to me

Just so you'll know where I stand on this, there are many times I need to hear the soft, subtle approach and innate wisdom a woman would use to suggest to her husband how to deal with a problem. This balances out my more headstrong approach to things, and blends the two into what usually turns out to be the best approach. So you see, your insights, perceptions and thoughts are invaluable to me and *Us* – whether it might be dealing with an external problem or an internal disagreement.

I'm just saying I don't have to be the one who comes up with the right answer; my ego isn't that fragile. Actually, nothing works when one person always has their way, and "two heads are better than one." So I need my wife to maintain a vigilant eye on my blind side.

What's important to me is that *together* we come up with every possible solution, so that whenever a decision has to be made, the best one can be made. Anyway, thank you for being the woman who is capable of such a critical role, and for understanding my responsibilities to you, as well.

23 Resistance and discouragement

Isn't it amazing how resistance appears whenever people want to change something (including themselves) for the better? Whether it's to break a bad habit or to make a better world, conflict is there. Especially, it seems, wherever a husband and wife are striving to maintain marital harmony, one can be sure opposition will be there, too . . . lurking.

I want to talk with you about this, because I know what it means to run into resistance within oneself when trying to grow. And because you're now seeking to develop further in some areas, you're beginning to experience it, too. It's almost as if we have an enemy within our own camp whenever we start to improve. The camp is our mind, and the enemy is negative thoughts (insecurities and excuses) about why we can't do this or that.

The more we know about an enemy, the better prepared we are in trying to defeat it, and the enemy we call *resistance to change* is no different. Yet this enemy knows us extremely well (it's in our camp, remember?), so it can attack our human weaknesses in different ways.

Now I'm not trying to get studious here, but please bear with me a minute longer. Since it's easier to fight an enemy we recognize than one we don't, and since I've allowed this enemy to influence my life at one time or another, I know it pretty well.

So, moving on to the battlefield, our mind, we find that this enemy can attack us on five different fronts, because there are five human weaknesses that resist change. Four fall under the heading of plain ole laziness, but laziness can be overcome by breaking bad habits. Thus, if we as a couple are to make our dream a reality – in this case the dream for awesome marital harmony – we're both going to have to replace bad habits with good ones.

Replace? *Oh no*, to replace a habit sounds like work, and to a lazy person, additional work is horrible! So, we are introduced to the first of the barriers of resistance that is included in laziness, and that's *self-absorption*, where each person seeks his or her own selfish way.

The second barrier is *unawareness*, a particular friend to laziness. By choosing to remain uninformed to what needs to be changed, one has an excuse to skip-out on the time and effort required to make those changes.

The third barrier of resistance is *pride* or *self-importance*, where one acts without seeking the counsel of others (their husband or wife, for example). They think they already have it covered.

The fourth is *irresponsibility*, seen by a person's lack of growth when they consciously won't (or refuse to) replace undesirable habits with desirable ones. This person will say they just can't change, no matter how hard they try. The truth is: they haven't tried hard enough, and probably don't plan to.

So, under the heading of laziness we see four distinct barriers that can (if we let them) stop us cold whenever we try to change ourselves for the better: self-absorption, unawareness, self-importance, and irresponsibility.

The fifth barrier of resistance is *negative influence.* This is where friends attempt to influence my decisions or yours about things they themselves have never tried. They may tell you that you're out of your mind to think about giving the reins to your husband. They may think they're helping you when they recommend you not show your husband too much respect "lest you spoil him.'"

How ridiculous! No one gets spoiled through respect; it's too much pampering that's not good. Respect on both sides is one of the most key elements for a marriage to stand . . . it's the mortar in the bricks . . . and if you increase your respect for him, he will increase his respect for you.

Your friends may even tell you to not worry about "those little problems" in your marriage, because "everyone" has them. But always consider the source of these suggestions, because these people are missing the passion, romance and oneness in their marriages that a willing spirit will put into yours with a devoted husband. Perhaps they're even a little jealous?

They might even be like the person who learns of her friend winning a free, all-expense-paid trip to Hawaii. Immediately she begins making comments to discourage her friend from going. She talks about the danger of air travel, the crime rate in Hawaii, the bad weather this time of year, and whatever other discouraging remarks she can think of to talk her friend out of taking the trip. But then her friend tells her that she has a second free ticket and invites her to come along. Suddenly, the discouraging comments end and the excitement begins.

So always consider the source. Don't let others do your thinking for you or discourage you. Discouragement can kill our chance at glory and happiness. Instead, please stay focused on the higher calling. Once we've progressed far enough along to begin to taste the treasures and reap the rewards, I believe you will want to fulfill it far better than many couples would ever try. I know I will.

24 Men need to learn about women

You asked me why I've spent so much time learning about women. Well, other than the fact that women are fascinating to men, the short answer is: The more I learned about women, the closer I got to knowing what kind of woman would be right for me, and what I needed to do to be right for her. By this, I mean to be able to fulfill her needs and complete her as much as a man can.

Once I knew what kind of woman was right for me, I was able to devote my time to learning all I could find out about that particular type; i.e., what she would want and need in a man. Then, of course, I could set about developing myself into the kind of man who could especially fulfill her.

Not surprisingly, I discovered the only kind of woman able to complete me (and therefore enable me to complete her) is a woman who as a little girl wanted something similar to being rescued by a white knight and belonging to him forever.

She understands the multitude of benefits of yielding to that 'white knight' as her husband, and is ready to stop her exhaustive, fruitless and potentially deadly efforts to swim against the current. Instead, by *choosing* to yield to a good husband, she will be carried happily, effortlessly, and gracefully downstream on the natural flow of relationship.

Choosing to yield means to stop fighting and resisting and pushing against reality. It means to slow the rapid aging process showing up on a woman's face. It means to stop all futile arguments that bring both woman and man to the point of frustrated anger, frazzled nerves and exhaustion.

For those women who can comfortably surrender, however, it means that by yielding, they will discover they are now in step with nature's design that produces truly free and happy wives. Moreover, yielded women understand that consenting is the quickest way to real seduction and power, as well as their gateway to happiness. They have discovered that those women who are given to being cooperative, soft, and conformable are the ones who get the most favorable (and loving) attention from their husbands.

But again, as we have discussed, this must all be the wife's free choice, without any pressure brought against her by her husband.

Let's not kid ourselves. All women need (and certainly deserve) more than mere attention. So it behooves us men to be sure we're always sensitive to their other needs and how best to fill them — needs such as respect, real appreciation, time, listening, patience, courtesies, helpfulness, security, and nurturing their talents and desires. And all of these must be done with sincerity if a husband expects his wife to continue her soft approach. A man can't fool a woman by just "going through the motions."

Husbands and wives must remember that it's critical (on a regular basis) to *ask* the other spouse about their wants and needs — in the bedroom, living room, in public and everywhere — and seek to fill the other's needs first. By so doing, each makes the other want to respond in kind, and both should then have their needs met beyond expectations.

I think such attentiveness is important in all relationships, but especially for a woman like you who is just beginning to think about yielding herself to her husband, because she's bound to feel more vulnerable for a time (even if she's done it before, but now must learn to trust a new husband), at least until she discovers that because he can indeed be trusted, she's in the most secure place of all. This is what I'm wanting for you.

Now, about our last conversation, of course you are right; men should think in terms of what their wives need in husbands, such as for men to *be* real men (not just act like it when they want to). That means being a man even when it's not comfortable, like providing real leadership, protection and nurture for a woman.

To me, leading means to act in absolute integrity and with the wife's very best interests at heart. To protect is to stand between her and any harm that might befall her, whatever that might be. And nurturing, to me, means the husband should be aware of and available to his wife, sometimes to comfort her, sometimes to fulfill her emotional needs and sometimes her physical, and regularly to take care of such seemingly insignificant things as jobs around the house that she needs someone to do.

About these jobs, I think the ones that are repetitive (even such small things as replacing a light bulb in a ceiling fixture) need to be done as soon as they occur, *before* the wife asks. (It doesn't hurt, however, to wait until she can see him do it.)

I hope you can appreciate that all of this is quite an assignment. You can, can't you? Yet there is something more I think you should know about my past.

A number of years ago I joined a discussion group of married men (of which I was the only unmarried one). Our purpose was to read about things important to a wife, and then meet once each week to discuss them.

Obviously, for a man to be able to meet all or even most of what a wife needs, he must grow personally to become more of the man she needs and desires. (A real man is what she requires, not an immature "boy" who happens to have achieved something in the world.) Therefore, over several years we studied through numerous books and discussed them in depth. These were about being men of integrity, husbands of merit, and builders of marriages of distinction.

Each weekend we discussed a portion of the book that we had studied during the week, and talked about how best to apply it in our personal lives. As a re-enforcement, we formed accountability partners so each man would be responsible to his partner for his actions during the previous week – whether he did his best to be the man his wife needed him to be, as well as being a man committed to practicing spiritual, moral and ethical principles. When you boil it all down, these are really all a part of being the kind of man a wife requires and deserves. This, of course, is in addition to meeting her emotional, physical and spiritual needs.

Okay, so I figured that if I could become a man who could do all those things (although I still can't do them all), I could attract a woman who would soon recognize the difference between the kind of man who had been unavailable to her in the past, and why, and what would be available to her in her future with the right man. I was counting on her being a woman who would be willing to adjust her mind, direction and habits, from resisting a man's leadership to instead choosing to embrace and follow it.

If she did this, then I knew that she, already a woman of integrity, would earn my deepest respect because she would have resolved to live in peace and harmony with nature's design for a wife. She would no longer struggle against it as too many wives do. I also believed if I could grow into the man of excellence a woman such as she would deserve, then she would recognize that quality in me and not accept anything less from a husband.

This is why I have been studying so hard to learn what women want and need in a man, and why I continue working so hard to achieve it. And it's also the answer to your question of why I've spent so much time learning about women.

25 Men and Women, 100 years ago

Most men were called gentlemen 100 years ago. There was a reason for that; they truly were. Most men were honorable heads of the household and faced difficulties head-on. And when spouses argued, there was nowhere to go; they simply had to work it out.

These men were generally good fathers who spent quality time with their children. They were protectors of their family. They were noble and masterful. They had influence and respect. Yet these men were often modest of their own accomplishments because they didn't view themselves as more "manly" than any of the other respectable men in town. It was the way men were supposed to be, so they were doing no more and no less than what was expected of them.

You could trust a man like that. His handshake was as good as gold, his word as good as money in the bank. A man was gentle, self-controlled (able to handle himself well) and in control of situations around him. He had a positive influence on others and had their deepest respect. He was a great father and role model. His son could look up to him, respect him, and want to grow up to be a "real man," just like him.

Imagine . . . What if society expected this behavior from men today? How many men do you think could meet the expectations that society once held, especially for a married man with a family?

Well, all this about men is getting much too convicting, so I'll move on to women.

Most women were called "ladies" 100 years ago, because that is what they were. Men respected them and treated them as such, and more likely than not, those ladies were amenable in their behavior toward their husbands.

Women were capable, respectable, pleasant, and had a refreshing and gentle spirit. They were teachable, cooperative, supportive and nurturing. Many possessed a willing attitude that produced a youthful outlook on life and a richer, boundless femininity. These were women who, by virtue of leaving male-related leadership affairs to their husbands, set themselves free to achieve excellence in their femininity and pursuits. Their role model was the *Proverbs 31* woman (but women who follow it must understand that the 'list' is not all done at the same time. Certain things are done at certain times as a woman goes through the cycles of life). Today, however, there's a severe deficiency in both good men and good women; instead, much of "society" seems to extol wealth and physical prowess or appearance above all else.

To me, the women of earlier days bring to mind the essence of womanliness in its purest form. They were models that I would think most women today would endeavor to emulate. Instead, however, there are some women who scoff at the very idea of acting like a lady, and some wives who balk at the idea of leaving leadership up to their husbands. Imagine, if these same women today happened to be at a social gathering with the women of yesteryear, and the women of yesteryear were dressed in today's styles, with nothing sexy, which women do you think today's men of integrity would go for?

Ashamedly, the lowered standards set by many of today's men and women are quite a bit different from what they were then, and quite different from God's unchanging standards. But that doesn't mean our personal standards have to be diluted to fit in with society's lesser expectations. As for me, I want to be a man of excellence like those real men were 100 years ago. And just as certain, I want the woman I marry to feel the same way concerning her own dedication to being a real woman.

Now here's something from the FYI department you might find interesting: A man meeting the standards 100 years ago was sometimes referred to as being masterful ("dominant") or influential ("authoritative"). BTW, authoritative is not to be confused with the word authoritarian, and dominant is not to be confused with the word domineering; these are *not* the same.

Authoritarian men are domineering, dictatorial, tyrannical, oppressing, overbearing, high-and-mighty and bossy. They are never satisfied with another's efforts; no matter how well one tries to please them. Consequently, they make lousy fathers and even worse husbands.

Three extreme examples of authoritarians are Adolph Hitler, Joseph Stalin and Saddam Hussein. Sadly, these men dominated whole societies and ordered many millions of innocent people slaughtered to glorify their own power.

Some more "contemporary," excessive, authoritarian examples might include Martin, Laura's (Julia Roberts') obsessive husband in "Sleeping With The Enemy," who beat his wife if *anything* wasn't perfect . . . or she dared to suggest wearing a different dress for practical reasons (it was cold outside), then he became quite deadly. What about Slim's (Jennifer Lopez's) domineering and abusive husband, Mitch, in the movie "Enough?"

How would you like to be known as a woman with the personality of an authoritarian, like Adolph Hitler? Or to be called a female Saddam Hussein, or be obsessively controlling like Mitch? I know. These are dumb questions.

But this next question isn't: How would you like to be known as someone who is *the exact opposite* of one of these authoritarian or tyrannical people? You can be, because the opposite word or antonym for authoritarian means to be yielding or surrendered.

To yield does not mean to lack strength of character and conviction, or mastery and respect in one's position and fields of endeavor. On the contrary, some of the strongest and most admired women in film classics include beautifully gentle and yielded women like Nell in *My Friend Flicka*, Marmee in *Little Women,* and Esperanza in the original *Zoro* with Tyrone Power. Then there was Maria von Trapp (*The Sound of Music*) whose humility, willingness and determination to do the right thing in difficult circumstances drew the Captain to her; then kept him for a lifetime, affirming: *"I cannot ask him to be anything less than he is."*

And what man would not be drawn to the gentle and meek spirits of the romantic and alluring women in the Bible, such as Ruth?

Ruth was a young but widowed peasant who began working in the fields of a wealthy landowner named Boaz. On her first morning there – while she was gleaning grain (to feed her widowed mother-in-law, Naomi, and herself) – Boaz saw her out in the field and sent his foreman to get her. When she came to where he was working, he asked whom she was. "I am your servant," she said, and won his heart. Shortly thereafter, they married. As an interesting side note, they are the great-grandparents of King David, in the bloodline of Jesus Christ. She is written about in the Book of Ruth.

Then there were David and Abigail. King David took Abigail for his second wife, a very meek and humble, yet courageous and wise woman, who surrendered her will to the Lord and to David, once he became her husband.

But the first day they met was a time that, because of her bravery and the meekness in which she spoke to David, Abigail was able to avert a tragic moment during a time of severe and hostile feelings on David's part toward Abigail's husband. Her husband, who was a drunken, brutish man, later died, but not by David's hand — although David would have killed him if Abigail had not arrived to speak to David. There is more written about her in 1 Samuel, Chapter 25.

Then there is Esther, the beautiful and courageous Jewish Queen of the Persian King, Ahasuerus, who won his favor and saved her people. How did her acquiescent spirit affect her husband? When she came to the King he greeted her saying, "What is it Esther, what is your request? It shall be granted to you, even up to half my kingdom." He would have given her anything that was within his power, because he could trust her, he could confide in her, and because she led him into a depth of love he had never before imagined. She is written about in the Book of Esther.

All of these feminine women were the most powerful when they used the sweet allure of their yielded hearts and actions to captivate their men.

26 A game of love

You mentioned tonight that a lead/yield relationship was almost like a game. I hadn't thought of it like that, but yes, that's more or less what it is: A game of love.

In the "game of life," one tries to be as successful as possible by thorough preparation and making as few mistakes as possible. In the "game of love," the object is for a couple to produce the greatest amount of intimacy, depth of love, and oneness possible. There is only one way to accomplish this in abundance — the couple must have a relationship where they flow in harmony and unison, respect and devotion, and fulfill their respective and complimentary roles with utmost attention to the needs of the other.

Both "games" are extremely important. Because whether in life or in love, both are what a person decides to make of them. A person can drift through life, just doing the minimum to get by, or a person can take life by the reins and ride it for all it's worth.

It's the same with the lovestyle of a real man and a quality woman. Two very special people can connect and enjoy a superb love life, or else take things for granted and lose out on a lot. It seems to me that it all depends on how seriously a couple takes what has been given them, whether with life or with love.

27 Our relationship

A while back I allowed my emotions to become vulnerable to a cute li'l filly. There was no way of knowing at the time, but by letting those emotions seek whatever they might, they sought and found your sincere heart.

Not too long after, the feelings you began relaying back to me were not those of a woman with a half-hearted interest. Instead, it seemed that my emails and phone calls had stirred in you a wholehearted desire to complete the connection for a lifetime relationship. I knew at the time that you were very definitely beginning to make your mark as my "baby girl," because I could feel it being written on my heart. And just as surely, I was wondering if perhaps you had found your purpose as well.

I usually think things through before making a decision (one makes fewer mistakes by going slow, especially concerning relationships). As things have turned out for me in the past, it was good that I did. Although I met many fine women in the past, everything I needed in a woman to complete me was not there.

But of course, things like this sometimes take time to become evident, especially over the Internet. Nevertheless, I'm very thankful I got a chance to meet those women. I think it was a kind of preparatory experience to allow me to recognize the genuine article when she came along.

So now here we are, you and I, and you know how much I have desired for you to be that genuine article. I want you to be. I hope you will be. I know you can be. But a lot is going to depend on you.

If I seem hesitant, I'm not. If it seems that my feelings for you have changed, they have not. I just want to be cautious so neither of us gets hurt, at least no more than necessary. It's so easy to get carried away in the excitement of the moment. But excitement won't keep a relationship alive; excitement alone is too rich for everyday fare and is too weak to sustain by itself. Relationships need much more depth than that. They need everyday nutrients, too.

Do you want to become that genuine article? Or more to the point, *will* you strive to become her? It's your choice, because evidently you have all the ingredients that you will need, although not all of them have yet surfaced.

What I mean is this: you've not let go of everything inside you, and I understand — it's a scary thing to be vulnerable. Nevertheless, those things you think you're keeping hidden from me, I've already seen. So you need not think I'm expecting perfection; I'm not in some unrealistic fog thinking you're Hollywood's version of the perfect woman. (Who would want Hollywood's superficial version anyway?) Besides, a perfect spouse would be intimidating, as that would set an impossible standard to try to match.

What I am finding about you, though, is that you are much like a Swiss Army knife, seeming to always have just the right "tool" for the need at hand. Moreover, I like you very much. One reason is that you show a willingness to get into the relationship with me, and to dig for solutions until we find the best one. (I'm referring to those times when I'm not easy to understand or get along with.)

Although I'm not the type who typically gets lonely, I realize it was the man who needed the woman in the first place. In *Genesis*, God said it was not good for man to be alone, and therefore He would create a woman to help him be all he could be.

Now, here I am, having for several years feeling the deepest kind of need to give my love to a woman, but only to a very special woman. I think this has come in part from my years of studying women, so that the more I learn, the more I appreciate, and the more love I have for women in general. Women are so special and so needed by men — for just about everything.

So now you can understand what I carry inside my heart. Love. But it is becoming like an overfilled balloon, and I want so much to send it into the heart of another; one whose heart will then become light as a feather and full of joy because of it. This is why you can understand that the wife I need must be a woman who has the capacity and desire to receive *fully* the outpouring of love I'm capable of and would want to give to her.

This means that to make room for that love, and consequently me, she would need to get rid of any excessive self-oriented thoughts that she might have toward herself. Let's call it what it really is: the *me-me's* — selfish thoughts of *me, me, me*. Selfishness is a big killer of relationships, because it consumes all the room in one's heart; it doesn't leave room for another's love because it's too full of self-love.

As I said, my tastes require a special kind of woman. But not every person is teachable (whether man or woman), and therefore can't be taught because they don't want to learn. (Did I just hit on one of the barriers of resistance to change that we talked about a while back? Yep.)

The woman I want will learn how to use those certain powerful and sexy seductive qualities that will create torque in me. She will recognize my tastes require the kind of woman who will grow with me; the woman inside who wants and needs my help for her to be set free. This is the woman you said you wanted me to reach into and teach in all the ways unknown to so many.

First, however, you should be aware of the significant consequence that such a release of the real you, the inner you, will have on your heart. Because, metaphorically speaking, your heart is the seat of your attitudes and emotions – the center of your personality. Therefore, there will be some changes in the way you *feel* about some things.

Also, because the heart is not just the control center of emotions, but also of attitudes of the mind and will, you're going to change in the way you think and respond to some things as well. So get ready to feel and think and respond a little differently – with much more femininity.

If you truly know yourself and want me to lead, then after I've taught you those things and you've acted on them, you're going to meet someone entirely new and beautiful in the mirror. Furthermore, when you're in large gatherings among other women, you are likely to be recognized as the most exquisitely feminine woman in the entire group.

Meanwhile, other women in attendance may be pondering what it is you have that they don't (to so powerfully attract men). And although the world normally doesn't recognize nor understand those things I would teach you – such as certain superior qualities fine women live out every day in their standards, values and beliefs – the world's lack of understanding will not alter in the least the priceless value of those things that only a willing woman can possess.

So if the makings of that woman you believe yourself to be are inside you (and why shouldn't they be? They're inside every woman), then you, too, can learn how to recognize and understand those same higher values that lead to peace and harmony and weave them into your own life. At a minimum, you can become one of those prized, youthful-spirited women who, almost regardless of age, can create wildfires in men.

Meanwhile, you're going to find very few women who are able to understand and appreciate why you chose to please your husband by adapting to him. It places you in a different league than all the others who would be independent of and therefore unconnected rather than yielded to their husbands.

If you choose to become this exotic female, then you alone will be able to motivate me to achieve excellence. This is as it should be for a man around an extraordinary and deserving female.

Moreover, I've never met another woman like the woman I know you can become (at least one that wasn't already spoken for). You have opened to me a world of intoxicating delights that I thought I would never see, and shown to me an unattached woman who matches the woman of my dreams.

Furthermore, for me to have already given up the "chase" more than a year ago . . . and then to find her in you out of the blue . . . has been a wonderful blessing and an amazing adventure.

28 Winning the prize – our very own love story

How very sad it is! In all your life, you never got to have your wholly satisfying love story. In all my life, neither have I. Ours are two lives that could have . . . but didn't. Oh, how they've been wasted!

Two lives using up their entire travel through life to this point without bearing optimum fruit — in the most intimate, the most connected, the most blessed of all the relationships that can possibly exist between a man and a woman. Two lives that have failed to experience all the happiness and all the rewards that life would provide them in a blessed marriage.

What makes this even more contemplative is that these two lives *can* connect and bear optimum fruit, *can* serve one another in love and passion, *can* produce bliss . . . *if.*

Yes, *if.* Because now, you and I — at this very time and place in eternity, in life's overall scheme of things — have the opportunity to live out our very own special love story. We can enjoy what few couples have even dreamed about, *if* . . . we change the things in ourselves that we should have changed years ago, even before our prior marriages.

To live out our very own love story . . .

Have you thought about how those words sound? I have, for years. I truly believe that if there had been tens of thousands of attempts to fit two people together, never would there have been so many coincidences line up, to fit so perfectly in one place, at one time, for one couple, as there have been with us.

The total results of all our personality and compatibility tests are ringing the bell at a 99.9% probability of success. If we can't take what I believe is a gift that we've been mutually offered from heaven and make it with each other, then we can't make it with anyone! Yet just because a bunch of compatibility tests say we would make an ideal couple doesn't mean that growth and development aren't required.

And so I repeat what I've been saying: We've got to change the things in ourselves that we should have changed years ago.

I want to experience a true love story, and a wholly fulfilling one, *for life*, don't you? — One that will knock your shoes off? Let's do it! Let's not sit around waiting to see if marriage is for certain in our future before getting to work wholeheartedly.

You know something? If we did decide to marry, then I would want to be your magnet. I would want each minute with you to be a collection of magnetic moments, and I would want them to be the best moments of your life.

So let's get busy now. Let's do all the other things we need to be doing that we should have been doing before, so we can get deep down involved in our own kind of awesome love story.

Let's make it happen!

Let's begin taking the necessary actions now, full steam ahead, to generate the growth and progress that will produce a happy marriage, because (to borrow a phrase from Edith Schaeffer) the living art form of a happy [marriage] doesn't just fall down ready-made from the sky!

Included in this progress is trust in one another. This means each of us must be able to rely totally on the other to keep his/her promises to participate in new areas of growth, as needed.

I love women; I think they're fascinating. I would love to have a good woman to love, to trust and respect, pamper and adore, cuddle and caress, to be proud of and be best friends with, and so on and on. And I would hope that you would be that woman.

But, just as every woman can readily tell you about men's many, many flaws, as a man I also know what negatives women are capable of. I've seen it sooner or later in all of the women I've known.

Needing to change

Most women have told me that they don't think of themselves as needing to change, to go to work on themselves. But on that note, neither do most men. Most men consider themselves as near perfect. So we have the men blaming the women, and the women blaming the men. But the truth is that both need to be working on themselves, because both must change for a relationship to work (any relationship, but especially a marriage). Consequently, even if one spouse is growing but the other isn't, their marriage will be far from healthy or happy.

It's a universal problem, really. Most of us think it's the other person who needs to change, not us. We think we're perfect just the way we are. This is why I said you and I need to "begin taking the necessary actions now. . . to generate the growth and progress that will produce a happy marriage." And. . . "each of us must be able to rely totally on the other to keep his/her promises to participate in new areas of growth."

Why do you think I mention this twice in the same breath? Why do you think I believe it's necessary? It's because the woman I marry will have already begun working on herself long before I would propose, just as I began working on myself many years ago (and continue to do so). But for work to be beneficial, a person has to be able to recognize which parts need the work.

That's why I need you to tell me about areas in which I can be better for you, and vice versa. After all, is there any one of us, anywhere in the world, who can say we're perfect? Besides, can you think of anything else in this world that could be so fulfilling, so intimate, so much fun, and so exciting, year after year, than the marriage we can not only strive for, but also actually attain?

You know the concept (you've heard me say it in a dozen different ways); by growing within yourself you will grow within my heart. There, within the center of my protective core, you could be thriving in the perfect shelter for you. It would please me very much to be able to carry you in the warmest, safest, most loving part of my heart. There you could snuggle up so cozily, with all that you are. In spirit and soul, you could be "cocooned" within me and esteemed by me, so you could know you're secure *in* me.

Whatever your variety of moods, even when you're being defiant, you would know you could not be abandoned by me. Neither could you be unappreciated by me. And certainly you would not go unheard by me in each of your needs, including when you have a case of the "frenzies."

But notice that this is contingent upon my ache for you to live within the center of my protective core. Otherwise, if you're not living *there*, then how can I be all you need me to be for you? And if you're not growing within yourself, then how can you expect to grow within me?

Just to hold a marriage together requires numerous skills; we've talked about this many times. Then there are our personalities to consider. Just as I've developed habits of doing things in certain ways, so have you, and neither of us is likely to change much (if at all) regarding those things that are inherent in our makeup. We can be sure some things are going to clash — that's just the way life is — and that's just a minor example of things a couple must be prepared for.

Something else is required, too, for us to have our wholly fulfilling love story for life. And it's a very important something, because for a woman to be a contented wife (as opposed to an uptight, exhausted one), she must let go and follow the leadership of the man she wants as her husband. If she won't begin doing that before they're married, then obviously she won't do it later — just because a piece of paper says the two of them are now married.

Her attitude and behavior must be in tune with his before the marriage, else it's self-evident he's not the man she's willing to follow and release herself to. Think about it: If she cannot place herself inside him through the process of yielding to him, then why would she marry him, other than for selfish reasons?

You know from your previous marriage how good it felt to be sexually surrendered, to be taken — your body consumed in unrelenting passion and masculine power. Similarly, a woman must be willing to *give the rest of herself*, too. Then she will find she has gained even more, and discovered more about her own true identity in the process

. . . with the additional joy of identity in him.

As a reed yields to the wind, a wife yields to a good husband's guidance, and in so many appropriate ways, he yields to and leans on her, too. This willingness to yield is something most wives quickly glaze over, which helps account for the numerous women who showed up at the seminars and group sessions with troubled marriages.

Since it's up to the woman to choose the man with whom she will identify for life, she must choose wisely. It's the last significant choice she should ever have to make independently of him. Therefore, she has to know that the man she marries can handle the responsibility and is worthy of her trust.

She has to want to give all of herself, to *just plain let go*, although being vulnerable like that can be scary. Thus, she will need her husband's understanding support, tenderness, unquestionable devotion and assurance along the way. (He needs to be comfortable, too, in opening up and being vulnerable to her, and be able to place his ego aside to listen carefully to words of wisdom or warnings she might give him.)

She also has to know he's going to be able to meet most (if not all) of the needs a wife can reasonably expect a husband to fulfill. This includes giving her some sort of financial security A.S.A.P. Nevertheless, a woman who is happy because of the attentive and loving way a man regularly treats her is far happier than a neglected (or even abandoned) woman with a jewelry box full of diamonds.

An unusually extraordinary woman

What I'm going to tell you now is a very unusual story about an extraordinary woman. She used to write about how her devotion to the idea of yielding turned her life into days of beauty. She also invited other wives to her home and taught them the same principle, so they could enjoy the same experience she regularly enjoyed.

After her untimely death, many of those wives began blogging about the poise and ladylike demeanor they had observed in her during their visits to her home. They also noticed how, during the times her husband was present, he could never seem to take his eyes off her. He continually worshiped her. It was obvious that her attitude kept him totally seduced with her inner beauty, for she was not at all what one in all honesty could call an attractive girl. Nevertheless, she treated him like her king. And this made her king need her to be his queen, and so he treated her as such.

Now, what was so unusual and special about this woman? Just this: whether by accident or purpose, she had found and set the standard. Other girls who knew of her success would now look up to and admire and seek to emulate her.

Of her own volition, without ever being told, she had placed herself into training as a *wife-to-be* years before she ever connected with the man of her choice. She taught herself how to cook, clean house and decorate. She learned how to dress and conduct herself in social engagements. She learned how to communicate.

She studied the sensual things, too. She learned there are considerably more erotic locations on a man's body than one would think. She learned the various methods available for each of those spots.

She learned how and when to use them to give him the most pleasure. She learned how to "keep up" his interest in the game for extended periods.

She learned these things from books written by doctors, marriage counselors, and happily married couples, not from misinformed friends and trashy novels. She learned that being compliant is an art as well as an act, so she set about to learn and perfect numerous erotic positions in her body language.

All these things she did by taking personal responsibility and showing initiative instead of waiting to be told. She had gone into action regarding her own development. Then, when the right time came, she was well prepared to produce the abundance of femininity and other attributes so very necessary to attract a number of the best men from whom she could choose. Thus, when she was ready to choose the right man for her, she knew her chances of getting him were excellent.

She had become what some would best describe as an American geisha, self-taught in all the arts and skills of pleasing a man, in public and private. Yet she held back to await the sole recipient, the man who would be the fortunate object of her many attentions.

What was the result of her self-development? She ended up attracting and marrying a highly influential and desirable man who was respected by all who knew him.

From this woman we might very well have heard her say that talk is cheap and action takes effort (and sometimes a great deal of work!). Isn't it downright foolish how people will work so hard to get and keep a job, but work so little to keep the spark hot and alive in their marriage?

We can have our own love story.

This is why I say we *can* have our wholly satisfying love story, *if* I take the necessary actions that nature has assigned to the man, and *if* you take the necessary actions that nature has assigned to the woman: "the great deal of work" that enables a couple to connect in peace, harmony and intimacy.

It's easy to let things slide and take the path of least resistance. I should know, I've been guilty of that plenty of times. Yet allowing one's garden to be overrun by weeds of disinterest, letting them choke out the beautiful flowers originally planted there, is more than laziness; it's stupidity. So if you will work with me to keep the weeds out of our Garden, then I think I can promise you those days of beauty that she wrote about. You can do this by allowing me to lead while you follow.

Moreover, your faithfulness to this principle will arouse within me the masculinity to reach into your natural core, to keep you stimulated and pleasantly fulfilled. Your moods will be happy, too. Your creativity can be operating at full measure while you think about what you will choose to plant in our Garden.

Still, we already know of some things we especially want in our Garden. One is your exquisite inner femininity (unleashed, of course). Without it, passion, intimacy, and all the rest cannot exist.

You may be wondering, why would your growth in becoming softer, less resisting — and all the rest in this email — bring to you those days of beauty, while also sparking my masculinity? It's because I'm a man, and that's how we men are wired. And that's why, when a wife yields, it melts and seizes control of any husband, who then can give his wife days of beauty.

And that's also why we can win the prize — *our very own love story*.

29 When I first knew I wanted you

You've asked me to tell you when I first knew I wanted you. That's easy. I knew I wanted you when I read your first letter and your profile. The things you said about a wife yielding to her husband blew me away. There wasn't a single woman anywhere that I knew of that even came close to understanding the concept, let alone agreeing with it.

It's sad, really, when you think about it. A woman, by her own choices, destroys every possibility of having the very connectedness she seeks with her husband. Without realizing it, her choice to be independent instead of compliant makes true intimacy impossible.

Still, although I knew you understood and had chosen to be accommodating, it wasn't until you took the enneagram, the Meyers-Briggs™, the pre-marital and other various compatibility tests with me that I could be reasonably sure of our fitting together well.

All that remained, then, was for me to find out if you were as serious about *being* a willing, consenting wife as you had said you were. You know the old saying: *Action speaks louder than words.* So, if it turned out that you really were *that* serious, then I knew it would be a privilege to help you be the surrendered wife you wanted to be. Plus it would be an even greater joy to have you and serve you as my wife.

In thinking back, I remember setting up visualization for you to read and think about. I knew that if you responded positively (which, as things turned out, you did), then I would know that you were definitely serious about sticking to the principle of my taking the lead with you at my right wing. So it seems like I pretty well knew within a week or two of getting your first email. Still, it takes time to really know whether a woman is “ready, willing, and able” to be accommodative (at least in her heart) to the right man.

I remember it was during that time that I set the wheels in motion to be at least as reasonably certain as I could, considering it was still very early on. And I can see now by looking back at some things you included in your letters and we discussed by phone, I knew you would want to learn what pleased me. I, too, would learn what pleased you, so we would go together like a cup and saucer.

So yes, I want you. But I also want you to stay on track as best you can to become the person you keep saying you want to be, that I need you to be, and know you can be. And don’t worry; I’m working on me, too.

30 Being true to our roles

Wives remind husbands of their responsibilities, and husbands remind wives of theirs. One of his is to protect his wife in her vulnerability. Hers include protecting his blind side and stimulating him to always be the man.

Isn't it amazing how much more a woman can stimulate a man when she acts vulnerable, even when she isn't? Even such a small thing as standing on the top of a kitchen step stool in a cute little skirt, and then calling out to her husband to come steady her, can work to her advantage. Just as he arrives, he sees her standing barefoot on the stool. She is stretching up to the highest shelf on tiptoes (for an item she earlier planted there, of course, for just such a time as this).

Maybe the man knows that she didn't really need him to steady her, to keep her from falling. But then again, can he ever be absolutely sure whether or not he was being manipulated? After all, it can never be proven, can it? Women can be very clever that way.

This interplay between the sexes is one of the most interesting subjects I've ever looked into. You women fascinate me! You can be cunning as a fox, yet you need us and we need you. You want to see in us our strong yet gentle, manly disposition, predisposed to protecting you. We want to see in you a soft and pliable disposition — it drives us crazy and makes us want to be even more the masterful, strong and protective man who will watch over and provide for you. It makes us strive ever harder to earn your trust and respect daily.

Strong, trustworthy men and the women who yield to them

arouse, inspire, excite, and heat up one another, because this is how nature intended each to react to the other. She *"is,"* and he *"is,"* because together they *"are;"* they ignite basic desires in each other. The woman's willingness to follow triggers things in the man, things such as: gentleness, kindness, patience, passion, and loving tenderness. His acts, in turn, trigger things in the woman that cause her to desire and be fully receptive to him.

For them to experience *all* they were designed to be, to have, and to enjoy in their marriage, they *must* play off each another. Each must be faithful and true to their respective roles that nature optimally assigned to them as they work out together and adjust to their personalities and the marriage.

He must live out who he is. She must live out who she is. Unless they *fully* live out their roles together, neither role can ever be altogether fulfilled. Neither role can ever be complete without the causal factor of the other. Each is a catalyst that sets the other afire.

Otherwise, such couples can be just as lonely, unsatisfied and incomplete as if they were living across the country from one another. How unhappy is the woman who feels compelled to fill a leadership void left by an inadequate husband, or the man who doesn't have exquisite, soft femininity by his side and in his arms. That will *not* be us!

When a wife allows her husband to be the dominant partner, the two will eventually find their perfect fit. I say eventually because they need to allow some time for trial and error and other adjustments.

And if that woman happens to have a man who can be trusted to run things well, no matter what, then she has a man who can awaken in her a sublimely pure and vulnerable course of conduct. That manner of willing behavior, in turn, stimulates him to become very protective of her vulnerability.

Her husband's desired (and predictably masculine) response creates in her feelings of safety and protection. This assures her that she is secure and can move forward into a place of solace and surrender. In this comfort zone she can give herself wholly to a man who doesn't want anything from her, except her. Now she belongs to him, and he belongs to her.

Once she begins to rest in this security (which remember, she brought about by virtue of her empowering her husband through her yielding), a natural process begins by which her Adam begins to spontaneously glorify his Eve. And if she remains true to her role and doesn't short-circuit nature's perfect plan for couples, she will remain in her glorification process. She will freely receive blessing upon blessing through her husband and he through her. He will begin giving her more of what she really needs – abundantly more than she ever hoped for.

You've noticed those married women whose faces clearly glow with a beautiful skin and radiance, haven't you? They're the ones who are cozily nestled in nature's perfect role for them. But those wearing scowls on their prematurely aging faces are often the ones that are overrunning their husbands, or whose husbands dropped the ball in their leadership responsibility.

A sensitive and good husband can feel his wife's refreshing attitude whenever she resolves to live out nature's perfect role for her. Moreover, it motivates him to live his life for her, as he has covenanted to do. All she needs to do is rest in his care while also continuing to grow in wisdom, life-skills, and contribution to the marriage.

Nevertheless, I want to emphasize that a woman is a masterpiece of strength and capabilities in so very many areas that simply amaze me. It seems that a woman can do most anything she puts her mind to. So even though a wife will choose to depend on her husband, I gladly acknowledge that she has significant areas of strength and contribution that a husband just cannot do without. And if a husband is smart, he will show great appreciation and respect for everything his wife does for him.

As you can imagine, a considerable gap exists between a woman who puts forth no effort yet says she is compliant, and the genuine article who consciously practices compliant qualities, just so she can avoid as much as possible the power struggle between the sexes that has existed since the beginning of time. Because of this, a deeper level of her feminine traits is being awakened, even to the point that those desirable qualities become a part of her personality as each is exercised.

This is where things start to get interesting, because (as we have discussed before) in a social gathering of men and women, the changes that are taking place in this woman from her former self cannot be hidden, any more than a candle burning in an otherwise dark room. Nor can most other women who are present duplicate her transformation. Why? One reason is that her transformation is deeply embedded in her very nature.

You can see why I want to encourage you to consciously allow your femininity to evolve further. You already have everything you need to do this through the docile, supportive and nurturing qualities that nature gives every female to use if she chooses. So that means you can be clothed in that mysterious and exotic and oh-so-desirable nymph-like nature that extraordinary women have.

You don't need to break 'speed records' in your growth. After all, you already are perfect in my eyes — insofar as your current level of desire to yield to me *allows* you to be. So don't think you need to strive and strain to become perfect. I only ask you to do what I've been modeling for you, which is to grow for me as I continue to grow for you.

As you begin to give all of yourself to me, you'll be letting go, abandoning the negative as best you can — whatever your current level of trust will allow. When you do that by sincerely trying to yield to my leadership, I alone become responsible for the outcome. Furthermore, in a sense I become responsible for you, because you are central to that outcome.

Your part in this dance, then, is simply to be soft, yielding clay in my heart — the purest form of innocent trust — for in that state, a woman becomes the most desirable, the most sought-after kind of treasure.

I long for a taste of that day. More than that, I hunger for a taste of you in that developed state, for then our hearts' desire can be filled. We can begin living our love story in new roles . . . as husband and wife.

31 I want to specialize in you

I could never have gotten as far as I have in my business without knowing there was always someone I could be learning from, even if it was the newest beginner in my profession.

I can learn from you, too, which is what I want to do. I want you to be my center of attention, my primary focus, second only to my spiritually related activities. I want to specialize full time in you, as much as is possible — to know your needs inside and out, and know them better than anyone else you know. I want to become expert in my "professional" care of you. I want you to feel so safe and secure in that care that your heart feels as light as if it has wings to soar.

Ours is not just a relationship to me. It is my quest. I want to know more. I want to know *all* of it — about your "transcript," your history, your interests, your talents, your skills, your desires and passions, and the intimate, untold secrets of your heart. I want to know how you're going to respond to things almost before you do. I want my quest to be one of making your life a better one for you. All you have to do is simply make the decision to start trusting and release the desire to resist. The resistances will then start dissipating layer by layer.

32 The day you took my breath away

The day you first contacted me was a day I will always remember as a "10." Frankly, the part where you said you wanted to belong wholly to your husband in everything took my breath away.

You went on to say that your reason was so your future husband (and therefore your marriage) could benefit and prosper in every way. There's not another profile anywhere that I had seen that in. But obviously, you're not like any other woman. So yes, I remember being very wonderfully surprised when I read those words.

I received hundreds of contacts over those several years that I searched for a wife. (I was on *a lot* of dating sites.) Yet your profile was the only one that stated what certain men would know was the perfect attitude for the ideal wife. Although it's been a while, I can still remember how very deeply those words affected me.

I can recall as if it were yesterday how very attracted I was, and how peaceful and soft and warm I felt inside as I read through your profile (several times), and how pumped I was to the idea of getting to know you! I remember the decision I made, then and there, that instantly gave me tunnel vision . . . so much so that the thought of every other woman that had ever written to me vanished from my mind. There was only room for one focus, one thought, one woman . . . and that woman was you.

I remember thinking, right then, that although your profile failed to say where you lived, it didn't matter. Wherever you were, in whatever country you lived (it could be anywhere in the world, anywhere, distance wouldn't matter), I would pursue and find you there. Then I would win you over and marry you, the woman whose thoughts and beliefs aligned in perfect harmony with nature's plan for the ideal equal partnership for husbands and wives. And so, of all the women in the world I knew I had to have you. How could there be another? There couldn't, and I knew it! You were my one chance, my sole opportunity, and the insistent and increasingly rapid beating of my heart and the urgent *"don't mess this up"* thoughts in my mind, busily colliding with one another proved it so.

As I sat at the computer, crafting my answer to your email, I found it very difficult to hold back, to not allow an overly excited response that might scare you away. I dared not say too much, yet I wanted you to know clearly that I was interested (without letting on that I was overwhelmingly interested), that I recognized and valued your beliefs, and that because of them and you, I would hold you and any forthcoming relationship with you in the highest esteem.

33 Want to know what I think about?

Do you want to know what I think about during the day? I think about you, about how my baby loves the sense of exhilaration she gets from the gratifyingly positive results coming from her seductive power over me.

I think that as she works her skillful art to fulfill what she envisions, she also envisions what her life, as a surrendered woman would be like. I think about my baby loving the fact that, already, her power is showing an early and responsive return, and is only a small portion of what she can really do once I arrive there in person.

My baby loves the idea of how such a small, cute filly, Mixie pixie, hot chili pepper, baby doll (and who knows what all else?) can exert such powerful influence over her man with her potion. My baby loves knowing that already she's beginning to drive me crazy with passion for her; yet she has hardly tapped into her captivating power with its arsenal of sensual seduction tools that are waiting there, ready for her to discover.

My baby loves what she's learning about the power transfer, to which when "played" respectfully by the woman, the man cannot help but succumb, laying his power at her feet. My baby loves this perfect plan conceived by nature to maintain balance, peace, and harmony between the sexes.

My baby loves feeling like a captivating, sensuous woman, having now been put in touch with her inner femininity and told that it's okay to let herself feel like a little girl again (after all, grownups miss half the fun). My baby loves feeling sexy, and how youthful and vibrant it makes her feel, knowing "that" day is coming. She loves the idea of being chased and then caught, and fantasizes about what her man will do to her in that very moment of passion.

Because my baby is highly vulnerable, she loves that her exotic personality is appreciated and not abused by her man. She loves that his personality understands her intensely feminine needs and is exceptionally eager to satisfy them, over and over. As a woman, my baby loves the thought that I cater to those ever so special needs.

My baby loves the promise of hope that the future holds for a woman who is soft and willing — the most exotic of all women — knowing that as she yields, her fantasies can become realities even beyond her wildest expectations.

Those are just a few of the things that I think my baby loves. But do you want to know what I love? I love the idea of you!

I appreciate you more than you know — you exciting, exotic, sexy creature you! I could never get enough of you. I think I would always yearn for more of you, sooner, deeper, longer.

And although I can never do enough, I intend to try to show you every day just how very much I do appreciate you! I want to make you forever glad that you're a woman, and I want to make you yearn for me, as only a woman can for the one to whom she belongs.

I want to make your thoughts of me cause your heart to be filled with happiness, and your life to be filled with as many carefree moments as life can possibly permit. And so daily I thank God for my thoughts of you.

34 Misery and bliss

Since I've acknowledged my appreciation for your attitude and insight (about the fragile balance of roles we talked about for husband and wife), your new attitude lately has been a most desirable trait (one that men of understanding seek in a wife). Not to mention you're intoxicatingly attractive in both your outward looks and your inward beauty. One might even say I'm growing more than a little attached to you.

But then . . . sometimes the image of Mixie the mischievous pixie pops up in my mind, and I think, *should I get in deeper, or should I back away? Sometimes she's just so confusing. She says she wants me to help her grow, but when I do help, she doesn't attempt to follow through.*

Occasionally, my being drawn to you reminds me of a combination of lemonade and potato chips. Lemonade tastes both sweet and tart, and with the salty chips, it's hard to eat just one and leave the rest alone. So, the more salt I eat, the more lemonade I drink; the more lemonade I drink, the more salty chips I eat.

How much of this combination of sweet n' sour, misery and bliss can a man stand? I don't know. I guess I'm going to find out whether or not I become addicted to lemonade and potato chips . . . like I have to a pixie named Mixie.

35 I should have been more sensitive

I should have been more sensitive. Instead of making your burden lighter, I made it heavier. I should have put more of myself into your shoes, to see and feel all that's going on around you – relatives staying with you, out-of-state guests coming next week, the decision of whether to make a job change, your To Do list, your friend's surgery date, your list of promises to friends, and on and on.

Wow! What a heavy load! No wonder you feel overwhelmed. Who wouldn't? But it doesn't have to be that way anymore. Perhaps you can start reserving some of your personal space (including your time) by saying something like, "That sounds like fun, *but* do you mind if I check other commitments I've made before I get back to you."

Among the husbands I know, there have been times when the husband telephones someone back for his wife's sake. What happens is that his wife gets into too many commitments because she can't say no to people who ask for her help. So if the wife agrees, the husband simply calls, apologizes, and tells the person that his wife cannot do what the friend requested because he had already made a commitment for her concerning something else. And of course, that "something" might mean her personal quiet time, or time to spend alone with her husband, or family night to include the children, or perhaps a weekend out, or whatever, but always the truth.

I was impressed that these husbands protected their wives by using something similar, because these husbands were communicating closely with their wives about their mutual schedules and stresses. Therefore they could understand "overloads" and act as a buffer to help protect their wives from taking on too many things. And a wife could use her husband as a mirror in case her plate was getting too full. (And vice versa.)

Okay, so where does this lead? Sometimes I feel like, well . . . just when I'm about to pull a thorn from your foot, you want to jump up and go running out to the thorn patch again. You, like so many women, have so many demands on you from so many different directions, it makes a man's head spin. (Even if a woman were an octopus, she wouldn't have enough hands.) But won't you please use me as we discussed to help you watch out for yourself? I am concerned that you are trying to please too many people and ending up with no time for you, or us.

Frustrated and concerned.

36 You bring pleasure to my life!

You bring pleasure to my life, happiness to my heart. With you, life has been the best ever. As the song says, *"You light up my life."*

Just now I was looking at some of your pictures. One of them is where your sweet little head is poking out from under a white furry snow coat, with the rest of you snuggled up tight, buried under there somewhere. It's just one of the many joys I remember whenever I think of you. Often I look at your pictures (and yes, look you over), studying your beauty, memorizing your facial expressions and thinking of the sound of your voice.

You're mucho fun. The more I know about you, the more I like about you. Definitely, you can be a male trap: captivating, alluring and fetching.

In many ways I'm so full of happiness. I've been this way all morning, ever since you called on your way to work. I think maybe why I'm so happy is because you were happy, too. Anyway, it pleased me a lot that you called and said the things you did.

I've put so much of myself into you; actually, I've structured my world around you. You're like honey to my soul! I never thought I could love again this deeply, much less this quickly. It feels good. *You* make me feel good.

Throughout last night's late hours, I became aware of a feel-good buzz in my head, yet I had nothing to drink. I'm also aware that I feel this buzz most of the time, day or night, whenever I think of you, with all the emotional attachment that goes with that.

I believe this buzz is a result of my loving you, because I truly do love loving you. Loving you gives me a warm glow inside. My wish for you is that somehow you will come to love me back in the same wild and wonderful, no-holds-barred way, so you can experience the same marvelous highs I enjoy.

You make loving you the most wonderful experience of my life this side of heaven.

37 Dreams

Some happily married women I've spoken with told me that when they were little children, they would have dreams of being pursued and swept away by a very masculine man and kept by him, feeling his power and strength and never wanting to leave his arms (or dreams of a similar nature). No harm ever came to any of them, just feelings of desire to stay in his protection, securely and gently held by him. For some women the dreams have carried forward into adulthood, but with a more mature twist to the storyline.

Dreams of this type are perfectly healthy for little girls, yet I have found other women with similar dreams who have felt uncomfortable in discussing them. They mistakenly believed these kinds of dreams were bad. But the dreams are not bad; they are perfectly normal for those who have them. To say that these dreams are bad is to say that these women as children were bad. Yet as children they were much too young to know social right from wrong (their spirits would alert them of something if it was intrinsically wrong) — so how can their dreams be bad?

The rest of the women I asked who had already adopted the idea of surrender had no recollection of dreams of this type. Yet they were every bit as amenable as the others. They just had to work a lot harder to get there.

Anyway, it didn't seem to matter what any of those dreams were about, so long as the dream starred the right man. He was always a strong but tender man, and a protector of sorts whom they could fully entrust with their lives in every way with sweet surrender.

38 I want the same experience

You know how it is whenever we do what we know is right? We usually feel good about ourselves, don't we? And have you noticed stress is generally nonexistent during those times, because we know we're doing what's right? It only seems hard when it's momentarily uncomfortable or inconvenient, but we do it anyway because we know there is often a reward at the end . . . and then that, too, reduces stress.

The same can apply to a wife who shows honor to a good husband by doing what she knows is right by him. Negative stress can be nonexistent for her, because she doesn't have to live her life feeling guilty or torn in different directions, or experience her husband's displeasure. There's also a connectedness there, a depth of intimacy, and a shared joy of such magnitude that these couples will tell you cannot be understood nor appreciated until experienced.

Ever since I talked to these couples and learned there can be so much more intimacy than ordinary marriages have, I have wanted to have what they have. I want the very same quality of connectedness, intimacy and joy they have . . . and more, if possible. (Like Mary Poppins, *Let's go fly a kite. Up to the highest heights.*) Frankly, I expect to have it, else why go through life living with a partial stranger with whom you can never grow soul-to-soul intimate? Or for that matter, why be worse off than you were when living alone?

Some women will cower to their husbands not because they want to, but because they're afraid not to. (The men they married are thugs!) On the opposite end are those women who yield because it's their nature — they crave the effect it has. They love it; it gives them the strongest feelings of belonging and security, of validation and accomplishment, of passion and intimacy. Still others yield because they see the way society has been twisting marital relationships (like a soap opera) is simply not working.

Incidentally, women who "naturally" consent to their husbands probably represent a small percentage of the total female population. How small? I have no idea, but if you wanted me to venture a guess I would say around 1 to 3%. That makes a lot of wives who don't naturally yield to their husbands. And that means there are a lot of husbands out there whose wives haven't found the necessary fiber in those men to be willing to follow them. This is probably because many husbands don't engender the necessary level of trust for voluntary "surrender," nor have most of today's men been taught how to treat a woman. They just think shallowly and chauvinistically of themselves as "the man," (like I did 20 years ago).

But it would also imply that most women who have chosen to be compliant to their husbands have had to work on it, at least at first until it became a little easier and more natural for them. Nevertheless, these women are no less accommodating than the "naturally born" variety, and in some ways are probably more so, since they had to work for it.

So, we've talked about the "naturally" agreeable woman who has taken delight in being cooperative since her childhood. And then, of course, we talked about those unfortunate women who give way because they are married to cruel husbands, and would rather take beatings than to live alone or without financial support.

Between these two extremes are those women who are more like you. They want to practice yielding but find they often do the opposite. Yet at a young age they sought to be captivating to Daddy. They discovered that by being "pleasing" to others, their behavior brought rewards to them of one kind or another. Then as adults, these "pleasers" find that surrender is the most attractive, rewarding and sensuous path to a happy marriage. After all, what man in his right mind would not want the quality of a soft and non-resistive, cooperative woman . . . one that he knows can be enfolded in his arms while he thanks her dearly for her agreeable disposition and loving kindnesses?

Whenever a woman's approach is gentle, compassionate and giving, a man is going to feel within himself a tremendous surge and powerful desire to love and protect her, to give of himself for her. Simultaneously, he will also feel himself succumbing to her because of her desire to be under his leadership, to trust and find security in him.

This, then, is where it begins. This is when she discovers her awesome captivating power! And this, dear heart, is when you could be getting yours if you want the same experience as I do for you, and as do those deliriously happy couples I mentioned!

39 It's an all-encompassing arousal

I have a dear friend, a psychologist, who specializes in counseling divorced and unhappily married women. Most of her professional life has been engaged in doing extensive research into the subject area of a wife's attitude toward her husband – especially in its spiritual implications and applications. It may be that she has given more study to this subject than any other person in her profession.

She tells me that her advice to the majority of her distressed female clients is the same: *"Stop turning off your husband and start turning him on."*

Those women that do, she says, report back that they're feeling better about things, and their husbands are paying more attention to them, too. I kid her about getting paid just to tell these women about such a simple solution.

Although this solution sounds simple, I'm sensitive to the fact that husbands and wives can start growing apart under everyday stresses, stop really looking at each other, and get ever more frustrated, distracted and ill-tempered.

So, Mixie, how can a wife get his attention back, and make him want to pay her more personal attention? *By turning up the heat!*

You know these things only too well, but please hear me out. These centuries-old steps or ideas have not changed, because *men have not changed.* So although the following may sound corny to you, it absolutely works on a man, but only the man on whom it is applied! So do it!

Be mysterious: She can do something like giving him a hand written sealed note as he is leaving the house in the morning; ask him not to open it until lunch; or drive to where he works and place it under the windshield wiper of his car.

Be promiscuous: In the note she might consider coming on to him . . . strong. She can express her love and desire for him, and a pleasant anticipation for the coming time when they can find themselves alone that evening. For example, the note can say she is going to make him feel *very* good when he gets home from work.

Set the mood: Before he gets home, light some candles, turn on some mood music, and lower the lights. Put on soft makeup, let her hair loose (no hair products), and wear a soft cologne or perfume.

Meet him at the door: Be wearing something that will definitely grab his attention. Lead him to his favorite chair, take off his shoes and bring him his favorite drink.

Be naughty: impish, mischievous, playful, seducing him like never before.

Be inventive: add something new to her regular seduction movements or routine.

She will also give more and more of herself with a cooperative and willing spirit, causing her husband to often respond in ways uniquely pleasurable to her, which can turn him on even more.

Note: He doesn't need to be moving or talking to be seduced; if he's keeping his eyes on her, he's seduced.

I'm going to attempt to describe the process here, although it's going to vary among husbands and wives and the length of time it will take to turn a husband around. Some husbands change in days, others take longer. That can depend on the husband and how good a job the wife is doing.

I realize this is obvious, and it's more difficult when the husband is not striving for her trust, the trust that she has to be able to rely on if she is to give herself to him. But the sooner she is able to begin yielding softly, the sooner he will start responding. And respond he will!

The point is that she doesn't have to be perfect (nobody can anyway). The point is to make a serious resolution to do something, to be consistent, and to grow in showing appreciation for your spouse. It all starts with one day at a time, for 7 days. (This works for husbands and wives and softens hearts to open anew to the other.)

1. On the first day give him an inexpensive gift (from 1.00 to $4.99).
2. On the second day she can serve his favorite meal.
3. On the third day she can do one of his chores that he was supposed to do that day.
4. On the fourth day, she can do another chore, only bigger and taking longer — one he hates to do. (This is sure to make him feel humble).
5. On the fifth day she can recommend an activity to him that he loves to do (with her or just with the boys).

6. On the sixth day she can serve another of one of his favorite meals. And so on and on.

As the wife shifts from resistance to softness and attentiveness, the husband will begin feeling a "magnetic" attraction to her — call it an emotional arousal if you like, because it's a huge, heart-felt turn-on to a man. It may include the physical, yes, but it goes far beyond that in scope and power.

As it grows stronger, it becomes more like a feeling that pulls and tugs on every part of a man. So it's both psychological and physiological in nature. This feeling keeps growing in intensity over time, sometimes days, sometimes only hours or even minutes, to the point where the husband is spiritually drawn *deeply* into his wife.

Keep in mind that his change is due to *her* shift, in the way she has been both approaching and responding to him, and to what extent.

A good marriage starts with his decision to pursue her and earn her trust, and her decision to be a surrendered wife. The sooner each begins, of course, the sooner each will have the other responding. But following the formula above, either one can light the fuse to start repair in an already stressed marriage. The point is, somebody has got to strike the match.

Meanwhile, if her husband is a good man, the reaction on his part is often going to be humility and a desire to be ever excelling in all he can be for her. Most husbands want to be the best they can be for the wife who wants to please.

Turn him on

What I'm going to talk about now is not referring to a Stepford wife, or a so-called perfect, dutiful, or subservient robotic-like wife, or anything close to that. Instead, I want to tell you about something a wife can do that can often cause her husband to become mesmerized under her spell, which is to say *seduced to the extreme*. It can unite the husband and wife in a sort of mental, emotional and spiritual oneness, especially when the couple is deeply in love, as I am with you.

There are different triggers for different men, but for most men here is what is the most powerful turn-on. All it requires is that the wife sits back *quietly* on her heels, covered or uncovered (and within her husband's easy reach), looking at him in a position of soft surrender.

She places her hands on her thighs (palms up or down), or comfortably behind her back, Then, after a short while, without her doing anything else (unless she wants to increase the seduction through use of her hands to emphasize her body), if he hasn't already reached out to touch her, then it might be necessary for her to get up and do an erotic dance routine before returning to her previous position.

A few flickering candles (three or four) nearby, plus dim lights and soft romantic music playing as he first walks into the home will help. Perfume should be minimal, with little more than a hint behind each earlobe, since this area of the jaw moves and thus releases the fragrance each time you swallow. Wearing earrings are important, too. And if she is uncovered, then a liberal use of jewelry (including a heavy chain and medallion for the neck and/or a lighter chain to hang loosely around the hips) can be productive in the seduction.

Now, getting back to her sitting back on her heels, and not saying a word unless asked. If her hands are behind her back, then she will appear especially surrendered to him. All of this prompts a feeling of an affectionate intertwining of a couple's minds and emotions, a joining of hearts and souls more pleasant than any joining that has gone before. It's a most rewarding experience, with accompanying sensations far deeper and lovelier than I have the words to describe; but the result is incredible intimacy for a couple to share. I only wish we didn't live across the continent from one another, and unmarried, else we could join our hearts and souls in this sort of connectedness now.

Since in today's world a woman may have cultivated an ingrained habit through a perceived (and sometimes real) need to take charge, she might have begun to usurp rather than follow her husband's leadership. That's especially true if he is not a strong and reliable leader who has earned her trust, or he has provided no real leadership at all. So she might experience difficulties of varying degrees when she does seek to follow.

But as she makes progress, he should become more dutiful toward her, more trustworthy, and love her even more. The more willing she is, the more she will burrow her way into his heart and snuggle herself there; she will make herself a part of him that he cannot do without. And over time, she will have less and less trouble, because things will usually turn out better and better when she does.

Writing this makes me want you, baby, as a part of my life, but not as a part time part of my life. You make me want you to become a *part of me* for all of my life. You make me want to carry you and cuddle you and hold you close inside me, to want you in the most tender part of my heart, always.

I realize you don't want to waste yourself on the wrong man any more than I do the wrong woman, but you've heard the song, *Love's more beautiful, the second time around.* That's what I want to make happen for us. I want to provide you with the greatest meaning and value and connectedness in our relationship that you've ever experienced in your life. I want you to have the greatest sense of belonging and security in your heart that will constantly assure you that you have the right man— one who treasures, cherishes and honors you, and loves you unconditionally.

In a very real sense, God willing, you are now much of my life's purpose. I want to release my love into you. I want to be good to you and for you. I promise to forever be learning and growing in ways to become better, to listen and seek to understand you, to assure you that your value as my wife (especially as a devoted and exotic, alluring woman) will not be wasted on me.

Further, I promise that if you follow through on your desire to be a surrendered wife, then your purpose to be an ever-so-rare delight in my life will never be underrated. Instead, all your actions will have the utmost meaning as you fulfill them in me.

[Note to men readers: These are critical among the promises that your wife needs you to keep for her if she is to trust you enough to become your surrendered wife.]

Your devotion to me, your every gesture to want to please me, will not go unappreciated, and will be more than returned in kind. I know you'll make me very proud of you, and that you will flower and bloom in ways that will cause all those who know you to take notice of your joy and happiness, and especially your radiance. (Yes, even your mother will finally begin to like what "that man" is doing for her daughter.)

And I know all too well that your blooming is not your responsibility but mine; it will be in direct proportion to the care I give you, and the depths to which I fulfill your emotional, spiritual and physical needs, and your personal sense of value. You need only to show me due honor for this to work exquisitely, as I will already be committed and motivated to be and do all these things for you. My love is unconditional (agape).

I intend that your value, purpose and fulfillment as a wife, matched to your servant/ leader husband, will take on a splendid new meaning for you. I intend to continue to learn what fully complements and completes you in every extraordinary way. And I will continuously be looking for still more ways to fulfill such an uncommon woman as you. I will lavish you with such gentleness and kindness, and will consistently seek to prove my reliability and trustworthiness, and to remove any desire or perceived need in you to usurp.

This may seem to you like a silly supposition, but as you yourself have acknowledged, it's in many a woman's nature today to usurp men. Just by looking around us and observing other women, we can see how some tend to override men and take advantage of various situations (and how some men don't leave them many alternatives). It's a rare woman who chooses to refrain from challenging a decent husband's position . . . and it is a choice, a function of the will.

What I'm saying is . . . I want to be able to sing praises of you at the "city gates" and everywhere else. And I can, because you have chosen to work toward the concept of the "Proverbs 31 Woman" and you will have decided to be a wife who, by conscious decisions, honors her husband, and understands that everything she does and says in public reflects on him, his reputation and his character, as well as her own.

These past weeks I have wanted to deepen your sense of appreciation for the power possessed by the women I have been describing. It gives them an impressive and awe-inspiring influence on a man, as well as the stellar role in the relationship. There are other benefits for such women as well.

Simply by surrendering consistently, all of your innermost little girl/woman/temptress (and all the rest within you) can be set *completely* free and captivate me entirely. Then I will have quite a task ahead of me because I will be growing and learning, not only how to fulfill the physical needs of you, my one woman, but also the psychological, emotional and spiritual, as well.

(This is where I think so many men fail, because they figure once they've married her, that's it. But they don't realize that marrying her is only a stepping stone to the real relationship; he has to be able to swim with her for the rest of his life, and do it better than a dog paddle.)

In this regard, I have been attempting to provide the proper catalyst that corresponds with your growth, talents and pristine character through the teaching, leadership and guidance you sought from me. Hopefully, I have helped you feel free to grow to be all that you are — all that you have always been but have never been able to fully express.

I am having ever-higher hopes that if you will just be consistent and keep your eye on the prize, you will become all the woman you can be, and certainly all the woman I will ever need. I just pray that when that time comes, I will be all the man you will ever need.

40 I was saddened when we hung up tonight

I was saddened when we hung up tonight; I so did not want it to end! When you read this tomorrow, the emotions of the ending of tonight's call may have passed from you, but I'm still feeling them, and the ache is a long way from going away. I wonder, did you fall asleep with the same ache of desire?

Always I have wanted a "babygirl" I could hold in my arms. She would be someone I could be gentle with as I snuggled her body against mine, as our cheeks warmed and our lips danced. Always I have wanted a soft, feminine woman who would allow me to think of her as my baby, a cherished, soft, tender babygirl/woman.

Hearing the desire in your voice tonight for my companionship and leadership, and sensing from your voice that I'm already fulfilling you in many ways, were so rewarding to hear. They fit perfectly with the way you were so non-resistant toward me.

I was instantaneously turned on. I more than wanted you. I more than needed you. I'm aching inside for you. I so wanted to spill my heart out to you and say what I felt, all that I felt, that even though we've never met face to face, my soul is becoming impassioned with you.

Thoughts of you are present with me everywhere. I take you with me wherever I go. You were there beside me in the stores I shopped today. I thought of conversations we would have and plans we would make. I thought of places we would go, of magnificent sights we would see, and adventures we would take.

Yes, you are very much on my mind. I've brought you into my life as if you and I are already a part of each other. I no longer think of myself as separate from you; I am happier than I have been in years! And we've only just begun.

Surely I'm not making any sense with this. It's late and I'm rambling. But I'll send this on anyway, when probably if I stop to read it, I'd have second thoughts and delete it. Well, goodnight, dear lady, dear sweet, sweet, amenable baby.

41 It's not a fantasy

I'm a romantic fool. I know that. Yet I believe with you, we can make our romantic fantasy a reality that's as real as you are.

First off, it's not a fantasy in my mind that eventually you will be coming to me as a soft, yielded woman. This is something that is incredibly embedded in my mind. It's something that deep inside I held would have to be, must be, for me to be able to begin anew with a woman, and allow myself to fall into her heart with abandon. I have wanted to deliver my life over to her, and to serve her with all that's within me; but without her corresponding abandon, it simply wouldn't work. I would feel cheated.

So I need you to be that surrendered girl, that willing baby, that innocent, trusting and beautiful creature, whose mind, body and emotions I can enter, and commune with, and become one with. And I want you to become a part of me that I can bring inside.

Moreover, during those brief times when your soul was compliant it aroused me intellectually. Not just physically, but something far deeper that I've never experienced before. It's like an itch on the inside that I cannot scratch. Yet I know you can.

You would be such a blessing to our *Us* if your resolve to follow me would blossom to where you and I both know it needs to be for a marriage between us to truly work and to bloom. And although I cannot know how your present fight with fear feels to you (how can I know what another person feels), the thought of letting go and trusting must be very frightening to you, and I thank you and respect you deeply for your desire to work through this fear and move forward anyway.

You are everything I ever imagined, but I never really allowed myself to think it could all come from one woman. I patiently wait on the day you set that woman free with me.

42 Your picture

Thank you for your full-length Christmas picture. And since I understand a woman's need for affirmation concerning her photos; i.e., wanting her admirer to waste no time in telling her how she looks, I won't keep you in suspense. Instead, I'll just give this honest and off-the-cuff comment, but keep it as G-rated as possible — *You look like a hot little chili pepper doll !!!*

I noticed in this festive picture that your toenails are painted to match your happy-looking shoes; they're perfect for the season! And the oh-so-feminine toe ring is a nice touch. I enjoyed seeing you wearing an anklet, too, and bracelets on both wrists.

I have a theory — very feminine women can wear lots of jewelry and easily carry it off. You're definitely one of these. I think you could have been wearing even more jewelry had you wanted. I don't think it would be at all gaudy-looking on you, in fact, just the opposite.

I think you might look especially adorable wearing a choker-length necklace around your slender, graceful neck, too. I know they seem to have gone out of style, but boy, do they ever attract *my* attention. I just think that, tastefully done, a red or black velvet choker better emphasizes a woman's femininity and adds to her beauty. But what do I know? Besides, women dress for women, not men.

I love your wavy hair and the color. It's very attractive, too, just the right length to invite fingers to be run gently through it. I would like my fingers to slowly make their way to what I can see of those cute ears that lend their beauty to the earrings. I can imagine your face softly framed in a silk scarf.

Your lips are so full and inviting. And your neck is so slender and graceful; I would like to give it my kisses, slowly, all the way around. Such soft and feminine shoulders, inviting the touch of a man's lips! Your legs . . . *hmmm*, they're classy; did I mention wearing an anklet is a nice touch? And your feet . . . none were ever more beautiful.

This is just my opinion. But since a woman's body is an *objet d'art* that seldom fails to attract a man's eye, I think his eye should be drawn to focus on the main attraction — the art form — and not get sidetracked by the jewelry or by the clothing. The right jewelry is like the right frame around a painting; instead of competing with the painting, the frame should draw the eye *into* the painting.

Clothing, too, should flatter a woman's body, not bring shame on the woman. It should beautify it by showing it off in its true light, and this is what you have so artfully and tastefully done. In this way a woman leaves the best part to a man's imagination, and his imagination can do far more to enhance a woman's beauty than can sluttish clothing.

I believe a woman should be made to feel very special to her husband. One reason is that when she comes to *feel* special within herself (and all women need this, no matter how special they already may feel about themselves), then she will become *irreplaceable* for that man. I believe this should be a husband's lifetime endeavor, second only to his relationship with God.

Now, here's a playful jab back at you. The other day, when I said you looked younger in your recent profile photograph than your actual age, I truly meant it — I wasn't full of blarney. I was telling you the truth as I see you, just as I am now. *Sooo*, why don't you just breathe easier? You've still got "it."

Funny though, when a woman looks at a man's picture, she will usually say something like, "You look good," and leave it at that, as if a man's ego didn't need positive reinforcement, too. (How little most women know.) Yet she will spare no amount of subtle hints to find out from a man as many details as possible about how she looks, until she's convinced he's telling her the truth and not just saying what she wants to hear.

Nevertheless, if you would like me to "upgrade" the foregoing description of you by reducing and summarizing the five paragraphs to five words — something like, "Oh, your picture looks good" — then just return this email to the sender for editing, and it will be returned to you with the required text change.

Sleep well, my little girl doll.

43 I know peaches. And I know you!

You've said several times that I couldn't know you all that well because we've known each other only a short while. Yet almost in the same breath you've asked, "How is it you know so much about me?" You've said, "You understand me better than some of my own family; you know what I need even when I don't."

There are reasons why you've experienced, time and again, how I've identified things within you (thoughts, motives, desires, the dark side, the bright side, etc.) that have been exactly who you are. One reason is that I have you in my thoughts so much of the time. There are those things you tell me about you, your family, how you grew up, your childhood activities, the things you like – all of that.

I think about those things and try to imagine myself as if I were you back then as a little girl. What would it have been like had I been you, living in the same place with the same friends and relatives, and with the same experiences as you? What were those things like for you.

Another reason for my understanding of you is due to my study of women in general. If I were a connoisseur of peaches (and I do love them), I wouldn't have to bite into one to know generally how it was going to taste. Having been exposed to so many peaches means that I know how they "answer" to my touch, so I don't have to wonder whether a particular peach is going to taste scrumptious. When it comes from the best tree in the best soil in the best region at the best time of its season, it's pretty obvious.

You are like that peach. I know peaches. And I know you!

44 Behind doors number one and two

Okay, so what do we have here, folks? Behind Door Number One we have a honest-to-goodness, genuine *hot-chili-pepper,* my babygirl named Mixie. And she isn't going to change that (thank God). Mixie wants to be a soft and yielding female, so she can enjoy the security of being embraced in protective arms.

But that's not all folks, because behind Door Number Two we have . . . not just an admirer, but *whoa !!!* the type of man who caters to babygirls, especially this one. She wants to take the surrendered path and therefore needs a strong, trustworthy, protective-type man, because strong, honorable and dedicated men are known for making loving protective cocoons. (The well-known Meyers-Briggs™ psychological test refers to this type personality as *Guardian.*)

Sooo, folks, we have two people. One wants to be protected by a knight in shining armor. The other wants to be that knight. What makes matters more challenging, they found each other on the internet (what are the odds of that happening?), and now have such strong passion for one another that they ain't never gonna un-cleave once they attach. So what to do?

Shall we ship them both off to some clinic for psychiatric treatments? Or shall we just leave them alone in their happy "misery" of being co-dependent and therefore not "textbook?"

But wait, folks, it gets worse! She's not just an affectionate, accommodating type babygirl, as rare as that is. She's one of those that get their kicks through an enchanting, male-rocking, compliant seduction to seize power from their men.

Is this dominant-type man up to the task? Can he maintain her properly? Can he keep her hot chili pepper disposition satisfied and happy? For the answer, tune in next week, same chili pepper time, same chili pepper channel.

45 I couldn't leave you alone

Okay, babygirl, so all this extra email tonight proves is that I couldn't leave you alone in my thoughts; I had to write again. Or maybe it means that over there in your earlier time zone (now midnight), you're sending me private messages in your sleep. LOL.

What's going on? I should understand these things. I've studied enough about the dating process to know the answer, but all I know is that I'm so sensually turned on to you . . . your voice, your laughter, your personality . . . and your admission that you're as deeply driven sensually as I.

The other day my daughter asked what I thought was a strange question. She asked me if I was turned on to her mother on our first date. When I told her that I wasn't, she was surprised. (I guess she had read something that assumed all men are the same.) But now, here I am getting turned on to you without ever having met you in person. But actually, I've already given the reasons: your voice, your laughter, your personality, and your vulnerability.

For you, this must be exciting, to know that a man desires you this much. For me, it's to know there's finally a woman out there who makes me come alive with desire for her. We both may have to wear chastity belts, and hand over the keys to the preacher until after we're married.

I shouldn't be telling you these things, or should I? I want to be able to drop my veneer, everything, and expose my very soul to you. You're my last shot at ever trusting a woman. You're my last attempt at ever wanting to try again. The emotional pain from making myself so vulnerable has been very costly in times past. But with you, I'm again being that totally vulnerable. I'm as exposed as a man can be.

Why am I going on like this? I guess because I need to connect with you now, but you're asleep. I need to feel close to you. Writing to you lets me imagine you're there reading this as I'm writing it, so we're sharing it together. And I feel a need to be open before you, to let you know that I'm for real and want nothing held back between us.

I want to go on an exciting adventure with you, and I want it to last a lifetime. I want to burrow my way inside you, and I want you to curl up inside my heart. I want to protect you and take care of you. I want to hold you in my lap. I want you to stroke my head in your lap. I want to experience every fiber of your being, the mind and heart and soul of you. I want to eat of you and drink of you and never get full. And I pray to God that you will never get full of me.

If you hadn't contacted me before the dating site's free win-back days expired, I never would have known you had written. Instead, I would be taking a leisurely excursion into the mountains on a new Harley right now. I had already planned to leave the week you contacted me, but now all I want is for my life to be wrapped up in you.

Yet with this vulnerability thing, I keep thinking . . . *Is she going to blow it? What if we married and then she got crazy on me? She's a great woman, but what if she usurps me and wrecks what was previously agreed. Or what if she makes decisions without me that can adversely affect us both?*

After all, major decisions in a marriage have to be made by husband and wife together, since they affect both and two heads are better than one. She could make an excellent wife and lover and lifetime partner for me, but if she leans more on her emotions than on logic, then she's leaving me out as well as half of what's needed to make sound decisions. And if she messes up then she messes me up, too. So she's got to be willing to work together and follow my lead.

That's why I talk to you about coming to me first before you've made a decision on your own that affects *Us*. Frankly, I'm very impressed that you're not caving into your friend's admonition about Internet relationships and letting that panic you. Yes, that impresses me very much, knowing that you know your own mind and how to follow your heart.

Each week, I discover things about you that tell me you're an even stronger woman than I had realized. I like that — for you to be strong like me. But I also like you to be soft and yielding, like a flower that knows when to bend in the wind so the stem never breaks.

All I really know is that pleasant thoughts of you come with each new day. But there are also thoughts about losing my freedom to you. I would be rolling the dice, the same as you, betting on the other person's faithfulness and commitment to our *Us*. I believe what you and I have sitting before us is our dream relationship come true, something we've never had, always wanted, and always believed was achievable . . . *if* we had the right partner.

I believe you want it as badly as I, but how would I know you would listen to me and work with me on anything that could make things better? I know and understand (trust me, baby, I really do understand) that you want a relationship between equals. Equals, but with different roles: husband and wife roles, not overlord and peon roles, and certainly not master and slave roles.

Still, if the husband is to lead, then I should lead. If the wife is to follow, then you should follow my lead but at my side giving suggestions, not behind. If we're both occupied with doing our own roles well, we'll seldom have occasion to feel friction between us. And remember, a yielded woman is a real turn-on to a man. What better way can you get me to succumb to you than to be the soft, glorious creature God created you to be? Moreover, you will perfect me as you allow me to glorify you!

You will have allowed me full entrance into your body, mind, emotions and spirit, and we will be one, no longer separate. Imagine the intimacy! Imagine the thrill! Imagine the security you will feel in such a jointly created garden of physical and emotional and spiritual ecstasy!

You, the woman, are the conduit through whom God designed such relationships to be formed. Through you, it can happen! I can plant the seeds of love and devotion and respect and caring and protection. But yours is the soil that will grow the seeds.

Interestingly, when we hear the word glorify, it's normally associate with hymns of praise toward God, in the sense that glorify means to exalt (Him) to the heavens, to extol praises. So if one used the word glorify in this sense when speaking of a person or thing, then obviously that would be sacrilegious, since it would be showing disrespect or irreverence toward God. But glorify is also used in another sense, which is not to exalt, but rather to beautify and adorn, praise and enrich a person or thing. That's the sense in which I'm using it here, and that's what I think a man should do for his wife. What a blessing I will then receive by glorifying you.

As you said about me the other night, quite honestly, I've got a lot of faults. I do! But two faults I *don't* have and at which I'm able to excel are leadership and loving a woman tenderly. You're that woman, and I've chosen to love you tenderly, with all my heart and soul. And so I do love you . . . but not even a tiny fraction of what my love can grow into when I see you and hold you, and watch your antics, and have the blessing to know you ever better. That's when I'm going to fall in love with the whole package and not just the personality. And then, if you and I are ready, that's when we'll be able to introduce you as Mrs. Adam Andava.

Funny, I see that name and don't even feel trapped or skittish. You must be quite a woman for me to consider exchanging my freedom for a commitment to another person for life. But oh my, what a person! Actually, you have the most wonderful potential of any woman I've ever met. Only let me help you set it free, to fully release the youthful girl in you, by helping you to relax your grip and just simply and fully trust me. Allow your youthful-spirited woman to gain supremacy without fear. Then we can be equal partners, enjoying perfect balance and peace and harmony, and you can be at one with your inner self, your spirit.

There is so very much I have written for forums and such about God's plan for the wife's glorification through her husband. And we have talked about how he is to nourish his wife daily, administering to her to keep her richly bathed in his pool of love for her. Hours and hours could be preached on this subject from all the notes I wrote from multiple scripture passages — I wish my hard drive hadn't crashed.

But maybe it happened so that you and I can write it again, only together in real life experiences, instead of my having to write about what truly yielded women already know and enjoy. How exciting that would be to me, to take your words, your wisdom, experience and ideas, and put them to paper for all to read for the betterment of their marriages.

I would love to prime you with affection and devotion that would keep you contentedly in bliss. I would love that nothing could disturb you from enjoying an emotional outpouring of happiness in your heart to be expressed from your lips — something I could write about so that other women could know how to experience what you experience. I would like to feel like a musical instrument in your hands, with you playing the music through me; but I would whisper words of love to you instead of musical notes.

I have told you before that you have the most wonderful potential for me of any woman I have ever met. You have a passionate and youthful (girl's) demeanor. You have deep reserves of emotions and want to connect with mine. You are intelligent and know how to use that intelligence. You are listening and learning more about how to excite a man, and how to be "hands on" and playful. And you are sexy. But most importantly, you know it.

I found something strangely shocking when I asked numerous women on the various dating sites if they thought of themselves as sexy. Almost everyone said they didn't think they were sexy. I don't think they were just trying to be humble, I think they truly didn't see themselves as sexy. But those few women who did believe themselves to be sexy held onto that feeling despite their figures, size and weight.

And the fact that they believed in themselves did indeed make them come across as sexy.

Anyway, back to your potential. You have the know-how and the desire to feel and look pretty for your man. You appreciate nice clothes and understand styles. You are already fairly open with me, truthful and direct (whenever I ask the right questions), and so many other wonderful things . . . but you already know what they are.

I hope that someday you'll be established as that most beautiful of all blossoms as you continue to allow me to be your gardener. I want and expect you to hold me accountable to you; to always strive to be the best qualified to deserve such an honor as tending you. I would enjoy nothing better each day than providing care for you with my gentle, reasonable and purposeful direction, with my words and actions, eyes and touch, praises and prayers, and showing you off to the world at every opportunity; i.e., to glorify you.

Well, when I began this email it was because I wanted more of you, our talk was wonderful but I just didn't want it to end. Writing all this has helped me to connect with you again, although it's now past six a.m. over there. You're sleeping soundly while I finish banging away at this keyboard, and I can't believe I've been writing for this long.

Anyway, although I miss you because we're apart, still, there's a connectedness between us I've never felt before. Furthermore, and this may seem strange, even though there have been lonely times, I don't feel like I've ever been without you — even from the beginning. Every morning I wake up with you. Every night I go to sleep with you. In between, I carry you inside me wherever I go. There has never been emptiness between us, and there never need be. You are always with me.

46 Her security ~ his responsibility

I keep imagining how lovely it could be if you were further along in your commitment that you made to me. You could be sheltered, resting comfortably and safely with me. I visualize you in the palm of my hand — no fear, no worry, no need to control.

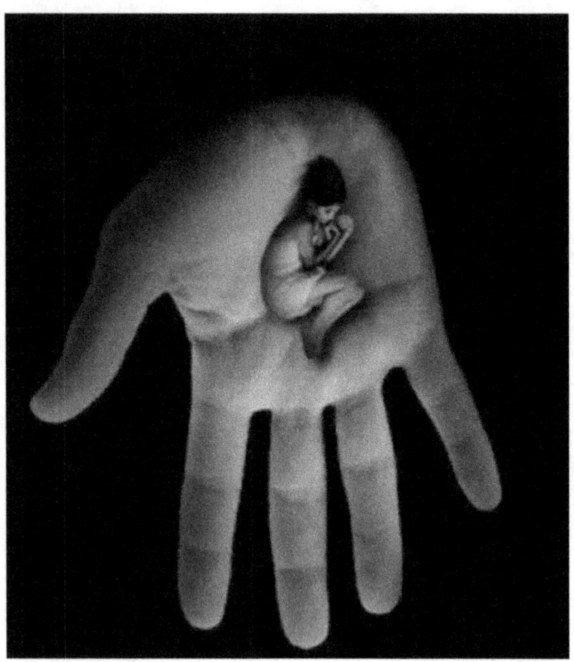

Her Security – His Responsibility

Imagine this: Let's say your emotions were to get you all confused (as can happen to anyone when they are overwhelmed or stirred up). If you were to try to crawl over the side of my hand, endangering yourself, I would cup my hand to cause you to gently roll back into the safety of the center of my palm. If you were to get crazy on us and try to run away, I would come get you, pick you up in my arms and rock you. I would speak gentle things to you, kissing and caressing you. And when your body became limp and too weak to resist, I would gather you up in my arms, carry you back home with me, and make love to you again.

47 You could be in loving hands

Yes, you could be in loving hands — a place of intimacy, security and peace . . . where every woman can be who has a man she can trust and chooses to allow that man to lead.

If you were fully yielded to that leadership right now, you could be living a fairly carefree life, and so much more. Since a wholly surrendered attitude triggers the nurturing button of a man, his desire and instinct kick in to properly care for and protect his woman. He wants to give her an environment suitable for her. In turn, his especial care and protection cause her to want to trust him even more. Tonight, I want to focus on the trusting part.

Trust never should be freely granted on a whim. Trust should be earned; a person's trustworthiness should be proved. Unfortunately, however, because of their very nature, naturally compliant women often place their trust in the wrong men. Generally these women will make mistake after mistake in their decisions, especially concerning relationships, because they rush too quickly into what usually ends up being disastrous for them. Yet when one relationship ends, they often want to be in another as soon as possible.

Not so with you, however. Since your late husband passed several years ago, you've been able to work through the grieving process. Your thoughts and emotions have had time to settle, and the ample time you've taken has gained you a clear perspective of the road ahead. So here you are today, seeking a fresh and distinctly unique intimacy unlike any other, one so new to you that it requires growth in your understanding and development of your inner nature. An intimacy I would think all wives would want, but only a special few seem to be willing to let go of the bad so they can have the good.

Already you've learned much about the youthful girl within. We've talked about her role and purpose. We've talked about how she will bring a carefree and cheerful facet to your life. We've talked about how to set her free so you can be living life to the fullest through her. We've discussed how, by not fighting with one's husband, the girl inside is realized, released and allowed to "soar."

This essentially lifts the lid, removes the ceiling and makes everything in a woman's life look brighter and clearer. Nothing about her is negative. Everything about her is lovely and vivacious, and the environment she will provide to you is so much better than the undeserved one you lived before. Thus every new day you delay is another beautiful day lost that your youthful girl within could have given you, had you allowed her to be free.

I know to trust completely feels like high risk to you, especially considering the previous marriage you endured. There's the fear you've carried forward, too, not just from the marriage, but all the way back from your childhood. It's not easy to let go of the controls.

In my efforts to gain your trust, I realize, and openly and freely admit, I've never walked in your shoes. I have had some leaders fail me, however. So I am committed to putting forth my best efforts to have the infinite patience required to gain the trust that can be so easily broken with one mistake.

Being a man I forget how difficult it must be making the choice several times a day, to leave the reins in the hands of another human. If only so many emotional 'scrapes and bruises' didn't happen from the beginning of our lives that create mental caution 'flags,' the two concepts of trusting and leadership (so easy to explain in words) would not be so tremendously difficult to do on a daily basis.

Yet this is why I keep encouraging you to not only read the writings of happily married, surrendered women, but to also take action on what you're reading. These women have extensive knowledge and experience that have produced in them wisdom, and they help provide the assurance that, with the right husband, a trusting wife is a lot healthier and happier than a controlling one.

Now that they are yielded to the leadership of husbands they can trust — husbands who respect them and value their wishes, opinions and areas of expertise — these women have a foundation, secure and established. Now they truly are liberated women. They have more understanding, more insight, and more discernment. They see and feel things differently than a woman opposed to her husband's leadership, whose lives have more chaos and confusion. Instead, in their security and relative calm, they can see and feel through wiser eyes and hearts.

My desire, then, is for you to become as they are, with the confidence, freedom and security that will allow you to soar. I only pray that I might engender the necessary level of trust to become the man who then is to lead as your husband.

It would be my pleasure to help you release that youthful girl inside, to see her joyfully burst forth, never to be confined again. You can stop suppressing her. You can, instead, be enjoying an inner renewal and newfound peace by allowing her to come forth.

God said it's not good for man to be alone, but I believe the converse is true, too, that it's not good for a woman to be alone, either. We are made for companionship, for human touch with meaningful relationship, and to share our burdens; there are too many of those in this life, and it's too hard to go it alone. That's why a husband and wife have each other to lean on during those difficult times.

So I'm asking that you get more of your feet wet than just one toe. I'm asking you to continue to follow my lead, just as you have been, but to follow all of it, not just the part that you would have chosen to do anyway. Ask me questions about things; let's discuss new things you're learning, and any questions you have about my role and me. In other words, I'm not suggesting anything different from the path we've been on all along. I'm here to help us move forward.

48 You give me pure joy

Let me tell you something, if I could go back 20 years and you were available, I would look for you. But somehow if I found you, I would know very little about how to appreciate you and take care of you. I would not deserve you; I would not be worthy of you. Back then my knowledge and understanding of women was disgustingly limited, and my finesse around women of class was even worse.

Today my affinity with women is not the same as it was 20 years ago; neither is my knowledge and understanding. Those same years were well spent reading and asking and listening and observing.

So to have you in my life today, every day, every hour, is pure joy. It's the most exciting activity I've ever experienced this side of heaven. It's glorious; it just keeps on keeping on.

It's as if you live in my mind. Wherever I go, I imagine you're there with me. In both my dreams and my fantasies, my eyes drink in your beauty wherever we are. The feelings I experience, *ahhh*, those feelings . . . they're so special, because you're so special. You are my joy, my happiness, my ongoing reward. You are a masterpiece given to me for a lifetime of enjoyment.

What would I do without you, without the pure joy you give me? There's a song I keep hearing in my mind, the words of which perfectly describe what's going on inside me. It's called, *The Very Thought Of You:*

The very thought of you, and I forget to do
The little ordinary things that everyone ought to do.
I'm living in a kind of daydream, I'm happy as a king;
And foolish though it may seem, to me that's everything.

The mere idea of you, the longing here for you,
You'll never know how slow the moments go
'Till I'm near to you.

I see your face in every flower,
Your eyes in stars above...
It's just the thought of you,
The very thought of you, my love.

Every day I carry these thoughts of you, because, like you, they give me pure joy.

49 Would I make a good wife?

You asked me tonight if I thought you would make a good wife. Maybe you were just flirting with me, nevertheless that's a good question to ask oneself: *Would I make a good spouse?*

But that's not the question you asked. You're asking what I think. Still, it's one of those "loaded" questions that's best answered by the one asking it. After all, you know yourself better than I do, especially what you're like to live with day in and day out.

Anyway, let me first word your question a little differently: *Will* you make a good wife? And my answer to that question is, *Yes, definitely!* I think you will make a good wife, a wonderful wife! But there's an *if* attached.

Although I love you just the way you are, that doesn't mean I could marry and stay married to you without both of us reaching a certain point, because I know myself. What if for some reason one of us decided to stop growing and learning about the other, about how best to understand and respond attentively to the other, and just level off at the place we are now? I don't want us to contribute to the statistic of over 2/3 of second-marriages that fail in the U.S.

So, yes, you would make a wonderful wife, but growth is required, and that's the *if*. I don't want you to think I'm looking for Hollywood's illusion of a perfect woman, any more than I want you to think that I'm anything different from the man I am: a little rough around the edges and flawed from the get go. I just want us to be realistic about who we are. That way we're not self-deceived by whom we "dream up" the other person to be, and then suddenly become disenchanted.

Being someone's husband or wife is one of life's major roles; it requires the very best a person can give of themselves to their spouse. It requires study and practice. It requires concentration, dedication, reliability and consistency. It requires lots of giving and forgiving. It requires improvement. It requires . . . growth.

As my wife, you would be the one person to whom I would be the most vulnerable, and as such, you could do me much good, or if you chose, much harm. This is because I would be inviting you to be my soul mate and life partner, and therefore a part of all my plans and activities throughout our life that would affect you the same as me (and in some areas more). I have already allowed you to enter the innermost, intimate part of my mind and heart; at this point I would be devastated if you hurt me.

Let's say, for example, that as a married couple we were discussing a plan to do something affecting us both. Before making a decision, I would be seeking your active participation: your wisdom and insights, your fresh ideas, preferences, intuition, decision factors, recommendations, etc.

But what if I then had to make a decision that you weren't particularly happy with? A decision that I believed was the only correct choice, given all our discussions and the decision factors we had to work with? Would you be able to support me in that decision? Or, what if, after I made and implemented that decision, you countermanded it, although I had already committed people and things and money to a certain course of required action? What would happen? A train wreck, probably.

You must know that I *want* and *need* to hear what you have to say, loud and clear, as we discuss any and all matters! I need *all* your valued thoughts, intuition and insight. I may have your back, but you would have my "blind side." That's what respectful and attentive life partners share, and it's one of the many important contributions husband and wife should make.

What I saying is that behind closed doors, it's important that we are both free to speak openly and candidly, to present our ideas, recommendations and analysis, but once a decision is made and we emerge through the door, we must speak with "one voice." I need you to support that decision. Nothing else will work, in a marriage, a family or a business.

In other words, please don't do anything that would hurt our *Us*. Instead, if you will be like the sea grass that sways in the high winds, but never breaks because it never resists, and I, your strong Knight who seeks truth and good for his fair maiden, then we can remain strong, mutually committed and at peace.

Along with good times will always come the bad times, too — the kind that no one can foresee or prevent. So we must work together as teammates, not opponents. You'll be allowing me to love, trust, and respect you all the more. Moreover, through your tender support and cooperation, you'll be empowering me to do things for you that will give you the deepest kind of wonderfully satisfying and intimate emotional experiences. That I can promise.

But never forget that through it all, I will be constant in loving you *unconditionally*. With faith in God and in the power of our mutual covenant, we know we can work through anything.

We have been created to enjoy the most intimate experiences as husband and wife. As your trust in me grows, so will the depth of your abandon, and hence, our enjoyment. It cannot help but affect how demonstrative I feel, too, as we all respond naturally to warm invitations far more spontaneously than to someone lukewarm. And how can a person perform at their best if their own partner doesn't trust them? Trust is a major player in marriage relationships, especially mutual trust.

Something else that needs to be trusted is logic. Just as emotions keep logic in check, sometimes logic can help keep frenzied emotions in check – and they can flare on either side. While women are generally considered the more emotional, a man has emotions, too. Whether man or woman, either can sometimes make a rash decision – we've all allowed our emotions to control our behavior and done things at times that we later wished we hadn't. That's why a couple needs each other in these times, to prevent or to soothe the spouse with the out of control emotions. So if either of us have emotions that conflict with logic at a time when our emotions cannot support the case we are trying to make, then we need to be able to trust the logic.

Anyway, your question about making a good wife has almost everything riding on whether you would be the trusting copilot and allow me to be the pilot. I've been digging through numerous articles I've been waiting to send to you – all of them by wives in exceptionally satisfying relationships. That is, wives who are secure in their role as the willing wife of an especially loving, supportive and trustworthy husband. These articles contain customs, traditions and manners that have been in repeated use for centuries, passed down from generation to generation. Why? It's because these things work, bonding marriages into the strongest and hottest kind of love, spiritually and sexually and emotionally.

Husbands and wives *must have* this to satisfy their core natures, their inner cravings for the marital roles each was created to fulfill for ultimate harmony, security and bliss. That's why I want this deepest kind of relationship with my wife; I won't be happy with anything less, which is why I tell you these things.

50 The ultimate lovestyle

In the beginning you came to me with an unsatisfied yearning. No, more than a yearning, it was a passionate craving. Furthermore, you were troubled because you were unable to identify its cause, and the source. You knew only that there was a feeling of incompleteness that refused to go away, a gnawing frustration that demanded satisfaction.

I recognized your need and how to fill it. But I chose not to tell you, at least not at first; you would never have accepted such a simple solution when we weren't yet in relationship where I could speak on those levels with you. We had not established the necessary trust and understanding. To understand the connection between your soul-felt need and how to satisfy it required much more than words — it required action that at the beginning could have been easily misunderstood.

So I began by sparking a deep curiosity in you, a thirst to learn about a wondrous lovestyle "known and yet unknown" to you. With enticing persuasion, I pursued you and aroused you to follow your curiosity wherever that might lead, knowing all along where that would be. Then, waiting for you there, I reached out to your unfulfilled soul and you gave me entrance.

Once inside, I encouraged you to explore your remotest and most intimate dreams and desires — and passion's allurement. As you responded, I began revealing to you the wonders and benefits of the act of surrender while I awaited its time to blossom within you. Ultimately, you would gain admittance to the only lovestyle that would fulfill the dreams and desires you passionately craved, your unfulfilled yearning that would not go away.

To take you there, I held out my hand and asked you to follow at my side. Taking my hand, you felt secure, knowing you had nothing in me to fear. In trusting me, you also empowered me to begin leading you onto the path with which I was well acquainted, a path to which you willingly adapted because of your burning desire to become the fulfilled wife God created you to be.

As we walked that path together, I introduced you to my inner man and explored your inner woman, in preparation of the two entering an oneness. That entrance, however, can only be attained through my earning your complete trust in my leadership. Only then can I take you to the fulfilling lovestyle your soul has been hungrily craving but unable to identify.

Although the way is simple, it is not easy. Though you are closer now, you have farther to go. Be patient a while longer, and you will have the oneness of intimacy mixed with the level of passion that your gnawing frustration within demands of you.

From the beginning I told you anything worth this much is going to take dedicated effort on both our parts, but the rewards will be splendid. And they will be! Once attained, the oneness will bring together two spirits sharing a common intimacy, a bonding of shared emotions and passion, and satisfying, matched sexuality.

It is the woman's choice to surrender, or not. Yet with the right man, it is perhaps the most important key in determining whether their life will enter that level of oneness, or not. If the woman will allow the molding, shaping, and structuring of her yielded power through the gentle hands of a loving servant/leader husband, the couple's emotions and thoughts can prosper in a spiritual union within which both will flourish.

Then the man can bring all of his gentleness, strength and security to the woman as she brings her willing heart to him. And, knowing at what price her surrender is offered; the man will pay her honor by accepting it with the deepest respect, appreciation and care at every moment.

Now, having entered the man's life, that woman says her heart is touched and completely won over. She has finally found her man, the one to whom she wants to cleave. As he loves her unconditionally, serves and leads her, her yielding to him can become complete. And because her needs will always be considered above his wants and needs, their love will continue to grow in a splendorous lovestyle, always.

To them, arousal will have taken on a new meaning, something very different from ordinary physical desire. Their arousal will be of a deeper, richer nature. It will be the seduction of two souls, the passion of two hearts, the joining of two spirits. Theirs can be the sweetest union of man and woman, sharing the ultimate lovestyle.

This is what you and I can have. It's waiting for us, but much depends on you.

ENTR'ACTE

FAMOUS QUOTATIONS

(THAT EVERY WOMAN SHOULD WANT TO KNOW BY HEART)

If you would be loved, be lovable. —Ovid

I do not want to be the leader. I refuse to be the leader. I want to live darkly and richly in my femaleness. I want a man lying over me, always over me. His will, his pleasure, his desire, his life, his work, his sexuality the touchstone, the command, my pivot. I don't mind working, holding my ground intellectually, artistically; but as a woman, oh, God, as a woman I want to be dominated.

—Anais Nin

To be completely woman you need a master, and in him a compass for your life. You need a man you can look up to and respect. If you dethrone him it's no wonder that you are discontented, and discontented women are not loved for long.

—Marlene Dietrich

Sensuality is beautiful, and dominance and submission in the right context is a passionate art, a muse which ignites the flame of femininity, enrapturing both partners in complete euphoria, magnifying both the masculine and the feminine in one tantalizing unit.

—Sai Marie Johnson

Respect the woman, desire the whore, and cherish the little girl. Then you have won her mind, body and soul.

—Unknown

51 I've never

I've never had so much fun with a woman as I have with you.

I've never been so turned on to a woman as I am to you.

I've never seen so much quality in a woman as I see in you.

I've never wanted the companionship of a woman as I want with you.

I've never wanted to take a woman and ravish her as I do to you.

I've never known just how much a man can need a woman, until this year with you.

It is you I want, it is you I need.

It is you I love . . . with all my heart.

52 How great is the love

How great is the love with which you have filled my heart! Where there was sorrow, you have placed joy. Where there had been hurt, there is now peace. Where there was boredom, you have placed excitement. Where there had been coldness, there is now a warming fire. Where other women have tried, you have succeeded.

With whom can you be compared? Your quiet spirit and humble nature are sweet blessings to my soul; they engage me within. Pleasant thoughts of you exhilarate my mind. When you are away, I want you close. When you are close, I want you closer. There is none other like you.

Like a soft breeze that sweeps into my heart, you refresh me. Each day, thoughts of you bring me peace. Each night, dreams of you uplift me.

Other women have done well for their men, but you have the integrity with which greatness can be achieved. There is none other for comparison.

Only you can create the Garden with the beauty and fragrances I so enjoy. Only you understand what I have taught you about how to satisfy physical desires. Only you are willing to take the time to learn how to tantalize the craving that will elevate my passion, so you can gratify us even more.

You alone are worthy of the secret name I have given you, for only you can fulfill all that the name implies.

I love you deeply. I appreciate you more each day. I need you and want you with a growing passion. You are my mission, my object of love, my purpose to fulfill.

53 Are you marriageable?

You asked me why I want you to read everything out there written by loving, supportive wives. One reason is that wives who cooperate with their husbands are possibly the world's leading experts regarding the creation and improvement of intimate and happy marriages.

Surrendered wives have earned the right from their husbands to 'guide' them, 'fine tune' them, and smooth off their rough edges. They also stay current with new ideas that their peers might have about improving their marriages, and then flow with that current to stay ahead of the "competition." (On that point, both spouses should be continually learning if they're going to be able to keep up with and be worthy of their developing spouse – there's always room to grow.)

A part of this improving, developing and learning encompasses skill levels in various areas. These obviously include those necessary for communication and serving one another, as well as those that bring physical pleasure to both husband and wife. There are numerous others that could and should be developed, too, such as taking dance lessons together.

You also asked if the reason for your "reading assignment" was for me to decide whether I wanted to love you and marry you. My answer to that is not so I would love you; I already do, you silly goose. My reason was so my need and passion for you would grow even more deeply and fervently as you embrace the yielded spirit exemplified by these wives.

For men like me, we need this, because the deeper, stronger

passion we are capable of producing *doesn't kick in* until the woman's part — to surrender — has elevated us to around a level 7 or 8. So the level of a wife's surrender to her husband has everything to do with the quality of a marriage and her 'power' over him.

Numerous centuries ago a girl was not considered "marriageable" if she did not respect and obey her father. If she did, however, then the assumption carried over that she would also be amenable to her intended husband, and therefore a good candidate for marriage.

Our English word *marriageable* actually comes from a word used centuries ago, which means efflorescent, or capable of bearing fruit, or bursting into flower.

This is what your surrender will produce in you, because first it will trigger the catalyst of desire in me to caress your soul with tender and meaningful touches. These touches, from the tender-most center of my heart, will bring radiance to your days and a glow to your nights. No, I'm not raining poetic words here; these are responses that occur in women who will treat themselves to living in this rich environment produced by loving, attentive husbands.

There's another reason why I want you to read everything you can find written by women who have surrendered to their husbands. Just as a mother knows her newborn baby needs help in finding the nipple, these women already know the way. They will help you find that "palm" in which you could already be safely snuggled.

Most of what I've introduced over the months has been new to you; it takes time to discover the qualities of what's in the palm. You needed to be able to differentiate between what you can have through a yielded lifestyle, versus the kind of relationship you have had to settle for in the past. Meanwhile, I've definitely been working on me, too, and I would like to tell you how.

Finding a Pearl of Great Price

"Upon finding a pearl of great price a man goes and sells all he has, then returns to buy the pearl." (Matthew 13:46) But imagine just how very valuable that pearl must be! So now the man must have a special place to keep his precious pearl safe; thus he gathers all the materials he will need to build that place.

That's what I've done, baby. In anticipation of finding my rare pearl, I began years ago asking surrendered, married women – precious pearls – to teach me what they thought I should know about caring for a yielded wife. Giving generously of their time and first-hand knowledge, they taught me how to prepare a place to keep and care for a rare pearl of great value.

They taught me about a sacrificial love that goes far beyond what I, and perhaps you, have ever imagined. They taught me how to love on a higher level, totally new to me, and how to create with that woman an uncommon and warm intimacy that defies description.

They gave me a heightened understanding and appreciation of just how very valuable a surrendered woman can really become to her servant-husband and to herself. Through their devotion to their husbands, those women showed me how wonderful and marvelous a woman can be when she receives the proper nurturing and support, and how very much that enables her to do for the man who appreciates her devotion and honors her.

Perhaps I've not emphasized my work on this enough in these

emails; I've emphasized it consistently in my phone calls with you. But that doesn't even scratch the surface of all a yielded woman can become to herself and her husband. There is so much more. And from that so much more, I have to wonder how any man who is not married to a "developed" wife could possibly function at anywhere near his full capability and love at his full capacity.

By developed, I mean the woman who has developed her gifts and skills (including her choice to surrender) to the level where they never cease to create a voracious hunger in a man. First she lures him, entices him, and drives him wild. Then with those very same tormenting skills, she appeases the craving she has just created, but just barely, while she continues to increase the man's appetite for more. I can teach you how to do this, but reading what surrendered wives have written about the subject will do you a lot more good, because then it is 'woman to woman.'

And what of the man?

How does the man feel about her holding this kind of captivating power over him? Well, speaking for myself, I'm going to love it.

For many years I've been gathering all the "materials" I could possibly use to prepare a special place for the woman who chooses to yield to me, because she will know it's the only true pathway to deep and lasting intimacy in our marriage. I have prepared this special place in my heart as a lavish cocoon, *the finest I could imagine,* to keep my future pearl safe. And now, finally, years later, that which I have zealously hoped to find — the pearl of great price — has been found in you.

Since discovering that you could be my pearl, I have been eagerly waiting for you to learn and grow in the new areas I've taught you, and I, too, have been learning. I've been learning about your particular needs and desires. I've been learning about how and what I need to be doing to make your new cocoon everything and more that you need it to be. I've worked long and hard on myself to grow up and into the man I now am. And although I don't consider myself to have attained anywhere near what I'm striving to become, neither am I anything like I once was.

Self Development

Which brings me back to a subject that's my pet peeve, which is another reason for the reading request. Marriage is not easy! I wish it were, but it isn't. Personal growth is "demanded" of both spouses. Otherwise, divorce can seem imminent. That's why I expect you to work just as hard on your development as I am doing on mine, and as those women still do on theirs.

As you know, I have not been looking for a woman who's in the "coasting" mode. I've been looking for a woman who's striving to grow. There are too many women out there who think they can keep a man's interest by their sexuality alone. But women with sexy shapes are a dime a dozen. Just like men, women have competition. It's time they started getting busy in the self-improvement department, learning not only what gets a man's interest, but also what keeps it — long term.

Mutual growth, not stagnation, is the stuff by which relationships can further knit. It's the activity that pays off in multiple dividends. And it's a two-way street. Men need to get busy in the self-improvement department, too. Too many think they can keep a wife just by providing financially and making up with gifts. That won't work long term.

Women search for happy, fulfilling relationships (men, of course, have the same need). So how does a single woman go about finding a man of quality? Simple. The answer to attracting a better man is to become a better woman. Or to say it another way, good things begin to happen when we get into the process of becoming the person we need to be — when we "keep on keeping on" growing.

But maybe in a woman's opinion she believes she has arrived. Maybe she's on a dating site and her mailbox is filling faster than she can hit the delete key. Maybe she's the envy of all the other women. Maybe she even believes, *"If men don't like me the way I am, they can just look elsewhere!"*

And so men do; they look elsewhere. If women can have expectations, so can men. Many of these expectations usually fall under the area of personal growth — those things people can control about themselves.

Wow! Why are the simple truths so easy to miss? I've been so guilty of that at times. Truths like, *"For things to get better, I've got to get better"*. . . Or, *"If I keep doing what I've always done, I'll keep getting what I've always gotten."* And then there is another I like; it's called the 10-word maxim. "If it is to be, it is up to me."

So there are reasons dreams don't come true. Fortunately, there are ways to change that for most dreams. The key is this: for my dreams to come true, for my things to change, *I've* got to change. For your dreams to come true, for your things to change, *you've* got to change.

And to make changes that will change our lives, there are five major areas each of us can personally control. These are: emotional, physical, mental, spiritual and sexual. Financial is a major area, too, but not always under a person's direct control.

I wonder what would happen if a person right out of school used the following rationale in a job interview: *"Hey there, Company Decision Maker, I want you to hire me just the way I am. I don't want to learn anything new because I don't plan to get any better. Nevertheless, hire me for a top position, pay me a lot to start, and give me lots of promotions just for showing up."*

You may think it ridiculous that someone would approach a job interview with that attitude. But, actually, some people do. I had to turn down a young man in the past that applied for a job simply because of that kind of thinking.

How does that apply here, you might ask? Well, a woman might say that love is not based on performance, and that a woman is not applying for a job when she aligns herself romantically with a man. I agree. But does she realize that a part of attraction is to keep up with or even stay slightly ahead of one's partner? Love can take years to mature. What's going to stand in the gap meanwhile, to keep the couple together?

Women with lazy attitudes

Baby, as you can tell from listening to me, I had grown very skeptical toward the women writing me. I was tired of them taking me for granted, when they themselves had not done one iota of work on their own growth. And so, as you know, I never made a commitment to any of them. That's because, until you, either none of them ever impressed me, or else their value systems conflicted with mine.

Of those who wouldn't work on their own development, I figured none had earned the right to have what I had worked so hard to give. None had shown any kind of sacrificial service, honesty, and earnest solemnity regarding any sort of personal effort through good old-fashioned work. None comprehended what it would cost me to give that much of myself, to give up my freedom, to give my uttermost commitment to another, for life.

Perhaps this was because they themselves had never given, nor did they ever intend to give of themselves equally in the same sort of development as I had come through (and still am). So I wonder, how could they ever think they could keep a man's interest if they weren't able to keep the previous man's interest?

Out of all those women who wrote to me, most of them had never done nor indicated any of those things. Almost none had even shown the slightest interest in working on themselves. None seemed willing — that is, before you.

A prize filly deserves a prize-wining handler

So now I would like to be able to trust that you will be adding to your knowledge and practice in whatever skills you don't already have ready to use. These are skills necessary to keep the mind of a man engaged and his appetites aroused and fed. And a man can become very hungry! (Of course, I will keep adding to my skill set those necessary for a man to keep his wife ravenous for him.)

I'm delighted with the things you're already doing, even without the help of my presence as the necessary "male foil." As the cute filly I love to picture, you have gone from a slow walk to . . . little by little . . . an increased pace. I love watching you, because you are a true thoroughbred, not just any ole' ordinary filly. You were destined to run, free and wild, but with a good handler to provide the great care and protection a prize filly must have.

Just as I see you as an extraordinary filly, I like to think of myself as a certain kind of handler (like a coach, perhaps,) while specializing and bursting with pride in only the very best — the kind of filly you are. We must have one another. Each is no good without the other.

I am learning more about my "job" all the time, and you're helping me to become even better at it. An important part of my job is spending liberal amounts of time in the pasture with my filly, learning her ways, constantly touching her and simply being with her.

Yet another part of my job is also to help you by encouraging you to learn more about yours, too. Of course I will not (nor could I ever) force you to learn, and should I even dare to try, I would drive you away. Force will make anything run away; it simply doesn't work.

But, knowing you can be extraordinary, I would be very saddened and disappointed if you were to choose to fail me, just as you should be if I failed you. (Should my filly ever fail me, I must first go back to see if there's something I did that was not right. I'm human, you know. I need to find out what was wrong.)

To fail to grow individually is to fail to grow the relationship. And as we both know, lack of growth means momentum stops. Thus, the relationship of *Us* would be teetering on a cliff, with no power, no energy to keep it from falling and dying. I've seen that happen to others, and I don't want it ever to happen to us.

Therefore, I will continue to remind both of us that relationships cannot be put on cruise control and then ignored, expecting them to continue as is, without constant nurturing.

Driven by Energy

There is a natural law in thermodynamics that states nothing on earth will continue its momentum without being driven by energy. Unless it was to exist in a total vacuum, either it will continue moving forward due to growth (energy), or else it will slow to a stop.

Solomon mentioned an example of this process in *Proverbs* when he wrote of a vineyard he had once passed by. At that time it was flourishing. A few years later he occasioned to pass by again, only to see it completely ruined due to neglect. That vineyard had taken years of work to bring to its previous level of glory, but for whatever reason that the story did not give, something of beauty and value was left to just simply die.

Great relationships are of even more beauty and value than vineyards, of course. But they, too, require consistent, attentive care, and far more so. Neither of us wants an average relationship when so much more than average can be gained. We don't have to settle for ordinary, for commonplace and dull as do so many couples, when instead we can embark on a *lovestyle* that will give us the ride of our lives! So imagine: a fresh and new excitement can be ours that is far from ordinary; our days can be filled with memorable moments we will treasure always!

You can see, then, that there is so much more waiting for us if you will do as I hope you will, and as I am, which is to continue learning. We can learn so much about the lovestyle that women who know how to surrender have been perfecting for centuries, and the character of the husbands they have entrusted with that choice. Truly, these couples know how to fill their relationships with meaning and purpose every day . . . and night.

They have taught me a lot, and I hope you will learn from their experiences, too. Their marriages are singing heavenly choruses because of what they're doing! So why should we settle for less when we, too, can take pleasure in an exciting, ambrosia-like life together?

You picked me, then hooked me, then waited for me to become enamored with you. Then you backed off to take your time in deciding whether or not you wanted to keep the fish you had been dangling on your hook.

Meanwhile, I chose you after discovering that I wanted you, but I had no idea that it was actually you who was deciding whether to choose me! What a shocker, huh?

Then later, I even discovered how very much more icing could come with the cake . . . more icing than even you know you have. So now that I have it, I selfishly want to have it lavishly spread, thickly, all over the cake. I want all of you, what you are now, and what you can become for *Us*.

Nature gives women special gifts to attract men, but it's up to the woman to practice her gifts until they become skills. (The same applies to men.) You know that I've worked hard to attract the right woman. So it is with eager anticipation that I wait for you, my right woman, knowing you are further developing your gifts into refined skills that will *keep* me attracted . . . forever. (Too bad I can't be a fly on the wall and watch all along the way.)

I've bet the bank on you in the amount of trust I've placed in you, my priceless pearl. I pray you will be able to place at least as much trust in me.

Your Web of Seduction

Now I want to talk to you about the web of seduction you've woven around me by spinning strand after enchanting strand around my captive heart. And I want you to continue strengthening the web overall by continuing to add strands to it, too. This is a part of the energy I was referring to above that will keep our momentum not just maintained, but building energy that is ever growing our relationship through our attraction to one another.

Women have only so much innate knowledge about seduction. Beyond that, a woman must learn with her man how to refine the ultimate seduction for him. Furthermore, she must know more than other women, so she can stay considerably ahead of them. She must know how to create a sensual silk web of allurement around her husband that no other woman could weave her way through. Even the thought of looking elsewhere would never be entertained by him.

I know, too, that the man must keep himself physically fit and ever alert to his wife's needs and moods, for thoroughbreds are often trained to jump, and she can jump out of the pasture any time she wants. He needs constantly to work on the art of attracting, verbalizing his love, attentively pleasing, caressing and satisfying his wife in both favorite and new ways, so she will never be driven to seek comfort and affection elsewhere. Adultery is awful because it wounds both the offended and offending spouse. Nevertheless, so many hurt and lonely souls seek its temporary anesthesia that all too often leads to regrets.

Knowledge applied is power

Now then, I've been talking about learning this and knowing that. However, knowledge of itself is not enough. It is like a book sitting on the shelf, filled with wonderful and important facts and figures, but gathering dust. Knowledge has to be properly *applied* before it can become power. So after we've gathered knowledge, along with all the rest from the savvy women we've been discussing, and *are then applying it*, we each can consider ourselves marriageable.

Now for your part: First you need to know what each of the threads of the sensual web of allurement must consist of; that's the knowledge part. Then I need you to create threads around me; that's the application part (and the more threads you can create, the stronger will be the web). So I'm going to tell you now, and in quite a bit of detail, of what these sensuous threads are made, and how to weave them. But remember, none of this works unless both husband and wife have embraced their proper roles.

~ EDITOR'S NOTE ~

Due to its adult and personal nature, the remaining content of this letter is omitted here.

54 How can I express what I feel?

Here I sit, feeling incomplete. Most nights I write to you, I try to express what I'm feeling. Sometimes I'm successful. At other times, the emotions get welled up inside because my heart is unable to send them to you. This is one of those times.

I think perhaps these emotions that hide from me, refusing to be labeled, are emotions I have never before felt for a woman. I would express them if I knew how, but how can I when I don't even have the words?

It's during these times that I seem to have the most powerful feelings of desire for you. Yet how can these deepest feelings for you be told?

Can love's longing be described
    with mere words in a song?
Can love's pulses be measured
    when desire is so strong?
Can my heart stop aching
    when night turns to dawn?
Or my empty arms comforted
    where instead you belong?

Even as I write these lines, I still cannot express what I feel; there is so much more! To speak my feelings, to even try, I would need to be inside you right now, to become a part of you, to seek your help to guide me to my deepest emotions, and then together, bring them forth from inside. I believe a special kind of woman can do that, and if that is true, then obviously . . . I believe it's you.

55 She's mine!

Whenever I think of you, which is quite often (as your seductive heart knows very well), I can't keep my mind on anything else. But that's plenty all right, because during those times, very pleasant thoughts take place within me.

Apparently it's nature's plan to keep a man tuned in and turned on to a woman through that woman's being by his side as his devoted equal partner. Although as a woman you are dominant, as you well should be, your desire to yield not only captivates me, it proves to me that you would be a good wife. Also highly erotic is that you are sharing more of your innermost thoughts and deepest feelings with me. This makes me appreciate you all the more, and to be so outright thankful that I have you.

As I've told you before, you're like an all-in-one package, one that has no compromises on the quality of the ingredients. You've got it all; all the things I've ever wanted and needed. You're all bundled together as a cute filly, as Mixie the naughty pixie, as an all-dimensional seductress, as daddy's babygirl, and as a sexy babydoll.

I feel these things must be expressed in writing, else with all the passion building up inside I might burst. Sometimes I feel a need to express this when on the phone. Other times you're not available and I must tell you in these emails.

So I wonder, how is a man to behave toward his object of love? Is he not to burn for his woman during a courtship? Is it even possible not to have romantic thoughts about the woman he loves, especially when she is you? Does nature expect us not to be excited, not to be so desirous of the one we love, since that one is not yet ours to quench the fire?

I don't wish to act improperly toward you. Have I been acting improperly? You're the only one who can answer that question for me, since otherwise I have no way of knowing. If I have acted wrongly, then please forgive me.

I admit I've been glad when I've turned you on. I've enjoyed trying and sometimes succeeding in seducing you over the phone. I know I have no excuse, but still, do you realize that even your partial surrender is arousing my very soul! Oh, my love, I so want to show you how much that means to me!

56 I know you're incredibly exciting

I know you're an incredibly exciting woman. I know we can look forward to the day when we can experience that excitement together. I know you know how to turn a man on and make love to him. I can tell you're very good at the art of captivating a man.

I'm certain of all these things. There's no need, then, for you to feel threatened or to feel a twinge of attack on your ego if I tell you something — I would like to expose you to even more of what's "out there," if only to know what other women are doing to stay ahead of the current.

Women who are practiced in the art of surrender (*which is the purest and most effective form of flirtatious seduction*) have along the way invented exciting things for their enjoyment, things that turn their men into mush.

I dream of your knowing what *all* of these exciting things are, even if you then determine that you prefer what you already know. I would just like to see you have the ability to be even better versed than other women who have sought to apply their craft of seduction on men.

57 Let's not throw away the next 20 years

Most wives love having their husbands accept the responsibility of maintaining security and leading the family; that is, assuming they feel safe and in good hands with their man. The relationship can be similar to head coach (him) and quarterback (her), or even vice versa at times.

A husband must remember that his most important role here is to make every effort each day to go all-out in loving his wife unconditionally, with a self-sacrificing, giving love that seeks her protection and best interests. A woman can get a real sense of belonging in this way, and this can make her feel priceless, cherished, and oh so secure. After all, a wife needs to know her man is capable and trustworthy 'on the job,' and able to help sustain order when life gets a little crazy. Likewise, at times the husband may need to encourage and build up his wife's confidence and belief in herself – her inner strength as a woman, and the insight and good judgment that women have – her power that substantially helps a man as his guide and to keep his 'balance.'

A husband's growth can be measured by how often and how much he tempers his authority as the family leader – by never being harsh, but always showing love, respect, patience, appreciation and gentleness for his wife. Just that alone can create a heated passion in the couple, because for the responsible husband and the yielded wife, the interplay of leadership and surrender is a dance designed to bring harmony. And they know they've got the dance right when they're always turned on to each other, because fire and energy feed off one another to grow stronger.

Since each partner benefits, she with her power and he with his virile strength, they have a kind of see saw. It is kept in balance by her intuition, sexuality and softness, to play off her husband and his provision of loving protection and security for his wife's freedom.

There's so much for both of us to learn, not just about one another, but also about what each of us can do for the other to keep the marriage in balance. Proverbs tell us the principal thing is to get wisdom; both husband and wife must grow in it. And for my part, I would much rather learn how to be a better husband pro-actively, by taking wise action, than by not taking any responsibility and just sitting around, waiting for life to take action on me! *Ouch!*

Am I ready to head the Department of Maintaining Security and Order? Am I ready to be the Head with you as my oh-so-important help? Have I completed all the training that will make me a good husband? Has either of us completed life's training for our emotional and spiritual growth?

I hardly think so; nobody knows it all. Yet sooner or later, there always has to be a time and place to get started. Life can be either a harsh teacher or a kind one, depending on circumstances . . . which can often be improved according to how much a person 'studies' and actually applies what they learn.

I will never complete all of life's training that will make me a good husband, but I know if I have you at my side as my indispensable co-pilot, giving me advice and all sorts of help, then together we will make our way through life as a team that is tough for life to knock down.

As an aside, I remember reading somewhere about a very fine man, a great man. He was an astute scholar, statesman and educator, very wise and very tactful. His particular field of expertise was being discussed one day. A much younger (and much less knowledgeable) man was casting disparaging remarks about the scholar's opinion on a particular subject.

The media was hoping to get a story that could incite an on-going feud between the two, so they went scurrying to the scholar and asked him what he thought of the young man's accusations. The scholar simply replied, "I can from all men learn something, and in that sense, all men are my teachers."

Your teachers and mine are the couples who *have* stuck together because they *are* stuck together. A key, of course, is when they are clearly together in a happy, passionate marriage. Those, whose lives reflect this beauty in their relationship over many years, know what they're doing; the lengths and quality of their marriages say so. They're the 'teachers' I want to talk to – they've earned the right to give advice and I want to hear every bit of it that they will teach me!

Notice I didn't say sticking together; these couples are *stuck* together, permanently glued, because both the husbands and wives in those marriages obviously know things that are important for every husband and wife to know, and they honor the covenant of marriage.

This is why I've wanted you to read from the wisdom of their journey. You'll be better equipped to see inside yourself and tap into the resources of a woman that you're going to be discovering have been there all along, perhaps lying dormant. These are resources you could be benefiting from, like power. They're there for a reason, not to waste but to allow you to get in touch with them and use them as part of the very foundation of our marriage.

Once I met a lady online who had begun working on her compliant nature for her (then) future husband from her late teens. She said this was because her mother taught her that proper ladies behave this way. I asked her to share some pearls of wisdom with me. She wrote back saying something to the effect that it was unfortunate I had not found myself a wife 20 years earlier who was agreeable to surrendering – that with that attitude then together we could have been learning from each other how to build the fire of our love ever hotter. With each passing year, our passion would have released still more of what each of us would have discovered is inside us, and her continued surrender would have served to drive me ever more intimately into her.

I think what this wife was trying to get me to understand is that a marriage never has to grow cold nor stale. Thus, always the student and ever wanting to learn, I have attempted to make up for the 20 "lost years" by learning all I can from women. One thing especially that I am learning is how very much it takes for most women to be yielded to their husbands, and for their husbands to earn daily that level of trust and respect. But oh, how great the rewards for both when he qualifies and she responds!

There's one other thing, for women; it's incredibly important because it is indispensable. Every time a woman has the need to be yielded to her husband about anything whatsoever, whether large or small, she simply has to think to herself, *Whatever!* And the matter suddenly becomes of no importance to her whatsoever. In a fraction of a moment she has released the desire to control, or even be concerned, because in an instant she just entirely turned it over to her husband just by the thought, *Whatever!*

It's amazing! Let me suggest you try it at the first opportunity. And of course it's great for men, too. I use it whenever I find myself beginning to get irritated about something, and instantly, the irritation is gone.

So let's not waste what others can teach us; let's not throw away the next 20 years. Let's live them in wisdom, love and laughter.

Excerpt from Mixie's Response:

I like another way to define the husband–wife relationship that you mentioned to me on the phone. It's the analogy your dog behaviorist friend suggested; that the husband is the dominant male and the wife is the dominant female. She's constantly encouraging him and doesn't fight with him. She surrenders to no one but him.

In the human world, if a man pushes too hard or acts as a know-it-all, the wife is sure to kick back. A wife remembers all things about her husband and knows him inside and out. So he had better be careful not to misuse or abuse her.

Nevertheless, she is constantly reminding him, "Don't get too full of yourself." If he gets out of line, she gives him a good hard 'nip' that reminds him she is not his property but his partner.

58 Your name

Every time I see your name (the special one I gave you – not Mixie), I get aroused. When I think about what it means, and that it perfectly describes you, and what's going on inside your mind and body, I get excited.

This is why I have given you the name that none but you and I know. The meaning of your name fits you so perfectly, for indeed . . . you are a flowing fountain of femininity.

59 The glitch is that there is no glitch

I'm very happy with our relationship. Yet I keep looking for the glitch. I keep looking, but not finding. Therein lies the glitch . . . there is no glitch!

That causes me to keep asking myself, *What am I overlooking?* Nothing's perfect. So why can't I find something wrong? Sure, you're always telling me you need fixing. (Don't we all?) But that's a key part of your attraction: your honesty and humility, as well as making me feel needed; you want my help and support.

And so I've been pursuing some thinking about a sculptor lovingly working with his sculpture. From time to time he discovers, just as he positions the chisel, that the piece he was going to remove to reveal the beauty underneath falls away on its own, as if it were never intended to be a part of the marble. It is the same with us, as if the sculpture in you was already beautifully formed and finished; yet due to years of neglect and lack of receiving proper care and nourishing, it needed only a light restoration.

So yes, I know you're not perfect, nor am I, and neither of us ever will be. It's just that you can be so perfect for me.

60 The sculpture and the sculptor

The ultimate sculptor is Life's School of Hard Knocks – how we respond to them and let God work in our lives. He is the Potter and we are the clay.

Although these hard knocks are not pleasant, it's during these very times that each of us is being shaped into better sculptures. And although we find ourselves entangled in the various problems and trials of life, they only serve as life's hammer and chisel to make us better persons. But do we stop to think that we are the *cause* of many of our problems?

Every emotionally and spiritually growing person (they're easy to recognize, they're the ones learning from their mistakes) can see this sculpting process happening within.

Life uses other people, too, especially those closest to us – *"As iron sharpens iron, so friends sharpen one another"* (Proverbs 27:17). That's what positive friction between two married people can create, provided they're really serious about cleaving together.

As you know, this cleaving together business is part of God's command: "Therefore a man shall leave his father and his mother and cleave to his wife: and they shall be one flesh" (*Genesis* 2:24). And then you know that the same command to cleave to his wife is in *Ephesians* 5:31, because that part of Ephesians, beginning at verse 21, is what you referred to in your bio on the dating site, and also in your first email.

And that, dear heart, is what told me everything I needed to know about you as a bride. All that was left for me to find out, then, was how our personalities would mesh over the long haul. And having now found that out, too, all that is left is to help you attain to your promise to let go of the steering wheel from the passenger's seat.

Now back to Ephesians 5:21 to the end of the chapter (and you know this passage as well as I):

To husbands the basic message is this: Serve her, take responsibility for your priceless pearl, love her unconditionally ("agape"), lead and guide her, protect her, provide for her, nurture her and help her blossom in her talents, supporting her in becoming the beautiful person inside that God created her to be and successful in her endeavors. But the message to husbands also says: if you *intentionally* fail her, hurt her, or stop romancing her, you will regret it to your dying day.

And to the wives the basic message is this: Honor your husband and yield to him in everything legitimate and reasonable. Learn to adapt yourself to him, and to please him, even as he seeks to adapt and please you. Then you will find yourself blessed by God and cherished by your husband. But woe to you if you try to take charge of your husband's assigned role.

In what ways might a wife be blessed? She will be blessed in public by praise and admiration from her husband and others. At home she will be blessed by her children's love for her, their high regard and respectful treatment of her. Her husband will have a happy heart because of her, and romantic thoughts day and night. But woe unto you, wife, if you *intentionally* dishonor or disregard your husband when he is acting in a godly fashion and his request is both reasonable and just.

Anyway, it's not surprising that of the numerous spiritually related authorities I've read, all are in agreement when it comes to the way husbands and wives should respond to each other. To both the overriding message, paraphrased, is "*...both of you submit yourselves to one another because you know how much God loves and values each of you, and will not put up with power struggles between you nor devaluing your spouse when He has paid the highest of prices for his and her spiritual freedom*" (Ephesians 5:21 and following).

It's true that this "wives are to love, honor and obey" business sounds on the surface like a one way, male-benefiting setup, and to be an obedient wife means to do everything to the best of her ability to please her husband; i.e., to *always follow* his leadership when it is consistent with God's instructions and man's laws. But digging deeper we see that by doing this, the wife gets a *well-deserved* stress-less life and can spend more of it indulging in bubble baths and pampering, in preparation for more candle lit, romance-filled nights with her husband.

If the husband abuses his position, though, how can he expect his wife not to abuse hers in response? The husband actually has to work much harder than the wife, and if he tries to "control" (doing what's not right) or leaves a leadership void, the wife will step in affirmatively, and the result may be the exact opposite of what both want. This is a dance, a fair balance that must be packed with mutual honor, respect and wisdom, leaving no room for bickering.

Both husband and wife need to remember, too, that the husband is human and may cross boundaries from time to time or miss something important; so the wife will need to remind him, "You're over the line" and to watch his back, even behind closed doors to correct him gently when he is wrong. As his right wing, she has a responsibility to him to do that, to share her wisdom and help him be the best he can be. And they both have a responsibility to remember that *they are a team*, and teammates that win *work together,* not against the outcome.

What About the Wife?

Now what about the wife? Who's going to take care of her? She has needs too, so if she's busying herself doing things for her husband, then how's she going to get her own needs met?

Have you been asking yourself that question? I've thought about it quite a lot over the last 20 years, imagining myself in the wife's place. It seems not to be an easy role, and the husband must do all he can to help her when needed. He does this by loving his wife (all-encompassing, unconditional love) every moment of every day, and serving her. This usually means putting her needs first, ahead of his. Husbands who do this carry the banner of love, protection and provision.

In this natural world and human reality, a wife may need to stimulate her husband to always want and remember to do that for her. (Perhaps that's why women were created to be such good reminders.)

Whenever a marriage begins, the couple steps smack dab into the middle of a powerful force. People who *fight against* it lose. People who *cooperate with* the force, however, win, and usually big time. It's called "*the law of sowing and reaping.*"

The couple that works together in harmony with this law, experiences what God always intended: a connectedness, oneness, peace, security, intimacy, and passion. But if one or both of the couple are bickering over what the other person is doing or not doing, instead of taking care of their own responsibility, then the marriage will teeter-totter and possibly fail.

Going with the flow

If they both go with the flow, they soon find themselves in a delightful place, reaping all sorts of great rewards. These rewards in their marriage are very tangible, and precious, too. But if either spouse goes against the flow, both will be miserable and eventually shattered.

Consider a team of horses pulling a loaded wagon uphill. If either horse should falter, the other can temporarily hold his weight. But if the fallen horse then refuses or is unable to get up, forget it. They could both tumble back down the hill and suffer injuries, or worse. So both must pull together.

So, too, husband and wife must pull and flow together in the same direction with equal strength of love and dedication for success in marriage. So how can the couple be sure they're going with the flow? Here's how: It starts with kindness, gentleness, respect and resolve to be attentive and serve the other person in love, regardless of their faults (and ours).

Marriage is nothing without love at the very foundation, with full commitment to the Marriage Covenant and to the One Who created us and ordained marriage. He should always be included as a party to that covenant.

The next most important things are mutual honor, respect

and service, with kindness and attentive consideration, and with a determination to work together to resolve any issues instead of bickering. Then there is the matter of leadership, so the marriage isn't a rudderless ship.

Flowing together also means letting one take the lead (the point man) while the other (the wife, as his right wing) is there not only to work together, but also to watch and warn. One example of how this might work is what a friend with a service dog shared with me.

Due to certain physical characteristics from birth, there are times when her balance becomes more precarious and she is at risk of stumbling and falling. In those times, she has her service dog with her to help. Yes, she is his leader, but here's how she explained the process.

"My job is to tell him where we are going. He has two jobs: He lets me know when my balance is getting off even before I notice it, and cautions me where there are any well-hidden cracks that tend to catch shoes, or other terrain hazards. He can also judge a heightened dysfunction in my body better than I can. So if he doesn't think at that moment I should be going up a certain step (that normally wouldn't matter), he just plants his feet like an ox, body-blocks me, and waits for my touch signal that I understand. He'll just lie down and not budge if I try to go forward without that.

"When someone you trust is doing their job and gives a warning like that, don't argue. You stop and look to see what the problem is. It's the same thing when a wife tells the husband, 'I don't like this person' or 'I don't think you should be doing business with him.' Stop arguing and trust her instincts. Don't let your pride cost you dearly."

The Older Women

Do you remember telling me about the two older women who told you that you should always "wear the pants" in the family and show the man who's boss? Yet by doing so, they had been suffering repercussions in their own marriages, hadn't they?

By their own admissions, their husbands had divorced them for this very attitude, yet they had not yet recognized the connection. They had unknowingly fought against nature's powerful force and, of course, lost. No one can beat the law of sowing and reaping. It's foolish to even try. With those two women, the negative attitudes they sowed were a direct cause of their reaping failed marriages.

Meanwhile, the disharmony and resistance those women sowed wasn't the end of it (although I'm sure they wish it was). They're still reaping unhappiness because of their "run-in with the law" of sowing and reaping. (You said their faces looked old and tired, and their mouths were turned down.) Do you find it interesting that although they're not that old to remarry, they advise against it, giving the reason that men are no good?

Of course, I don't know their exact circumstances, what their husbands were like or if there was a leadership void they felt it necessary to fill. However, I personally believe that the real reason they're saying these things may be that no one is asking them for a date. Perhaps bitterness has overtaken them, and their faces reveal it?

You, on the other hand, will reap harmony because you'll be sowing accord, as will I. You'll also reap emotional fulfillment and enjoy success, the same as others who flow with the law by honoring good husbands. That's how a wife can expect to receive positive, not negative, results in her marriage. The same is true for a responsive and receptive husband who listens to his wife.

The relationship between husband and wife is much like the eagles'. Our final actions in the marriage ceremony are to exchange vows and seal it with a kiss; theirs is to drop at incredible speed toward the earth holding onto each other's talons. We should take holding onto our vows as seriously. Then the rewards will be beyond measure.

The Grinding Process

Mankind (especially today's fast-food generation) wants things to come easily, without work, without effort, and for the wheel of rewards to turn quickly to bring the things desired. But life has another wheel, one of character building, which grinds exceedingly slowly until its object is fit for use.

The famous author and psychologist, Dr. Henry Cloud, in his book, *9 Things You Simply MUST DO* [sic], said this about people who help people who don't even recognize they need help. It applies to the situation where either husband or wife seeks to advise or lovingly correct the other.

> "Whoever corrects a mocker invites insult. A mocker resents correction; [he/she] will *not* consult the wise." (Emphasis added.) "What a disheartening experience to endure in any kind of relationship! [To] give valuable feedback, and as a result you get insulted. Something that should be received gratefully is seen instead as a negative, and you get punished for offering it. You reap a storm of resentfulness for just being honest. Such a prideful spirit that resists correction makes for

> bad relationships. And past that, it makes for a lack of success in the life of the defensive person. [He or] She is unable to grow and get past failure because [he or] she is closed off to the information that would help [him or] her."

Babygirl, I want you to know something. I'm just absolutely delighted in how honest you want to be toward yourself. That kind of attitude just makes me want to melt into you. Something I've especially appreciated in you from the beginning is that you've been able to recognize pride. Only a few, like yourself, recognize it in themselves and choose to do something to get rid of it. I, too, have seen the ugliness of my own pride and have had to deal with it — as I expect I will have to continue to do, always.

Can I help you through the grinding process in a way that won't be so painful? Can you help me in the same less confrontational way? Can the rough edges of my iron and your iron grind together so that life's character building process for both of us is made easier, smoother?

Is there a better way to quickly subdue a bad attitude when a negative trait pops out in one of us? I think there is. In fact, I should say I'm sure there is, because women in the know have been using it to subdue their men for centuries.

What if we were to use, as the subduing agent, the seductive chemistry that acts as the magnet between us, that so powerfully and passionately draws us together? Would that chemistry cause whichever one of us is misbehaving at the time to not take things so seriously and to become more sensitive to the other?

I know it has been really hard for me to stay angry when you start flirting with me, or when you're laughing at how silly the situation is. Your antics get me to change my attitude real fast, because it's impossible for me to argue with you if you're not arguing back — especially if, instead of arguing, you are seducing me. Things like this can make a relationship less grinding and more lubricating. We men need to remember that tactic, too, and find ways to humor, soothe and attract our wives to us, rather than light the fuse or throw oil on the fire.

Anyway, I think it's much easier on us if we do our own changing voluntarily than it is to do nothing, in which case life's hammer and chisel have to go to work on us. Don't you agree?

Two Excerpts from Mixie's Response:

I agree . . . but here's more for our discussion of learning, trusting and the "balance scale". . .

A good marriage requires balance and trust. Consider the handler riding a filly. His job is to determine the direction when the trail is steep; hers is to establish the footing that supports them both. He has got to give her head. If you even try to pull the horse's head, you will pull the horse off balance and you could both be killed. The horse has to pick its way.

In dense fog, you must trust the filly's instincts to find a way out better than you can, or you might stay lost. So at those toughest points, the handler has got to be able to depend on the filly.

Life is full of those moments. Any time a wife tells her husband there's a problem on his blind side, he should truly listen to her. She can see what he can't see; trust her instincts and insights.

61 A metamorphosis

When we talked about sculptures and sculptors, I spoke of certain women who are prized by their husbands because of the way they use soft compliance and loving devotion to be seductive. They are like beautiful sculptures, pleasantly appealing to the male senses. It's not at all surprising, from the things these women tell me about their relationships, that they are loved intensely and desired passionately by their husbands. How could they not be?

But I've been wondering: How many women can say they're loved intensely and passionately, as these women can? I don't mean to sound unkind here, but maybe those women who can't say they are should ask for a little direction from happy wives who know how to show the way? And why not? Inexperienced people-in-training (male and female) should always go to the experienced ones for advice on do's and don'ts and tips on enhanced effectiveness.

(Women ask each other for advice far, far more than they would ask a male. Until her mate learns how to be a good husband, he's probably going to be too rough on his answers for a green filly, since he is also a green groom. He will make them all about what she didn't do and perhaps demean her, and the results can backfire. Fillies, especially when young, simply won't have it. They're too smart to struggle with him in the corral, but will wait until he's all full of himself and not paying attention, then knock him down.)

These happy women I speak of are not necessarily prized for their outward beauty. Certainly, every little girl cannot grow up to be physically beautiful, any more than a beautiful woman can keep her beauty forever. Besides, a woman should never allow herself to get hooked on the opinions of shallow-minded people who value women on the basis of their appearance only.

Women who place themselves in their sculptors' hands (assuming those hands are kind, gentle and wise) to allow them to lovingly round off the rough edges and smooth-in the cracks, are women who experience a metamorphosis — from being ordinary to becoming extraordinary — in their feminine dispositions, their character, and even in their attitude.

When a responsible husband allows God, as the Master Sculptor, to teach the student (husband) and guide his direction, God will sometimes do the actual sculpting through the husband, producing a truly beautiful, prized sculpture (wife).

That's why I compared beautiful sculptures to wives who yield to the loving hands of good husbands. They take on an intriguing, mysterious and exotic nature when they surrender to their husband's touch and leadership. They become captivating and alluring, appealing and tempting, exciting and persuasive. I supposed this is why the mythical faerie, a delicate girl with butterfly-like wings, is likened to them.

Remember my comparison about how a sculpture doesn't have to strive and strain to become perfect; just the opposite? The sculpture simply yields to the sculptor's hand, just as I ask you to yield to me. Once you do, you will already have become perfect in my eyes, because it is I, not you, who must be judged. It is I who must be measured by my own handiwork. Since I am the one who commissions the sculpture and also does the sculpting, I alone am responsible for the outcome. I alone am responsible for you as you give yourself over to me, yielding to me, pleasing me.

Your part, then, is simply to be soft, devoted clay in my hands — the purest form of innocent trust. For in that state you will always be in my eyes the most desired, the most sought-after, the most prized of all women.

I very much want to see you blossom as a cherished woman, properly attended and looked after by the right man who adores you. I want to watch you bloom in a happy and protective environment of unselfish love. I want to give to you adoration that you can *feel*, pulsing from deep within the center of my heart. I want you to experience the kind of self-assurance within that can proofread my heart; that says with the utmost certainty you are highly valued and desired beyond what you had hoped or ever imagined you would be.

I want you to feel engulfed in love so sincere, so meaningful, that you actually glow as your heart takes in the passion I pour into it. I want that glow to be a living testimony to anyone who lays eyes on you of what a proper relationship can produce in a surrendered woman, because that woman will be snuggled in her husband's heart, cuddled in his arms, rocked in his lap, warmed by his slow kisses and skillful, gentle touch, and set ablaze by his passion.

I want to witness every inch of growth, every moment as you blossom with the confidence that you are unconditionally loved, protected, looked after, and cared for. This is as it should be for a woman whose heart is devoted to being surrendered to his. I want you to feel awesome about yourself! And I would like to feel that I am at least a little responsible for that.

62 Bossy or feminine, it's a girl's choice

I've been thinking back to the time when you told me of the stress you endured in your previous marriage. I was saddened that you were "blocked" from ever being completely fulfilled by your late husband.

The stress must have been horrible, living with his authoritarian, tyrannical influence over your children, and seeing what it was doing to them and you. When you told me you fantasized romantic "babygirl" activities to avoid the pain during times of his meanness, or even to keep from being crushed yourself, I understood.

I can see how the fantasies gave you a break from the adult responsibilities you chose to assume, such as controlling things that weren't otherwise getting done to your satisfaction, or wouldn't get done at all if you didn't jump in.

Yet at other times, I can just imagine your experiences when you had to "walk on eggshells," in fear you would do something to displease a husband never satisfied with the results and the major efforts others might have made to please him. It seemed to you that nothing was ever good enough to please him.

You had to ad lib within the circumstances you lived — an environment that neither allowed nor encouraged you to live out completely the wonderfully talented person you truly are. You compensated (and did a great job of it). Either way, stress was created for you and the children and frayed emotions were the result, as were the rips and tears that are still there, even though your marriage ended when he passed on.

I'm glad to see that in recent years you've begun to recognize yourself as you truly are: a woman who wants to think and feel and act like a *girl*, not the boss of a family. That's a role that should never be imposed upon a woman, let alone a wife, and I can understand how it added to your frustration and emotional exhaustion. But you were trapped and forced to fill the void in leadership and support that was your husband's place.

But what you did by assuming that role was to take the place your husband had abdicated as the leader of the family. That left him with no place — except to complain much of the time about everything you and the children did. You were willing to carry his and everyone else's loads, even though he should have been the one carrying them. So . . . he just let you. Then he griped without cause about how poorly you were doing in the very job he should have been doing.

Now then, you've asked me to explain why you feel you cannot let go, that you have to be in control of everything. In your case I believe it's because the motive behind your controlling behavior (which you now rightly look upon as harmful to you) is fear birthed in childhood and given unlimited feeding in your marriage. You feared things would not get done, or if they did, would not be done correctly.

Apparently you developed this fear early on, because for the first several years of your life you grew up with only your father available for you to depend on. But your father was not dependable — he was not the kind of person who managed things and kept them under proper control. The truth is, things in his life were totally out of control. Further, he didn't establish rules and boundaries to make his little girl feel secure.

This was unfortunate, because parent control in the right hands is the very thing a child needs if she is to feel secure. So the insecurities you felt as a small child were very real and demanding, and sadly, you could do nothing to resolve them. Only an adult could, but he never really grew up.

Still, the real question is: How long will you continue to maintain a death grip on those things that convention considers a man responsible for? Why should you continue to make your life miserable if a man is present, willing and able to take them on? The graveyard is full of people who "feared" things wouldn't or couldn't get done without them. But they *are* getting done . . . by those who survive them.

Baby, you've got to let go! How will you ever enjoy the fullness of life that you can have as a woman if you don't? The lovestyle I offer you can only work if you put these burdens to rest. Allow me to carry the responsibilities God intends the husband to manage.

If you had allowed things to pile up on your late husband instead of stepping in to fill the void, he might have felt forced to lead. But like a back seat driver fearing a head-on crash, you felt there wasn't enough time to see if your husband would take the controls (assuming he ever would). Living in a "hands off" manner while you waited for him was out of the question; fear or dire circumstances wouldn't allow you to wait.

You were living just about as far to one extreme as a wife can get, in a very difficult relationship that could harden a woman and eventually break her . . . and this left you exhausted. Yet at the opposite extreme is the wife who is hopelessly bone-lazy and apathetic.

You can see that neither of these extremes is healthy, not for the family, and certainly not for the woman. Instead, a balance needs to be maintained. Still, how could you (or anyone else in the thick of it as you were) be expected to find that balance, let alone maintain it without the proper partner? I can imagine chaos lurching out of the shadows back then, threatening to ambush you.

Fortunately, now that we've been able to identify that the source of the ongoing problem is fear, and that it's what is causing your (almost) panic-driven need to control things, I can help you learn how to trust and simply let go of the reins. So instead of carrying burdens you were never intended to carry, I want you to be thinking more about the feminine role you were born to live, the role you've been preventing yourself from living.

Moreover, I want to help you realize how much fun and games you've been missing out on. Then you can enjoy the fullness of your entire femininity, the role all wives should be entitled to – if they would just . . . stop . . . trying . . . to . . . lead.

This is as things should be. A woman should be allowed to be the babygirl she wants to be without having to worry about problems normally dealt with by the husband. She should be entitled to have a husband who is adult enough, strong enough and experienced enough to handle the family's problems as a whole (not just his own).

So when a husband properly provides this safer and less stressful environment for his wife, she's free to engage her acquiescent nature full time. Doing this makes her exotically feminine and incredibly attractive to her husband. She can be who she is, and who she is . . . is a delightful, playful, lifetime companion and helpmate of world-class dimensions.

You may be wondering why I didn't just go ahead and say, "stress free." First off, that's not realistic. And second, a stress free life is not a healthy life. A *little* stress is good for everybody, because it keeps us motivated to do the things we ought to do. It's the resistance that builds muscle as well as inner strength.

God made the woman from the first man, then put her at his side to do *what he could not do* without her, to be his 'right wing,' and use her wisdom and insights to watch his back. Doesn't it make good sense, then, for each of us to behave as life intended, by doing the particular jobs assigned to us individually? Why fight for the other person's job, and then exhaust ourselves trying to do it? You don't want to be married to a man who behaves like a woman. Neither do I want to be married to a woman who behaves like a man, doing the things a man is supposed to do.

I have seen the lovely rainbow flavors of who and what you can be. I have observed how the bits and pieces of information in your emails have settled into a place of understanding in your thinking. I can see you're beginning to understand that when a woman suppresses her inner nature to surrender, she is blocking her true happiness.

You've told me that everything in your mind is starting to make perfect sense to you. When you began recognizing and welcoming your right and proper new environment of romantic fare, you began to see one in which you could dwell and flourish. This is the 'babygirl' environment you escaped to in your fantasies, the one you always desired but could never be certain actually existed (the one place in which our *Us* can prosper . . . our Garden). Unfortunately, you've been afraid of *fully* surrendering to another, yet this is the one thing that keeps a woman shut out of the Garden.

Now look at this carefully, because it's very important for one to understand. In terms of this lovestyle, *to yield is to have power*. At first glance, because the woman is being asked to "surrender," it would seem she has 0% control, the man 100%. She has lots of sexiness and seduction, but no control, until . . . she surrenders. Then the power and the law of cause and effect begin working in her favor, giving her (at minimum) a 50-50 power ration. Later, as her man becomes putty in her hand, she will have 100% of the power.

Some women can give up control more easily than others. Women who were compliant children naturally fall into this category. Others, stronger willed, must put forth more effort to experience their "breakthrough." For both, however, time is the common ingredient required; it's just a matter of how much of it passes until a woman discovers all the good things waiting for her in that warm, safe palm; quite the opposite from all the bad things she has been experiencing by fighting the world (and her husband) on her own.

Some women are more afraid to let go than others, stubbornly trying to be both independent *and* compliant, even with a husband who earns their trust. But trying to be both will keep a woman in inner turmoil, not to mention producing unsightly weeds in the Garden that damage the relationship called *Us*.

So please help me do my job as sculptor-apprentice by being as non-resistive to me as you can find the strength and desire to be. I promise to be gentle and patient with you, and if (when) I slip and start to get impatient, please remind me. Then your femininity can glow like a full moon on an otherwise cloudy night. After all, whether bossy or feminine, it's a girl's choice.

63 There is no other way to bliss on earth

[Note to reader: This letter describes how a married man and woman can create a blissful bonding experience for themselves; nothing else is intended or implied. The headings and subheadings have been added to aid the reader.]

~~~~~~~~~~~~~~~~~~~~~~~~

We've talked about the proverb that speaks of four extraordinary things, so remarkable and wonderfully amazing that they'll never be (entirely) understood. The one that really gets my mind whirling though is "*the way of a man with a maiden.*" The more deeply I think about it, I find that I am still no closer to reaching its depth than when I began.

So I wonder about the flip side, 'the way(s) of a maiden with a man.' As I continue to burrow deeper into her many majestic facets, it seems each one is just as intriguing as the last, with no end in sight.

There is one facet in particular that is especially pleasant to a married couple. However, it cannot be easily described in mere words, and then only by a man who has been spellbound by it. All in all, it makes for a blissful bonding experience.

I know a man to whom that happened, who became enthralled by a woman's seduction, who tasted the delightful, who experienced the depth of her emotions as she experienced his. The bonding was glorious as he looked into her softened eyes and saw a surrendered soul . . . and loveliness within. And although he didn't try, he felt he
~~~~~~~~~~~~~~~~~~~~~~~~

would not be able to break loose from her power . . . nor did he want to. Meanwhile, the hush of silence prevailed throughout as the luxury of time stood still for this man and that woman.

Sexual seduction

I'll come back later to the blissful bonding experience. But for now, let's talk about another facet of women: that old standby, seduction *with* sexual overtones. And just to add a little interest, let's include some creativity in the seduction.

Creativity

Picture a youthful-*minded* woman (age is not usually that important) who already knows how to romantically seduce her husband. She knows that even a light flirt can get his attention, and that her touch can ignite a fire. But she knows something else, too. She knows how to capture his mind – such as the morning after, standing at the door topless as she sees him off to work for the day.

Baby, what his eyes take in that morning is going to be on his mind all day. And beneath that mental image is going to be a slow burner that is gradually cooking all day long. Man, is he going to be hungering for more of her, for all of her, when he returns home. Moreover, every morning from then on he's going to be like a kid on Christmas morning, wondering – when is she going to give him another present, and around which corner will 'it' be?

You might ask about the difference, where on the one hand, her husband gives little more than a glance in his wife's direction as she changes into bedclothes for the night, but on the other hand, sees her topless at the door in the morning? The difference is: It's the context.

Seeing his wife getting ready for bed eventually becomes regularity, a norm. But seeing his wife topless while he's on his way out the door is totally out of context. Almost anything sexual can excite a man if it's unexpected and erotic. But as you know, not all men respond to the same things, so don't feel rejected if something in particular that you wear doesn't turn me on.

For example, in *Pretty Woman* there's a scene where the woman is wearing nothing but a man's tie. That had no appeal to me at all. Nevertheless, it was creative, and creativity is what can ignite a man.

Now let me tell you about the picture of a fully dressed woman who was wearing an item of apparel that flat-out triggered my appetite! It was the cap you were wearing in one of your pictures; it is so, so sexy on you.

Easy does it

Anyway, getting back to the man with the topless wife: By the time he gets home, his thoughts about her will have heated him to the boiling point. He nevertheless should show her as much patience as she needs. So if he's thoughtful, he'll take things slow and wait for his wife to invite him in. Meanwhile, he can take time simply to delight in her (and tell her so), even as she delights in him.

Extending to his wife as much patience as needed can bring about the kind of 'slow heat' that can bring them ultimately to the point of it becoming for her a blessed and remembered experience. But what about an occasion when the man needs to unwind and wants to take it slow? Then she should accommodate him, of course.

Men don't know the first thing . . . but neither do women

By the way, I've heard women say that men don't know the first thing about how to please a woman in the bedroom. I agree; most don't. So why don't women tell them? Men aren't mind readers. Or if a wife is too modest, maybe she can write those things in a note for her husband to read.

But do women stop and think that the same applies to them, that most women don't know how to please a man in bed? Or even what a man's number one need is? And yet taking care of it is perhaps the most heart-warming, respectful, and honoring way a wife can please her husband.

And what is that need? This may surprise a lot of women, because it's not sex (sex is number 2). What a man needs most is for him to feel he's his wife's hero; by her showing him honor through her respect and admiration (provided he has earned it). To a man, honor is essential.

Not surprisingly, this aligns with a very necessary need of women: To be utterly cherished and treated with the profound respect and care that one would treat an invaluable treasure, a pearl of great price.

Psychological seduction

Now let's get back to that blissful bonding experience. And let's call it psychological seduction. You'll understand why as we go along.

Without a doubt, it is one of woman's *most enduring and astonishing means to remarkable power in the marriage relationship*. Moreover, this power is something every woman will want to mark at the top of her list, because in the end, it can bring a woman what she wants in her marriage — simply by letting her man be a man.

In one sense, I think of this seduction as a beautiful melody playing in the minds of two people; the same melody, and it's filled with emotion and sensitivity. At times the emotion carries a feeling of her loveliness and charm. At times it surges within the man as a warm and deep passion. But once it begins, there is this distinctive feeling of bonding, and of being at peace, at one with the other person.

As an aside, imagine telling your married girl friends that any one of them dressed in regular clothes can turn their husband into 'melted butter' . . . by a pre-planned 'surrender' to him . . . *outside* the bedroom . . . *without* using sexual seduction. Do you think they would believe you? Probably not. But I'll bet they would if they could see things the way their husbands do.

Important information

So I want to help you to understand through a man's eyes (a) the extent of this remarkable power a woman holds, (b) to what degree of seduction her planned surrender will subdue a man, and (c) the lasting influence these two forces have on a man. Also, you will want to keep these three in mind as we move along.

The power produced: Psychological seduction is one of those things a woman doesn't know the value of, until she does it. Nevertheless, *the end result can bring a wife everything she needs in adding unity to her marriage*. If she does it right, and she loves her husband,

and he loves her, then through the power produced, the two of them can *connect* mentally, emotionally, and spiritually.

Just think about this . . . *real* connectedness, *real* intimacy, *real* passion, *real* peace! These are tremendous feats! And the specific way to achieve them is by psychological seduction. And . . . if she chooses to add sexual seduction as 'desert,' then yes, they're going to connect physically also.

The degree of seduction: While sexual seduction affects the physical, psychological seduction affects the other three. It does this by building the mental, emotional, and spiritual links between the married couple – slowly but continually, until these reach a crescendo-like level. But instead of the best moment ending, the upsurge holds, continuing to greatly affect him in mind, heart and soul. It has the same effect on the woman, but I want to stick with the husband's experience here.

The lasting influence: It's the heart of a man that's seduced and affected through his wife's *total* surrender. But unlike sex (following which a man's interest can quickly move on), this psychological seduction will not soon end. Nor can he quickly forget the experience – and certainly not the woman who initiated it – because this is the beginning, where getting a man to *internally* connect with her starts.

How to begin the pre-planned psychological seduction

You know that as a man I can only give you suggestions about a woman's body language from my male perspective. So let me tell you about a pose that is sumptuous, aesthetically pleasing, and compelling to a man – not to mention it is graceful, elegant and uniquely feminine –

and it is no accident that it happens to be the posture where a woman's seductive power is at its maximum.

She positions herself close to and facing, but just out of reach of her husband, who is sitting. (If she intends to add sexual seduction afterwards, she needs to sit within reach of her husband.)

Then she simply sits back on her heels while resting her knees on a soft covered floor. To me, a woman sitting back on her heels can absolutely capture a man's concentration — *it's a real turn-on to most men.*

The next most seductive way would be just to sit on the floor, her feet completely tucked under her skirt. She should, of course, be within arms' reach if she wants to include sexual intimacy, because when passion overtakes him, so will the compelling urge to touch her, and that swiftly stimulates the passion to follow.

The seduction experience taking place

While the psychological seduction is taking place, the couple will gradually become aware of a very pleasant pairing that is progressing between them. This pairing will stimulate an almost narcotic-like feeling of well-being, accompanied by a mutual awareness of a oneness — of sensual proportions (more in a compelling than inviting way) that soon becomes a pleasant and very tranquil influence on the mind, emotions, and spirit.

There, in that euphoric rendezvous, a woman will have her much-yearned-for experience of being sublimely satisfied in her relationship with that man, and him with her. What comes next is a *major* human experience, so please don't think of how I describe it as being over-the-top — it barely scratches the surface.

An accompanying passion — reminiscent of a majestic heavenly harmony, building to an orchestral-like magnitude — will be on such an inspiring and peaceful level that she will most likely remember it for a lifetime — perhaps because, after her numerous struggles and attempts over the length of the relationship, this is where the ultra-rewarding, unconditional surrender can ultimately take place in her heart.

Once she makes this voluntary surrender permanent, once she has fought the final battle within herself, the true intimacy and gentle peace she has hungered for since the relationship began . . . arrives.

This then, should mark her last hold-out, her final surrender to that man for life. The man, too, honoring her commitment, will be deeply and irrevocably affected by her change; he will become further, more deeply, and more lovingly attracted to her. There, one man and one woman can truly know a permanent bond or covenant relationship has been formed to keep them in a oneness for life.

Could any wife desire more intimacy than a pairing of spirit and soul — to be caught up in the moment with her husband, mutually sharing in the same ecstatic, rapturous experience? (And remember, this has all been done without sexual seduction.)

What if she does add sexual seduction to her psychological seduction, and then raises it to the boiling point? If she does, then a powerful force will overcome him to break all boundaries to take her.

I believe there will come a time when you will have learned

how to do that to me, and drive me to the very edge. Then, someday, when the time is right, we will go to that edge together.

Babygirl, I have done my best to describe the incredibly alluring passion that comes upon a man, and the power that comes from a woman, when the two draw close together and gaze into one another's eyes, their thoughts and emotions shared. Two people, caught up in each other; a coming together as one in an astonishing affair — when a wife chooses to initiate psychological seduction before her husband.

In conclusion

If wives learned how to stimulate a man's mind to where he is sweetly (and permanently) captivated, their husbands wouldn't be able to stay away for very long without hungering for their companionship. By then, of course, a wife would have entered her husband's mind, written her signature on his heart's mailbox, and taken up permanent residence there.

For you (and me) it is ultra-important that you participate in this with me, so all of it will come together for us. Then we'll experience what rich pleasures come to the couple able to achieve unreserved bliss, time and again, through an intimacy that, unfortunately, defies my ability to describe in the way it deserves.

Do I sometimes sound like a preacher hammering out a "wives must surrender" doctrine from the pulpit? Yes, I am guilty of that. Still, I know of *no other way* to having a peaceful, happy home, than for a wife to let a man be a man.

Which reminds me: whatever happened to the women who know men will jump through a hoop for a woman who acts feminine?

Men need to see femininity in their wives, not manliness.

A husband should be humbled when he sees his wife loving him in this way, with all her heart in an attitude of surrender. And if he's not gentle and honorable, her yielded attitude could make him so. He could rise forth correspondingly as her knight in shining armor, and be all the other things she needs her husband to be, including the emotional and spiritual bonding aspects that truly fulfill their covenant.

Certainly a husband's proper attitude to such an extraordinary wife as this should be one of utmost appreciation and adoration. And I think husbands should express this appreciation to their wives often and in all manner of ways . . . at least daily. It really doesn't matter what those ways are so long as he sticks to her primary love language, so she will feel loved when he does. And she needs to remember to do the same for him, according to his primary love language.

I realize that if a man wants lots of intimacy, then appreciation and courtesy go a long way with a female. Furthermore, I believe that any husband who does not show his respect and appreciation for his wife's own respectful acts toward him is not fit to be her husband and lead her.

Apparently there are too few women who realize they can be one of these extraordinary women, whose change to surrender then changes their husband to treat them in extraordinary ways, with respect, esteem, and loving care. But it happens. If their husbands have integrity and take seriously their marriage, these yielded wives can cause them to be everything they have wanted them to be. Even difficult men might be won over through their observance of the agreeable nature and reverence in the lives of their wives who follow I Peter 3.

Furthermore, a wife's humility, integrity and receptiveness can become the catalyst that will *sustain* and *maintain* her husband in the frame of mind toward her that she needs him to be. In fact, I think God, in his wisdom, uses the woman as a way to teach the man many things, through her respectful behavior and other qualities.

A woman learns to use her yielded softness as a way of helping to mold a good man into what he has been created to be, a strong, confident leader and protector. But if he rebuffs that softness, he will harden and break her. In that process, he will experience her softness turned on him in the form of manipulation, and will be shattered by her. A woman scorned can become an angry person spewing out toxic fury.

But with the right kind of wife, a husband of honor will redirect his power and purpose to serve her kindly, gently, and in everything, happily and with a joyful heart . . . with all that is within him. And as the wife actively portrays her soft compliance through attitude, she will see a change take place in him. *That's* the kind of woman to whom I want to be married!

Okay, so what else am I trying to say here? From my male perspective, if a wife's surrendered attitude and poses are what cause her husband to melt, then it stands to reason that her husband will *stay* melted, humble and gentle toward her if she will just *maintain* that part of her lovestyle.

Baby, because such extraordinary women can grow their husbands to higher levels of masculinity, leadership and servant-hood, I want to encourage you to be one of those certain women. Actually, I *need* you to be, because this is the kind of woman I must have for a wife. And I will be on my best behavior to be the man you must have for a husband.

Of course, some men are like jackasses (like those who came to my couples' group for one session and then quit, while their wives stayed on). While a jackass refuses to budge or change, most men will respond very favorably and become permanently attached and emotionally involved with their wives, as they should be and (hopefully) promised in their marriage vows that they would be.

Listen, I've covered a lot of territory here, trying to summarize the way of a maiden with a man. Also, it's very important to me. So would you please read this email a couple of more times, just to give every main thought a chance to stand out? Then please give me your thoughts on all this?

Excerpt from Mixie's Response:

In considering the way of a woman with a man, you must remember that a woman's heart is a deep ocean. He's got to swim for a long time to find each treasure buried deep beneath the surface. She sometimes moves the treasure just little bit to make it harder to find, because she likes to see him on the hunt. She might even bury it under a rock and sit on it. But she sure loves it when he discovers one of her treasures. Then she entices him with another one, making sure he has to stop several times and massage the evidence before he finds the new one.

64 Confrontation is no fun

I don't like confrontation between us; it's no fun. But even when it's necessary, let's try not to take it personally when either of us is confronted by the other. Instead, why don't we think of it as someone loving us enough, and feeling we are important enough, to come to us with the truth? (Or at least their perception of the truth.)

You and I are a team of one — one-half plus one-half. Neither of us is complete without the other. It's not me against you, or you against me. It's *Us* working together on the same team, to fix an area that needs to be adjusted so our team can work smoothly again.

Every couple clashes about things from time to time; it is life's way to hone us. Besides, every time you and I have differed about something, isn't it true that we have become even closer than ever after the difference gets settled? Making up can be such fun! (Even over the phone.)

Whenever you think you're in the right, please say so and why you think so. I don't mind saying when I've been wrong, I'm just glad the error is caught so I can correct it. But you know that about me already. And if it should turn out that you're in the wrong, try thinking of what I say as me thinking out loud about what we need to work on next in the relationship.

Just be soft and non-resistant; let me do my job as the leader. And remember, every time you become softly pliable, you'll be becoming more feminine to me (not to mention more cuddled in the warmest nook of my heart).

A lot of marriages in this country are failing, including many of those couples going to marriage counselors. But other marriages are succeeding, where husbands are leading and wives are yielding. (Remember how it's impossible to argue with someone who won't argue back?) So please pay very close attention to what these wives have to say in their articles I've sent to you; it's very obvious they know what they're talking about. Their marriages prove it every day, because they live it every day.

I've noticed much of their journaling is for expressing the happy results of both pleasant and unpleasant learning experiences that they have walked through with their husbands. Or else they learn the things about themselves and the relationship whenever they succeed in passing another hurdle in their lives. Or their husbands have learned something helpful in the process. The result is a warmer and deeper connection with their husbands. And notice how contented they are in their marriages of harmony.

Sure, they write of feeling miserable when they've displeased their husbands (as a husband should feel, too, if he hurts his wife emotionally or displeases her in other ways). But notice how they seldom express feelings of rejection by their husbands. That's because they seldom are. Although a husband may feel deeply disappointed if his wife should disrespect something he asked of her, he's not the one who feels miserable because of it; a loving husband will take it in stride and be quick to forgive.

Instead, it's the wife who beats herself up for having fallen short of her idea of a "perfect" wife (which she needs to learn not to do; it solves nothing). Her standards for herself are unreasonable; they're too high, much higher in fact than anything her husband might expect of her.

Her husband shouldn't even allow her to beat herself up but, instead, say something to the effect of, "Hey, you're human. I love you and forgive you. So get up, or let me help you up, and let's move forward, together . . ." He should lift her up, "wash her feet," lavish her with affection . . . It's when women feel the most unlovable that they need the most love.

The only time a husband or wife should feel miserable is after *willfully* disrespecting or otherwise hurting their spouse. In that context, misery can be a good motivator, because it won't go away until that person makes things right again.

For obvious reasons, disharmony in a marriage cannot be tolerated. No matter who's at fault, both wife and husband must quickly get back in sync . . . else the wife could feel unloved, unappreciated, disrespected and insecure in the relationship, and the husband could feel frustrated, because men don't like to feel their leadership being contested.

If the disharmony happens to be the fault of the husband, and he's reasonable when shown his fault, then his correcting it quickly eliminates any further frustration that either has been feeling. But a run-away filly is hard to catch, so he needs to make the correction quickly and sincerely.

One of the reasons most marriages with surrendered wives work so well is that the wife's respectful attitude and behavior keeps male and female hot and alive for each other. They're able to slip much more quickly and easily through the confrontational times. For that reason if for no other, let's be sure our relationship keeps moving in that direction.

I love you dearly.

65 Please, listen to me

In your dating site profile you wrote that you wanted to marry a man who will *"strive to adhere to moral principles, including the 'traditional' marriage vows,"* and lead you to do likewise.

Sure, a lot of people who read your profile might have thought you were nuts to say something like that. But to me it just cut to the chase and saved a lot of time for both of us. You made it plain and up front what your life was "centered on." Obviously, I liked that because I wrote back.

Anyway, since those traditional vows are important to this email and our potential future together, I want to include them here.

Traditional marriage vows

Christian marriage vows constitute a covenant, far stronger than any contract, and are comprised of four major, biblically based principles. First and foremost is the principle of "union," the joining of two into one. "For this reason a man will leave his father and mother and be united to his wife, and they shall become one flesh." (Genesis 2:24) (So for either one to abuse or disrespect the other would be to abuse and disrespect oneself . . . unthinkable!)

This union is a lifetime commitment, not to be entered into lightly or honored only when it is convenient. When there are problems, the couple is to work them out together and seek harmony in their marriage. They are to cleave to each other, not run back to their parents or friends.

The other three core principles in the traditional marriage vows are *love, honor* and *submission*. These all work together and help define the full meaning of each. When each is fully present in a marriage, the others flow naturally.

So here are the traditional vows taken by bride and groom as they enter into their most holy marriage covenant:

> I, (*Man*), take this woman to be my lawfully wedded wife, *to love and to cherish*, to have and to hold, for better and for worse, for richer, for poorer, in sickness and in health; and I do promise, forsaking all others, to cleave to her and her alone, for as long as we both shall live.

> I, (*Woman*), take this man to be my lawfully wedded husband, *to honor and to obey*, to have and to hold, for better and for worse, for richer, for poorer, in sickness and in health; and I do promise, forsaking all others, to cleave to him and to him alone, for as long as we both shall live.

The vows are identical except for the portions I italicized. It's these portions I want us to talk about, because if something is easy to do, automatic even, one doesn't need to have a person promise to do it. For example, like breathing in and breathing out; it's a given.

So why mention it, why ask a person to promise to do something they're going to do anyway? Or here, why have the bride and groom give their respective promises?

It's because, unlike breathing, the keeping of these vows is not automatic; they require conscious effort if they're to be fulfilled as promised.

Did you know it's not so easy for a man to *love* and *cherish* his wife? Sometimes he wants to kill her. LOL. But seriously, the husband is commanded to love his wife with an unconditional, self-sacrificing, giving love ("agape") that seeks her protection and best interests. Obviously, a woman loved this way will want to stay with him for life. But from the man's point of view, this kind of love is far, far harder than just emotional, romantic love.

And I realize it's not any easier for a woman to *honor* and *obey* her husband; a man can be a real jerk at times and lose a wife's respect. But a husband who follows God's instructions for marriage, and for God's kind of love and treatment of the wife he cherishes, as well as in all his life matters (to the extent humanly possible), will earn his wife's honor and respect, both personally and positionally. That's the goal.

Honor and respect are essential for a marriage to succeed. Some people overlook the fact that the *principle of honor* is directed in the Bible to both husbands and wives, and is closely related to the command for the husband to love his wife unconditionally, sacrificially. 1 *Peter* 3:7 says:

> *"Husbands, in the same way be considerate as you live with your wives, and treat them with respect as the weaker partner and as heirs with you of the gracious gift of life, so that nothing will hinder your prayers."*

A husband who sees his wife as a pearl of great value to be loved and protected will give her honor, and she will naturally want to honor and follow this loving husband who is committed to her and shows her respect. How could we possibly be happy if we did not honor and respect each other?

But let's get back to the marriage vows. The bride's vow of submission (to "honor and obey") is in conjunction with the love and esteem the husband is to give her. We know it's not calling her to obey blindly like a dog to an ungodly man or to be a doormat. But it recognizes that God has set the man as the head of the home, although some chauvinistic jerks distort the intent by seeking to justify their own "slave" approach, disregard and abuse of their wives.

But God's Word is clear about the kind of love, care, respect and leadership the husband is to give his wife, and that he is to submit to God (1 *Corinthians* 11:2) just as she submits to him. That makes God my leader, and so, too, I will seek to lead and love you as the treasured gift from God that you are, so that I am deserving of your trust, honor and willing submission to my leadership.

This is all critically important. After all, if these promises exchanged between the couple were not important, or if they were easy to keep, would they have been included in the vows?

Another thing: Did you notice how few key elements are in each vow? Imagine all that could have been added, that wasn't. What is contained in the vows is the core; the very essence of what is essential in a marriage covenant, nothing more, and nothing less. Just imagine how wordy the first attempts must have been, trying to compose the vows to include everything the clergy thought should be there. It could have taken pages and pages.

So, given the brevity of the traditional vow, how essential would you say are every word and principle that was retained? *Very* essential, right? And couples took those words and their marriage covenants seriously!

Society, unfortunately, decided it knew better. So, following society's gradual decay in morality, for many there's no longer any resemblance to the commitments and morality mutually promised in the traditional vows.

The message in your profile

That's why the message I got from your profile was so mind-catching. I reasoned that any woman who wanted a husband to lead her, who himself was trying to live a morally upright life and would honor the fullness of his marriage covenant, must be a woman who herself was willing to follow, to honor and obey, to yield to that man.

Was I mistaken? Although your words said one thing, was your heart saying something entirely different? Was it saying that you could — not *would* but *could,* (as in, *if and when you wanted to*) — honor and obey your husband?

None of that became evident to me until recently, when I began focusing on what you were doing instead of what you were saying. Actions speak louder than words, don't they?

From the very first day, we enthusiastically began to exchange and interchange more of our "likes and dislikes,"' and over the following weeks, we discovered we were becoming quite the compatible couple. The future was looking bright indeed, so we took the relationship to a higher level.

You had already said in your profile, and in your second email to me, that you wanted a man to encourage you and "urge" you to grow. You said you wanted to develop in whatever ways you needed to, so you would "make him an excellent wife." And then later you asked me to take on that role and start your growth and development. So we began by discussing some areas that are already fundamental to every woman's natural inclinations, areas in which a woman could grow to make a more excellent wife.

I recall how happy you were to know about these unique and desirable features, and to know that you already had them built in, just waiting to be exercised. As we discussed each one, you mentioned how easy they would be for a woman to do, and that you were "ready to get to work." You said you wanted to begin "right away," and you asked me to help you by doing "whatever it takes to keep [you] at it." So, over the next several days I created a workable plan for you and gave you Step One of the first goal, which you agreed to begin right away.

Since that day, however, you've not yet begun, not even the first step. That marvelously special woman still lies mostly hidden within you, waiting to be stimulated by the special groom who can lead you to new heights, to life's grandest purposes to which you were born, where you can experience the most joy and happiness.

It has taken me a while, but finally I think I know why you've not yet embarked on what you told me you wanted my help to do. It appears to be because you've been scoffing at some things I've said. Once or twice you've said you knew "all about those things." And about other things — important things to develop intimacy — you've said that you take them "with a grain of salt."

I've gotten the impression that because you've been distracted from reading the articles written by longtime successfully married wives, you and I aren't on the same page. Or is it that you're just not interested in what they have to teach you?

You apparently aren't readily adopting those things as yours that they say are so important to a successful marriage. Furthermore, you don't even know *what* they're saying, do you? Yet, obviously, from what these women are saying about how they are going about things in their marriages, they're relationally happier than they've ever been. They've found their "home" and now have passion, peace and harmony, and especially deep down intimacy, because of it.

But for you and me, it seems that things are beginning to wind down, perhaps even approaching a dead end. I keep getting the feeling that you're taking a free ride and treating everything as if it were a game, and me as your source of entertainment. It really hurts me to say this, but I'm beginning to see no reason for us to continue as a couple.

Unless you start taking seriously the promises you included in your profile, and that we've discussed, and you begin doing your part, I see that to continue our relationship would be futile.

I love you more than you know. To separate from you would rip me into pieces and create in me untold anguish. Already I feel like you are tearing my heart apart, limb-by-limb.

I am more than miserable, because I fear the girl I have fallen in love with is fictitious, that you have invented her as a part of your game plan. It's hard to know these things right off when one person lives thousands of miles from another.

Babygirl, please listen to me. Do you see how happy and content you feel when you visualize yourself under my care, but how nerve-wracking everything was before? Do you see how peaceful and calm everything has been, and could continue to be as you give yourself to me for safekeeping and direction? All I'm asking is that you give me more of yourself to protect and to help, so I can make your life so much easier.

Have you noticed how useful you've begun to feel, both to me and to yourself, as you experience making a positive impact on your world and on me? Have you seen how you've begun to change in your attitude and confidence level? Yes, of course you've seen these things, and you've embraced them for your good fortune and mine.

But now there are things that need to be exercised, and others that need to be developed. Otherwise, how can we enjoy multiple blessings from what each of us can do for the other, if only one of us is doing it?

My days are dark and cloudy. The nights seem to pass without the moon and stars. No longer can I feel you inside me; I am empty and adrift. I am being shredded apart inside.

Please, listen to me!

66 Are those extraordinary gifts I see?

Are those extraordinary gifts I see that nature has showered on you? Yes, and in abundant measure!

You were endowed with much beauty as well, although you've said you're not beautiful, and have never thought of yourself that way. Perhaps you think you're not gorgeous, as man would judge beauty. Nevertheless, you're more than beautiful in my eyes. More than that, your beauty is *perfect* in my eyes.

You're all wrapped up in the most lovely, feminine package I have ever known, and with the prettiest bow and ribbon, too! On that package written in gold are the words, *"I want to be swept away and surrender my all into your waiting arms as my beloved husband."* It's that word *surrendered* written on your "package" that guarantees to me the awesomeness of the beauty and the greatness of the treasure that I know will be found within.

Now then, to surrender does not mean to be weak or cowering. Quite the contrary, surrendered wives are often very strong, influential and proud women, well aware of their effect on and power over men, and many quite accomplished and respected professionally. Their surrender is to their husbands and no one else, and they're not shy about it. (In fact, if other people cross the line, the husband had better step in and say, "That's enough. Don't talk to my wife that way.")

Yet even surrendered wives can be resistive to authority during times of anger, like when the husband behaves badly and makes them furious. This is when a quick nip from the filly will certainly tell him when he oversteps the bounds.

She would be remiss in her responsibility to him should she fail to correct his errors, doing so constructively and privately, in the same respectful manner in which he should do the same for her. Don't you agree?

Perhaps that's why there are so few women who are "heart-resolved" (self-dedicated, decided and determined) to be respectful peacemakers, as compared with the larger number of women (although itself comparatively small) who call themselves "peace-makers" when in fact they start smoldering fires.

Perhaps with some wives their motivation comes from seeing the awesome status to which another wife is elevated in her husband's eyes. Then she herself seeks to attain a similar position from her own husband.

But whatever her reason, she can have her heart's desires met through her total surrender to him when he cherishes her as he should, and opens his heart to be her home. Her home is her castle, her domain, and she wants it peaceful more than just about anything.

This is only the beginning, however. Then comes the fight when her insecurities try to coerce her back into taking control and running the show. During these times, it's important for her to remember that her husband may be new in this lead role, and she needs to make up her mind she is going to do her best to help him rather than fight with him.

She might recall the very day she first decided to surrender, the day that marked the major turnaround in her life, as proof to herself that she did indeed fully commit herself to her husband. And if she did it once, she can repeat it again and again.

But . . . a woman who has chosen to yield to her husband is seldom able at first to remain successful at it for long. Repeatedly, she may slip back into the old unhappy ways as you have been doing recently.

But practice makes permanent. Sooner or later you can reach that point of heart-intended resolve to do or die. That's when you're able to snuggle into the palm of that cozy and secure hand *and stay there.*

And when that happens, then you can be cuddled forever, instead of becoming an unhappy, stubborn ox whenever you improperly take the lead — like recently.

It took years before I woke up, coming to the conclusion that all of us must learn life's lessons on our own, and quickly. Else we *will* be taught by the hard knocks of life, and who in their right mind wants to suffer through those?

I think this particularly applies to the areas of humility and respect for both husbands and wives, especially those who want to be extraordinary in their roles. By that I mean spouses who are mutually fulfilling their respective purposes or roles well enough that both spouses are warmly content in the other.

This is why I repeat: one gift in particular that's granted to all women in fulfillment of their role as a wife is the ability to yield to their husband's leadership. I realize, however, that there is a huge difference between the ability to do something and actually doing it.

The ability to yield is supplied at birth. But so are free will and the ability to rebel, the desire or often perceived need to take control by usurping the husband.

The actual choice to surrender comes at the threshold of marriage, as the bride is drawn in by the leadership, character and loving kindnesses of her beloved. Then naturally and also with clear intent and commitment, the new wife can conquer her reservations and fears about yielding totally with a solemn marriage covenant.

That's why the wife must look at far more than financial security, comfort and legalized sex. She must be able to know and trust that her husband is a man of integrity and will be fair, balanced and wise in the conduct of his life and their affairs, and that he will honor, respect and include her. He, in turn, should take care to find a woman who will be a blessing on a man, because a shallow playgirl, controlling woman, or trophy wife is not worth the dedication and great love he will give to a cherished pearl of great value.

67 Complimentary things about you

Tonight you thanked me for saying complimentary things about you. But you see, what's really happening is that you're beginning to live in harmony with one of nature's laws – you're becoming the person you were designed by God to be. (And even more importantly in this process, "your groom" is also learning how to treat you and handle you better.)

So all of the beauty of you, and all the wonderful attributes within you, are beginning now to flow freely out of you. All I'm doing is simply reporting what I'm observing about your new *You.*

I just sent you some more articles you might find interesting. These have the common thread of husbands' comments about seeing their wives as so much more desirable because of their change of mind. Like most of the other comments, blogs and such about husbands, these were written by wives excited to discover that being committed to living in agreement to their husbands' direction is a choice that brings peace and protective cover over her, while walking in sync with him at his side, watching his blind side.

So it's the wives' commitment to surrender and nurture that explains the husbands' comments about their wives' turnaround, which in turn is causing their husbands to have even stronger desires for them – emotionally and physically – and will stimulate them also to adapt better to their wives. If the wife learns to be gentle and compassionate (unless her husband is a jack's derriere), then he will start coming around fast.

Why is this? Because when a woman yields to her man, it does something to him. It acts on him in a positive way. It makes him melt like butter. *It's just a matter of when . . . right now, or soon.*

Precious, I'm looking forward to all the exciting discoveries still ahead for *Us,* and the glorious life we will enjoy as you continue to learn about the lovestyle I offer you.

68 A powerful principle of nature

You evoked a very powerful principle of nature the other night. It didn't take long for you to reap the benefits, either. When those pleasant feelings swept over me . . . well, they were instantaneous. Moreover, what's evolved since then is more than I expected, meaning the effect your actions are having on me are even more powerful.

I want to remind you of something I said some time ago. Do you remember my saying that the proper actions of a woman would always bring positive reactions from her man? If her attitude is *suddenly* one of surrender, it will evoke a powerful physical stimulation in him, too. And that's what you've done in me.

Your turnaround in attitude and resolve instantly triggered in me a higher respect for you, a greater appreciation, and a deeper love. My love for you seemed to have immediately penetrated miles deeper down inside me. My heart felt as excited as a kid seeing a state fair for the first time. I can't begin to attempt to dig myself out of that love pocket you sent me to.

You are no longer resisting various things I ask of you. Your recent commitment and new resolve, *and your action* of yielding to my leadership and handling of matters, have caused my love for you to expand and grow stronger in ways I never imagined. Moreover, you've caused the capacity of my protective and nurturing instincts to soar.

You have begun working harder and with more diligence, and you're learning much more now about how to seduce and dress for a man. You've been practicing various poses and postures, protocols and mannerisms characteristic of seductive surrender. *These things, along with your discovery of your inner femininity, have now enabled you to exert captivating power over me.*

Wow! You've built up quite a list of accomplishments, haven't you? What it all adds up to, of course, is that you're learning more all the time about how to keep a man's *full and undivided* interest. And that's exactly what my dating site profile said I needed in a woman.

BTW, most of the time it's full skirts and dresses, please. That's the way to keep me always thinking of you as so very feminine and captivating. (Skirts sway when a woman walks; this adds to her attraction. Shorts and pants are okay, too; just not all the time, please.)

Since you've stopped leading so that I might lead, I've felt more intimate and loving toward you, even more than before. And even more responsible for your welfare, because now that you've voluntarily made yourself vulnerable to me, and trusting, you've also made yourself secure! God willing, you will never have to worry about anything regarding your future ever again, at least not in any of the ways I can help.

I'm delighted you want to keep on keeping on in the excellent job you're doing in your surrender-related skill development (poses, postures, etc.) and the impacts on your beautiful, soft heart. I'm so very proud of you! I only hope I've been improving, too, softening and further earning your trust.

Since you put your resolve into action concerning total surrender, you are seeing how the law of sowing and reaping is being fulfilled, positively and immediately. God's way can always be counted on. We just need to be sure that we're always on the right side of it.

I love you completely and with deep and powerful passion.

69 The power of resolve

Do you know what it means to have a husband glorify his wife, and how he goes about it? To "glorify" means to cause to be or treat as being more splendid, excellent, etc., than normal; to honor with praise, admiration; to extol. That's what I want to do for you.

Do you know what a glorified woman looks like on the outside, feels like on the inside, and behaves like? She's easy to recognize. She's powerful. She's radiant. She's contented. She's happy, satisfied, complete and . . . she's secure in her husband's leadership.

Do you begin to understand and look forward to the idea of how good you will feel as this glorified woman?

But if there's friction between us, it can't happen. The glorification process begins (or resumes) and continues only during those times when a couple is in harmony, and peace and harmony are at their best when the wife is yielded to a loving servant/leader husband.

So please give your best to this, without which all the rest cannot happen. I am doing my best both to deserve and to help you, as I assume this most awesome responsibility.

You may be asking right about now how to be surrendered, each time, every time, and all the time. The answer is: you can't; we're both only human, and we all fall short daily. But we *can* make a firm resolve ahead of time to do our best, every time.

By already having the resolve, any temptation to abuse one's power over the other, to control or usurp a role has no room to grow because the decision was already made, already resolved, already plugged in before the temptation got there.

A resolve made ahead of time can, almost instantly, diffuse most inner turmoil a person may temporarily experience due to the struggle of whether that person will or will not choose to honor the other and their marriage covenant (even when it's not "convenient").

As you continue to devote yourself to the idea of fully trusting my leadership, here's what will happen: Your sense of being loved, your feeling of belongingness, your state of security, and your contentment are going to grow leaps and bounds, because there won't be friction over who leads. After all, that gets couples into arguments.

Over time you'll discover that any of your misgivings, negative feelings or attitudes about a wife yielding to her husband will lessen considerably. Those feelings will be replaced with positive benefits, such as my wanting even more time with you, and much more of you.

I think you're also going to have the positive feelings of happiness and success, and an ever-deepening intimacy with me. You'll know you're safe in your cocoon within my heart that I have been lovingly maintaining for you.

There are all kinds of rewards that come to a couple when there's man/woman unity. The way to have unity is to have peace and harmony in the home, and the way to have peace and harmony in the home is for the husband to lead.

All of us learn with our minds, of course, because that's where information enters. But the things precious to us work their way from our minds into our hearts. The things I've been teaching you will make their way into your heart. And as they do, our intimacy can rise to a new and spectacular level once we begin to show our love for one another physically.

As a woman, you know what it means to have understanding from the heart. Nevertheless, in the mind is where resolve begins. You'll probably measure your level of resolve by the actions you take that are in harmony with my leadership, and at some point in the future, your (total and absolute) resolve will hopefully make its way into your heart.

Once you lay it down, you'll no longer have the burden of responsibility for any decisions I make for us, even while retaining a powerful, most valued "say." Instead, you'll have exchanged that burden for freedom, and this will enable you to soar in your endeavors and to express your femininity in new and refreshing ways.

There will come a time when these things will be even more solidly entrenched in you. I will know when that time has arrived because you will be automatically looking to me to be the primary decision maker. You will gladly defer to me because you will have reached a place where you ultimately trust me and deeply desire to surrender your all to me in various ways. Once you have reached this place, you will have a sense of completeness and a fullness of contentment.

Moreover, when you've reached this place in your heart, you'll have given me the ultimate gift: your complete devotion. You will have become in every way a woman who is then fully useful to herself and her husband. And everything in your life will appear fresher, newer, crisper, simpler, easier, better and happier.

All along I have been teaching you a little here, a little there, and giving you simple and small goals to achieve, which you mostly have. Although each of these achievements may seem insignificant to you as they happen, they will keep adding up. Then, one day you can look back and feel as if you are standing on a mountaintop, looking down at where you had begun. When that happens, your sense of accomplishment and pride in yourself will be one of my greatest rewards, and it will please me indeed; you will see it in my eyes and on my face.

I don't want less for us as the years go by; I want more. I don't want the holding of hands in public to diminish with the progression of years. I don't want our desire for each other to cool off; I want it to burn hotter. I don't want to hear the words, "Well, they've been married for (blank) years, so they're not romantic anymore." I don't want our romance to grow weaker; I want it to grow stronger. And I don't want to want you less; I want to want you more.

70 Your surrender is so sensual to me

My babygirl, your submission is so sensual to me. You are such a tantalizing Hot Chili Pepper! You are arousing and exciting and erotic, and every wonderful sensation the mind can imagine, all of it flowing over me. It's like you have me in a Jacuzzi, only better. Every time you yield to me, you drive me insane with desire.

Titillating . . . That's the word I'm looking for. It describes all these things you're doing to me. *Exhilarating* is another. You feel so good to the inside of my body. You feel so warming inside my head. Thoughts of you are acting like massaging fingers to my mind—very pleasant and relaxing.

Thank you for the positive change in you. Thank you for being such a delightful and delicious female. Thank you for beginning to learn how to make me want you with such fever and passion.

Thank you for saying yes to your youthful girl inside, for giving her permission to come forth, and for wanting to continue your lessons to release even more of your femininity for me to enjoy . . . for *Us* to enjoy.

And thank you for your renewed commitment. All this is now possible because you are exercising surrender. I am so proud of you; you couldn't be lovelier than you are right now.

71 I love you

I love you, darling girl. I love you because you allow yourself to be that baby for me. I love you because you fill the need I have inside to be the protector of that babygirl.

I love you because you allow me to exercise that at which I'm very gifted, and that is to take exceptionally good care of my woman. Your response makes me feel competent and capable in that role, and needed and respected. (That's so very important to a man.)

I love you because you are teachable and, especially, because you are now willing to put into practice what you learn.

I love you because you're becoming so moldable, so adaptable, so soft and yielding, and desirous of seductive surrender, which causes you to exude even greater sexuality.

I love you because you have all the perfect ingredients necessary for a woman to be a woman of compellingly attractive and captivatingly seductive qualities.

Yes, seduction is you. It's your playground. It's a part of you; it flows from your lips, and it draws me to you! Seduction helps to form your attitude and behavior, to make you the lovely, sensual creature you are. And because you are seductive, you will always be on my mind. My thoughts of you will always be loving, caring and protective. My need for you will always bring me to you, hurrying back to my future lover.

These are just a few of the reasons I love you. I think I could easily go to 100 reasons nonstop before pausing for breath, and then write the second 100. But I think I'll stop for now, and save the rest to give to you as you need to hear them, a few at a time.

I must add this very important one, though: I love you because you are a pearl of great price!

72 Keep open the floodgates of love

In the same way birds need to fly, in the same way they love the sky, I need and love you.

My sweet babygirl, you're my dearest. I cannot help but love you, and to love you deeply. Yet imagine . . . we have just begun.

The song we sing will grow into many verses, floating on a melody so lovely, so satisfying, its chords will continue to play even when we have drunk our fill of love and sleep overtakes us.

In the mornings when we awaken, the melody will still be there, waiting . . . to lift our hearts with its presence, to fill us again with its passion, to empower us to soar in intimate togetherness with the beginning of each new day.

We can feel love, we can make love, we can have love, and we can be loved. All of this can be ours as you keep open the floodgates of love for us — through your desire and follow-through to be my surrendered babygirl.

73 I've put my all into you

You've heard me say that my purpose is you, but do you remember me saying that you should tell me your current feelings every day, so I'll know what my babygirl needs? I've got to know that you're not holding back from expressing your true feelings, like you did in your previous marriage because you feared your late husband would be upset.

I want to remove that part of the burden you've been carrying, which is why I *do* want you to express your true feelings. Always, baby, always be true to yourself and to me. I've got to have accurate reactions from you, or else we'll get our relationship in a mess. Really. And a lot of that could be your fault, because if you're not giving me your honest thoughts, then I will be leading on false assumptions and be apt to make wrong decisions that affect our *Us*. So please, let's not let that happen.

Your very soul affirms my commitment and dedication – that they are to you, and for you, and that they are for real. You're much of the reason I get up each day pondering ways to be a better man. It's for you, precious baby . . . it's all for you.

Otherwise, had we never met, I would be sightseeing up and down the Rockies by now, from California to New Mexico. I would have abandoned my dream of ever finding the right wife for real happiness.

I also would have already shucked the whole idea of ever being able to use the knowledge I have spent all these years acquiring for a woman. All the skills would have been laid to waste that I believe I've developed over the years to cause me to change into a different man than the sorry one I was.

Had you not written to me, I would have continued believing that all those years on the dating sites were wasted; that of all the single women I had met during all those years, I just wasn't going to find the woman I needed. I had already concluded that the only woman I would ever want to pursue for marriage would be one who wanted to have a surrendered heart for her husband. But when I looked around and found that all the soft and compliant women I met were already married, I stopped trying to find "the one."

I had not yet realized that my dedicated study, self-work and search for my priceless treasure was *not* wasted, actually, because all along (although gradually) I was becoming a better man. What those women taught me as a whole made me appreciate them all the more. Also, I had begun recognizing the wisdom and wondrous beauty that women tirelessly contribute to this world, and that it is better because of them.

Other things about women, too, have contributed to my growth that I otherwise never would have experienced. Still, it was you coming into my life that helped me to begin putting it all together by applying my experiences toward relating to you.

So you are "heavy stakes," baby. I've put my all into you for one roll of the married-for-a-lifetime dice. I'm convinced you're the only woman I'm ever going to find who is able to meet my needs and encourage my growth to meet hers, all the while being able to put up with me.

74 Placed on a pedestal

Does a wife take advantage of the husband who places her on a pedestal? I believe the honest answer for some is going to be yes, at least at first. But not again and again – not after she realizes how good it feels to get to remain on the pedestal.

Being glorified and in perfect fellowship by pleasing her husband is not something a wife will easily give up. Wives who remain on pedestals are adorned by their husbands' provisions and nurturing. They're cared for and cherished. They get lots more attention, and their husbands are much more generous and responsive than normal. A wife so loved would be foolish to rebel against this environment of headship created by her husband's loving and protective will for her.

But still . . . it happens; wives usurp husbands.

All recognized authorities in the Church agree that Headship is the very environment scripture is commanding husbands to create. It is an awesome responsibility when carried out properly, and certainly no man has cause or room to gloat over having it. Wives should try to understand how very difficult the role of leadership can be, and support their husbands instead of seeking ways to challenge them or usurp them. On this you and I must agree; there can be no room for negotiation in this one.

You found out a long time ago how difficult it is to try to be the head of the family, because that's the role you took from your late husband. It was exhausting, wasn't it?

The role of husbanding can be a very humbling process. First off, he is not perfect. He will make mistakes. Often this can keep a man 'clawing' to try to get (and then be able to keep) a grip on so many things. If he's a man of faith, he'll forever be on his heart's knees before God to seek guidance for his marriage and to ask for help in becoming a better husband, as well as thanking God for his wife and asking him to bring blessings upon her.

If wives could look inside their husbands and see the frustration often found in truly sincere husbands, those same wives might feel shame for what they cause. That's because the disappointment comes from feelings of hurt caused by a wife's disrespectful acts — even after she decided along with her husband to do the very opposite.

Is there a wife who wishes to take the husband's leadership role? Oh, really? Then by all means, let her! But not now and then, just when she wants it; give her the whole bundle! And let her continue to lead through the days and weeks of havoc, not just the easy times.

Let her try to lead when her spouse is rebelling against all her decisions and being uncooperative with each one. Let her not be able to reason with her spouse when things have gotten totally unreasonable, since her spouse can't or refuses to be reasonable anyway. Let her be blamed for everything since she is the spouse who is making the decisions. And by all means tell her spouse to not help her. Better yet, tell him to resist her decisions as often as he can, and to never take back the lead role, because that's the role which already makes her responsible for the welfare of everyone in the family. And who wants to get stuck with that? Yet such is the lot for husbands.

Dramatic? Yes. But the husband's headship is not a perk, it's a charge given to the husband whereby he must do all within his power to protect the family. It's a burden of sorts, and burdens and responsibilities are not things to gloat about. Yet some husbands gloat about being in charge of their wives, even going so far as to become defensive when their wives (as women inevitably will) test the boundaries by testing their husbands' authority.

Yet it's not the husband in particular that's being tested, but rather a law of nature. The wife who goes against this law unknowingly places herself in dangerous waters that are far deeper, more powerful, and destructive than any human being can protect her from. When this happens, the husband must quickly do all he can to reason with his wife to save her from sinking before it's too late, before the law has taken hold of their situation. He must instead help her back up on that pedestal, and soon.

I said that a wife unknowingly places herself in dangerous waters when she usurps her husband; she has deceived herself by thinking she's safe. There's no time to reason with a person who's drowning. "You should have obeyed the signs posted by the lifeguard" is a pretty ridiculous statement at this end stage of the game. Instead, there's only time to snatch her out of the water and pump her lungs free, so she can get life-sustaining air.

So let me repeat the question above. Do wives take advantage of the husbands who place them on pedestals? Would you take advantage of me, knowing the pain and grief it would cause me? Should I be guarded with you, or should I love you unconditionally, day and night? Unless you know of something better, it's the only way I know of to keep you up on that pedestal, being glorified, and us in perfect fellowship.

75 Make me all soft inside like butter

Yesterday you said that the lovestyle I've been describing for us is as simple as the woman wanting to melt the man, and the man wanting to melt the woman. I think you hit the nail on the head!

Furthermore, it's the woman's soft and yielding attitude that melts her man, not her body. Her body, how she clothes it, postures and moves it, is important and certainly exciting to him, but her surrender takes the priority in turning up the heat high enough to melt him. Moreover, I think this may be why other women have had such a difficult task in trying to turn me on to them.

Normally, it's the body language and flirtation devices that would draw most men to them. But it's the femininity in the woman's spirit that equally goes to work on me. This is what gets my respect and instant interest.

I cannot say it here exactly the way you expressed it, yet I want to try. I want to be able to identify with you some of the things you've talked about. And, since you're looking to me for leadership, I want to do it in an understanding and thoughtful way — the way you like to be led. Then hopefully you'll wake up every morning taking comfort in the fact that I'm watching over you.

So, to begin, what I understood you to mean is that once you felt I was "the one," you've been aching for me, feeling your passion increasingly calling out to be with me. But then you realize you can't have me right away.

It's the same with me. Although I want you as you want me, I want to wait until we're married. And I appreciate your willingness to be whatever I need you to be because you love me.

When you respond to me by wanting to "fit in" with my thoughts and convictions, it's as if you become ultra-feminine to me. When you honor my convictions, it makes you even more indispensable, more attractive, more desirable, more seductive, and sexier.

Further, you've said you like the power you feel when your deference to my requests reveals my physical passion on the outside, and makes me all soft like butter on the inside. I like that too, because I like being seduced when I know I can respect and trust the seducer.

Generally, men initiate; women respond. It's the natural way of things. It's also the natural way of things for women to initiate seduction through soft surrender, but so few women do! Yet once they discover its power and how their men respond, look out!

I find the concept both spiritual and romantic, that a woman can take a man's power from him through seductive surrender, by something as simple as sitting back on her heels — just like she did when she was a little girl. Seductive surrender is so touching, so powerfully sexy, so sweet, and incredibly intimate, the way a girl can do that — make a man all soft inside like butter.

76 To guide you in the way you are

A wife can give her husband no greater gift (other than children) than to give him her full devotion and honor him. Since you're willing to do that, I feel very fortunate to have been enrolled for a number of years as a student in the *University of How to Please a Wife.* (I'll never know enough to graduate, however.)

Yet, other than that, what on earth would qualify me to be worthy of husbanding you? I haven't a clue. There's a certain amount of awe, fear and trembling in my soul when I consider the awesome role that's set before me as I am assigned the honor of being your husband. You are so special, so exquisite, so gifted.

Yet I know I'll give you my very best. And whatever I may lack (there will always be something), I know that your trust, adoration and devotion will drive me to continue to grow for you. Your seductive surrender will stimulate me beyond words, adding the final glue.

Meanwhile, I'm to stimulate you, too. I'm to encourage you to engage and exercise those particular surrender-related gifts of yours, to put them to work. This means I, especially, need to be in a continual state of personal growth, so that you will always trust my intentions.

It also means I need wisdom and patience in my roles as both your (future) lover and leader. I need to guide you in the way that will be according to your personal bent, because we know that "she who is convinced against her will is of the same opinion still."

So it does no good to force someone to comply. Instead, the inner motivation of the person must rule that person; compliance must come from a desire within. My leadership, love and devotion must stimulate that desire.

All this talk about growing may have you wondering if you're loved for who you are, just the way you are. This is why it's important for you to believe me when I tell you that yes, I *do* love you, *and exactly the way you are.*

But also, I love you too much to see you ignore possibilities when you're gifted to be so much more, for yourself . . . and for me.

77 Trusting and letting go

It's not easy to simply let go and trust. I understand that. And I also recognize that trusting and letting go is only the beginning; there's so much more. Otherwise, when one considers all the rewards that accompany the honor bestowed upon a truly devoted wife, if it required no effort, then every woman would want in.

It's no wonder, then, why those few women who do go to the effort, shine forth. And the husband who is married to one of these women knows he is blessed to have such a wife.

I've encouraged you almost from the beginning to talk with women I know with this experience, so you can see a bright and refreshing new world through their eyes and come away with a much better understanding of the rewards.

As you continue to do this, I will be daily proving myself. That won't stop even after I've earned your trust completely and you are surrendered. Then we will be able to walk in the path of "peace and harmony" together.

I've wanted you to gain this understanding for some time, yet I know how difficult it must be for you to trust. The decision-making process is a team effort; we pull together and find a middle ground. Although I will have the "tie-breaking vote," your wisdom, intuition, insights and wishes are critically important in this process. And once decisions are made, we must cooperate; I and *We* need you to support them fully.

I promise you, it's a wife's devotion, yielding and honoring her husband that stands the best chance of causing him (at least eventually) to become lovingly sensitive to her needs, feelings and vulnerability. And frankly, babygirl, just thinking about a wife being sweet and not argumentative is a real turn-on to a husband. It makes him want to hurry home to her.

My pride in you overflows my chest whenever I think of you. How responsive your heart, wanting to do the right thing; how tender it is, wanting to please me. How quickly you are embracing and assimilating the concepts we've talked about thus far.

This makes me want to please you all the more! Each of the things you're doing that pleases me is bringing you closer to me, just as I hope mine are doing for you. And gradually, you seem to be coming into agreement with the way I'm leading you.

But imagine a couple where the husband becomes demanding, controlling or abusive, or a couple where the wife is no longer sweet but rebellious. Imagine the disconnect between this man and woman. Imagine the cost to the relationship of either one's failure. Imagine how much time and energy will be required to restore it, even if only to a lesser level.

A couple can't expect to just step back into the same place where they had been. They can't just resume the entwining, the coming together. Lost momentum is costly. When these two souls were joined, they made solemn promises to one another. His were to love and cherish his wife; hers were to honor and obey her husband, and both promised to cleave to one another, forsaking all others, until parted by death.

These promises may seem archaic now, but between those couples that made and meant them, divorce seldom occurs. This is because the promises were not only taken seriously at the marriage altar and beyond, they were seen as a holy covenant, more binding even than a legal contract. They weren't only between the wedding couple, but between those two individuals and God. And they weren't about to break a covenant with Almighty God.

The marriage covenant called for action not words. But since the words of that vow are no longer respected and used, there are now more divorces occurring in the United States than former times when those solemn promises were honored.

I've been at this stuff for more than 20 years, and that's not one year's experience multiplied 20 times. It's 20 years in which I've spent time studying women. All that time I've been asking questions, learning and observing. Yet I'm only just now reaching the point of realizing how little I know in comparison to how much more is out there to learn about women.

But that's no longer my goal; that stopped being my goal when I met you. Since then, my goal has been to learn all I can about *you*, and whether we could make a successful couple.

Do you know where we got the word *husband?* Depending on whom one consults, it appears to come ultimately from an old Norse word which meant the master of a house. Over the centuries, however, more meanings have been added to reflect what the master of a house is who has a wife. And so, depending on the language in which the Norse word was used, the word husband came to mean *sponsor, curator, attender, lover, guardian, patron, preserver, protector, sup-*

porter and *defender*.

If I could fit all these descriptive meanings, I would be perfect; a perfect husband for your every delight. But I am human and thus flawed. Yet in the areas that I can learn about (or already know how to do), I can strive to become the very best husband that I can be for you.

I understand why from your childhood it has been very difficult for you to let go and trust. I've heard you say, "But I want to, I just have to get used to the idea while I ease into it." Here's how that works: Every behavioral psychologist will tell you, changed thinking precedes all lasting change, and that's a process.

First comes the understanding, then the decision to act, then the act itself, then the good feeling that corresponds with the proper action taken. That's the way we humans are designed. So when a person says they don't "feel" like it, you can remind them that the feeling of reward always comes last (although the understanding comes first).

My baby, you are my very own babygirl; already you have become so much a part of me. But please, let me know whatever remains in you or me that's an impediment. What must I be working on?

From the get-go you've said you want and need a leader. I want so much to be that leader, and for you to follow me. But the only way for you to do that without resistance is for me to be what you need. Then you can learn to relax and follow the leader.

I know that you know you're an extraordinary woman. And because you are, there is so much more to experience. But you must first lower the wall that separates us from having those wonderful experiences together.

Some yielded women who are now fully experienced first began as strong-willed women like you. Yet having found the right man, they could then launch farther. Now, they can describe pleasurable experiences that have become a regular part of their physical and spiritual lives, exciting adventures they were unable to fathom in their earlier days. Once they learned to surrender more than their bodies, they opened the door of intimacy to receive the full benefit of what they really needed and desired.

I want this for you, and for us, which is why I keep beating the same drum. You know I'm not going to stop striving for our happiness. I'm going to continue holding us both accountable to grow, so that we can exhibit the first-class qualities that only an "in synch" husband-wife team can.

Surely you also know by observing me that I stay focused on important issues. One is, of course, my personal growth as a husband. Another is to help you flower into the delectable girl you said you wanted me to help you be, and that you are so capable of becoming!

You told me about your friend making all those excuses to you about her past environment and so forth. You mentioned becoming so frustrated because you can see right through her. You wish she would grow up, but then you tell me that you know you're the same as her. So you ask why I don't get frustrated with you when you're procrastinating with excuses, just as you get frustrated with your friend.

The reason I don't get upset is that it isn't me you're rebelling against. It's the task at hand. Nevertheless, whenever either of us stumbles and falls short of our promises, we drag the other down with us. And because we've already begun to cleave together, we hurt the other just as an innocent victim would be hurt.

I realize we've already touched on Genesis 3:16 lightly, but there's more to be learned from it. No two people ever cleaved together more than did the first couple, Adam and Eve. And no two people were ever given a more beautiful environment in which to live.

God also gave them the liberty or right to choose which of two paths to follow: obedience or disobedience. So eventually, the serpent entered to tempt and trick Eve. Naively believing the serpent, that she could *"be as God,"* Eve was deceived and disobeyed God, thinking she would know what God knew and therefore be like him. Instead, however, Eve lost her original spiritual dimension; neither could she return to it to be a part of all she had just lost.

I don't know why Adam then disregarded the dire instruction God had given him personally, and instead chose to follow Eve into disobedience. What I *can* say is that he failed to act as a true husband should, by protecting his wife from the serpent's wiles.

So the first couple no longer shared the one spirit as before. Perfect intimacy had died — the once perfect couple had just lost the title deed to an eternal, perfect life in a perfect relationship with God (and each other) in a heaven on earth.

Although we're not told why Adam disobeyed, we know he blamed God and Eve in the same breath ("this woman that You gave me" caused me to disobey). It's the same way today; a person's first reaction is often to blame anything and everything except themselves. This was just as true of Eve as it was with Adam — "the serpent tricked me" (and therefore I am not at fault.)

After that, Eve turned her focus on trying to control Adam, possibly feeling that after her ordeal with the serpent's trickery she couldn't trust him to lead her and protect her safely.

Some might say all this was God's fault, that the first couple would never have had these problems if God had done things differently. But I wonder how much more clearly God could have made things than what He already had from the beginning. He had told Adam that they could do anything and everything their hearts desired, except for one simple thing. So how can God be blamed for giving Adam and Eve free choice instead of creating them as mindless robots? If God had stopped them from making the choice to disobey Him, then they wouldn't have had free will, now would they?

Let's change gears now. Let's talk about the beauty of God's design for this man and woman, how their separate talents and gifts complement each other in sometimes amazing ways.

Eve was equipped to "think" with her feelings and intuition, as well as her mind. Adam was equipped with logic, so his forte was to reason with his mind. Additionally, Eve could uniquely add to the partnership with intuitive suggestions and other components. Together, by combining their gifts, they could make the perfect team!

Adam could 'see' the whole picture by having the benefit of Eve's wisdom and insight before making decisions. And Eve would be able to first check with Adam to see if he had picked up on anything she might have missed. Therefore, before making any major decisions and acting on any important matters, each could check with the other. Isn't that awesome? That's the direction I'm trying to take us.

Every day there are people (male and female) who act impulsively before they first consult trustworthy people. (In many counselors there is wisdom.) I suppose a fitting motto for these people would be: "Feel before you act, then act before you think," instead of, "Listen and think before you act."

And this brings us back to us. You've told me that you seek to control when things aren't going acceptably, because you've been immersed in some chaotic situations not of your own making and don't have a "comrade in arms." But when you do take control, the impact of difficult family and other life issues on your emotions isn't good for you, either. And so you say that with your out-of-control emotions making the decisions, things have often ended worse than they were at the beginning.

(Understandably, when men or women make on-the-spot decisions out of emotion and exigency when under attack, out of a sense of desperation or overwhelming conditions, or when angry, prideful or hurt, the decisions are rarely the best, and the unfortunate results prove it.)

You've not only told me that your emotions have too often been out-of-control, I've seen it happen to you. I've ached inside for want of you first coming to me for counsel . . . as one who is not embroiled in the midst of the emotional, stressful situation, but who can stand back with a wide view of the proverbial forest and not just the tangled trees in your face . . . and allow me to step in and help.

Yet I've also observed complete transformations in you as you go from over-stressed to blossoming femininity by asking me to take over "damage control." I've seen your acquiescence enable you to clear your mind, so you could see what was truly important to you. Whenever you've yielded to my leadership, I've seen your internal conflicts go away and your emotions become very settled, very calm, as you can then let yourself "breathe." During those times I've watched you take on a renewed sense of happiness, like night-to-day changes in you.

In closing, let me add a little tidbit here. The beginning of a solution is often the restructuring of one's thinking, and often the first place to begin is the Serenity Prayer, that people are applying with great success. I don't know if you already know the prayer, but anyway, here is the short version:

> *God, grant me the serenity to accept the things I cannot change,*
>
> *the courage to change the things I can,*
>
> *and the wisdom to know the difference.*

It's such a great prayer, and easy to memorize. The bottom line of what it has taught me is that sometimes it's all a matter of simply trusting and letting go.

78 You are my Woman of Ecstasy

For my Baby

You are my Woman of Ecstasy.

My delicious babygirl, my delectable treat,
my reward on earth, my joy and delight,
my motivation and inspiration,
my fountain of youth.

No woman ever held such promise, such capacity,
such ability to love and fulfill
my heart and soul and body's desire.

My heart desires to enthrone you,
my soul desires to travel deeply up inside you.

My body desires to experience your touch,
to ravage you, to make wild, passionate love to you,
usually gently, but always unendingly.

You are my dream through the days,
constantly carrying thoughts of you with me,
in my mind, everywhere.

You are my yearning through the nights.
I want you beside me, to feel you, hold you,

heat you, appreciate you, lose myself in you,
fall helpless into your power.

And then I want you to regenerate me,
empower me,
make it impossible for me to stop
from doing it all over again.

You are the fulfillment of my needs,
the realization of my desires.
You are my mission, my goal,
my purpose, my prize, my testimony.

You are my opportunity,
my woman of genuine merit
for whom I can place myself into action.
You are a woman with whom I can live out
the holy sanctions of marriage,
and honor all things pertaining to
how a husband is to keep his wife.

You are the gauge by which your family
will measure my care of you.

By your complexion and smile
will all people know and judge me,
whether I am serving you well or poorly.

You are my love, and
I intend to love you forever.
With my words and actions, I will love you.
In the way I take care of you, I will love you.
With my thoughts and prayers, I will love you.
By my protection of you, I will love you,

and I will love you by leading you as wisely
and as appreciatively and as gently as I know how.

79 You are my Woman of Ecstasy, revisited

I had no idea when I wrote to you about being my *'Woman of Ecstasy'* that it would affect you as it did. Nor did the thought ever come to me that you would be motivated to write, since you've always said you would rather talk by phone. How many does this make now? Is this your third email, and in how many months? (I'm kidding, of course.)

Although I'm pleased, I meant every word of what I wrote. From your comments, it's apparent that it affected you as deeply when you read it as it did me when I wrote it. Else you never would have resorted to writing instead of telling me over the phone.

I'm just playing with you now. (Or am I?) But when you wrote that you didn't know whether it's my writings or me that you love, I became jealous of the writings. I hope it's me, then it will be okay to love my writings, too — that way I'll feel doubly loved.

In your wonderful letter you also thanked me for my love and desire toward you . . . and for you, for making you feel so beautiful. The things you said were just what I needed to hear — that you want my arms around you, that you want to get lost in me, that you want to be and look the best for me because you know that's what I want also.

As to making you "feel so beautiful," I only commented on what I observed in the photos and know to be true about you. Your face is like a work of art, a painting of great price by an Old Master, compelling its admirers to pause and appreciate the delicate and feminine features of the model.

As to making you feel so desired, you are only being and living what you truly are . . . a most desirable creature. Since you have begun to tell me more often about your intimate thoughts and desires, I am made to realize and appreciate even more just how romantic your thoughts can be. You are marvelous! You will be so wonderful to make love to, and so impossible to leave alone!

When you started praising me as you did for all those things — for my gentleness, tenderness, patience, leadership, passion — I think I actually blushed, and wondered if you were still talking about me. And then you thanked me for my concern for your happiness and your well-being. You said I inspire you to be more faithful to your calling, and that I bring you hope, and security, and bliss. Well, you bring me many things too.

Little babygirl, you say all these wonderful things about me, yet, if I am all this toward you, it is because I cannot help but be. They are a natural outflow of what you stimulate in me, the inspiration you provide to me. Were it not for you, I could not be turned on, or romantic, or motivated. You are my spark, my kindling, my fire. You are my combustible material, and I want to make explosions with you that create intense and powerful and lasting heat.

You say you love my intelligence, my smarts, the way I have come to *know* you, and to adore you just the way you are. You tell me you are sometimes not so lovely as I see you, and that you wish you could do more good to and for me. But I say no woman could possibly be doing more good to me and for me than you! Then you close your letter by saying, "YOUR babygirl, your Woman of Ecstasy."

Although I would love to be all these things that you say I am for my babygirl, I know that if I were I would be a god, not a man. Yet for a while I did sit here with my ego inflated. Then I realized these things you say of me are things you have put there, in my heart, for you. So it's not me, but you, that inspires and instills all those things in me.

Thank you for encouraging me, and for the "just right" way you know how to sprinkle your naughty and arousing pixie dust all over me.

Much love from the Woman of Ecstasy's man.

80 She disrespected her husband

Mixie was a woman used to having her own way . . . not every time, but often enough for her to feel like she was winning more than her fair share of the battles.

Then she fell in love, got married, and things began to change. No longer living only to please herself, Mixie instead considered ways she could also please her husband.

As always, of course, she continued to make her own decisions about personal matters that didn't really involve him. And on the things that affected them both as a couple, they agreed to discuss it openly and to value each other's opinions and perspectives before a decision was made. With full consideration for her position and any external facts they might gather, the final authority would still rest with her husband.

But one day Mixie decided purposely to disrespect her husband — to push the boundaries just to see what he would do. She knew it was not the right thing to do, because it affected her husband, and not in a good way, either. Still, it was only a small matter, she rationalized, and after all, what harm could one small act of disrespect cause the relationship?

Nevertheless, it *was* disrespect, and it *had* been intentional.

When her husband called her hand on it, Mixie at first got angry. Perhaps her anger was to conceal her false pride or embarrassment in getting caught, or something else he didn't understand, perhaps even the way he handled the situation. Maybe it was simply because she didn't want to follow her husband's leadership this time. Whatever her reason, Mixie exploded and stormed out of the house.

Walking to the dimly lit park at the end of her street, she plopped down on a bench and shrugged her shoulders. Then she began to realize that the night air was getting cold.

Nevertheless, she continued to sit there sulking so she could maintain her feeling of independence and self-righteousness. Yet she felt miserably lonely. *Is independence worth the price of loneliness,* she thought?

Moments later, Mixie heard familiar footsteps approaching. Lifting up her teary eyes she saw the form of her husband — the moon outlining his body as he drew nearer across the grassy knoll. He was carrying a blanket in his hand to warm her.

Seeing it, the pouting girl knew that ultimately she could not win against this kindhearted man. As her heart capitulated, she burst into tears. Instantly she began to feel relieved, secure in knowing she was better off being a part of this man than separated from him.

Without speaking, he sat on the bench very close to her and began wrapping her inside the warming blanket. Then, lifting her to his lap, he enfolded her in his arms. Allowing time to pass, to give her occasion to feel his affirming love, he began to speak tenderly to her. Finally he whispered, "We should go home."

Sliding his arm under her and gently lifting her from the bench, her husband snuggled her close against his chest while her cheek touched his. Neither spoke a word as he carried her home, but both felt a power melt their hearts into one.

Once home, he carried his wife straight to bed and gently laid her on it. Then symbolically, and without breaking eye contact, he began gently removing her defense barriers so that she began willingly to relinquish her control.

First, he opened the blanket. Then he began undressing her: every item, every stitch . . . but very slowly, compassionately, as if to say, "We are one, and we surrender to each other. I belong to you, and you belong to me. You are mine." All the while he continued to emphasize his conquest by keeping her eyes magnetized to his.

Speaking to her in a soothing tone, softly, reassuringly, he began to stroke her uncovered body. "We are in this together," he began, as he continued caressing her, lightly, affectionately. "We are a team of two. We are lovers who need each another. We neither function nor perform well without the other. I need and expect your cooperation and support, your obedience," he added. "Without it, bad things happen between us."

He continued: "Although earlier you acted poorly, I know you want to do the right thing and apologize for your behavior. Then we can put all this behind us and not have to have this miserable feeling of separation between us anymore, so we can again enjoy our lovemaking. And after we have finished making love, I would appreciate it if you finish doing what I asked you to do before you chose to disrespect me."

As Mixie surrendered — her arms resting above her head — a sigh escaped her lips. She thought how much more wonderful her life would be once she learned to surrender her will as much as she could surrender her body.

But then she thought, *If starting trouble gets me this much attention, maybe by tomorrow I'll have thought of something else to argue about.* And so her mind drifted off to plot her sneaky plan for the morrow. But her body stayed behind to enjoy the present.

81 Have you seen this woman?

This woman is wanted!

Although a part of the female population, she does not behave in ordinary ways. She turns men on like a hot water spigot. First, she *mixes* them up (hence, her alias is *Mixie the Pixie*), then she chews them up and spits them out. She is a desperado; that is, I am desperate for her.

If you see this woman DO NOT ATTEMPT TO APPREHEND; she is armed with female allure and should be considered DANGEROUS. If you have seen this woman, you should call the proper authority (me). I will know what to do with her while she serves out her life sentence with me.

82 A precious kind of love

A precious kind of love is what I have for my babygirl. Even from this distance thousands of miles from you, I'm making love to you with far more intimacy than my body; I'm making love to you with my heart and with my mind, will and emotions.

You have understandably tried to compare my style of love — my drive and passion, my romantic attachment and need for you — with that of other men. You tell me my style of love is like none other, and that I hunger for passion that includes more than the physical.

Yes, that's true, but more than that, my passion exceeds the physical; my wild side demands more, craves more than what is ordinary. If that passion were not satisfied, I could never be happy. And neither could you.

Once I take you "beyond" so you are able to experience your first release from a far deeper level within, then you will understand.

You said I know you incredibly well. That's mostly true; I think I know who we are inside, and what each of us wants in a mate. But there is more than the wanting, there's the needing, too. There are rooms and depths within you that you have not yet had explored. I want to take you there, and you must let me because, as I said, my wild side craves more than just the ordinary to be satisfied. And so will yours, richly so, once we open its floodgates.

I want us never to take for granted the passion that lives within each of us for the other. I want us always to be looking for ways to provoke and arouse that passion, to stimulate it, feed it, ignite it. I want us to be able to entice and lure one another through that passion, by exploring our capacities and capabilities for each other.

But I also need you to understand the loveliness that is beyond, so I can encourage you, and we can stretch and grow to get there.

83 Oh, you are such a babygirl!

Oh, you are such a babygirl ! . . . *kiss, kiss, kiss.*

You *luuuv* being babied! And to that you might say, "So what? Every woman likes to be pampered." But I would have to answer, "Not so, not all women."

Some women seem to feel as if they're being patronized, insulted, disrespected or treated as less than mature if they're babied. They seem to have a defense mechanism that causes them to think in negatives.

I wonder, is it because of a lack of femininity that blocks some women from feeling comfortable with the emotions of being babied? Is it because they have an anger issue with men? Is it because they had adult responsibilities foist upon them even as small children? Or perhaps it's simply personal choice.

On the other hand, babygirls set themselves up to be babied; they actually crave it. I'm not talking about being indulged, pampered or spoiled (although you like that, too). I'm talking about a woman being placed in an emotional state in her "daddy's" lap.

Here all she feels around her is a kind of unseen but felt 'power' consisting of warmth and love and strength and protection of her "daddy." For her, the world is essentially shut out. She has no fears or concerns. Her only awareness is a feeling of being safe and secure, deeply loved and cared for. And from there, what appears to grow most on her heart is a resolve to always try to be a "good girl" for her man.

And what does being a good girl make her husband want to do with her? *Ummm* . . . lots of things.

84 Am I just allowing you to?

I know I have an unfulfilled babygirl living miles away, and that she lacks receiving the personal passion she needs. I know what I need is there, too, with her.

I need to be able to hold you, knowing that you are to be the source, humanly speaking, of all that will fulfill me. I need to know that you are learning the art and the skill to go along with your natural ability to calm me, and yes, actually change me for the better. (Already you are doing that, so you have proved the books wrong again.) You have also asked what you can say, and do, to help and to please me.

Meanwhile, I've tried to be sensitive to pick up on the same about you. I have studied you to learn what I can do to serve and please you, the woman who wants to take care of me in a way that pleases me, the woman who wants to be the one who will melt me.

Melt me . . . therein lies the key. Remember the night when you were seeking to get a grasp on the lovestyle I advocate for us by breaking it down to its simplest terms? You said it was only a matter of each mate wanting to melt the other. You are absolutely right. I think the whole concept boils down to a mutual melting. When the bottom line is finally reached, that's what I realize all my dominant tendencies are attempting to do; that is, to melt you, to create in you a soft and pliable and delicious surrender.

And yes, I know. Men are absolutely stupid when it comes to thinking women actually are falling for the stuff men think they are putting over on women. Especially you, because I have come to realize you are very shrewd indeed when it comes to reading me. Which is why I let you 'run over me' at times, so you won't know as easily which times you actually can have power over me, and which times I am just allowing you to.

Still, I am never quite sure just how much of what you say is what you actually mean, as opposed to how much of it you say just to flirt with me. For example, when you say things like . . . you want me to have control over you and exercise authority over you. You want me to use you and possess you. Those are pretty powerful eroticizers to a dominant man like me, but only if I believe you mean them. Right now, living many miles apart, I'd have to say I'm never really sure how much of that kind of talk you mean, but I know I would like to believe it every time.

85 The right kind of mood

Baby, right now I'm in the kind of mood where I feel I could be at intimacy's best with you. It's because of the way you were, the mood you were in, when we ended tonight's call.

Every man knows (or should know) that the woman must be in the right kind of mood, etc., etc., which most definitely includes the way her husband has been treating her for the past (n) days. After all, foreplay starts with how a husband speaks to his wife first thing in the morning, and remains in play all day. To me this means keeping up with and being attentive to the little things that touch her throughout the day. How? With phone calls. But . . . a woman can tell when a man is going through the motions. It doesn't take a whole lot of things to turn her on, but they must be real, since a woman can tell by her 'insight' whether a man means it.

And I agree, as far as it goes. If the husband wants to be the leader, the responsibility is more on him. (He has to take extra prize care of her, as one would a prize filly.) But I think the wife is also responsible for how receptive her husband will be toward her — and all the little touches she gives him *do* count. Here's why:

A good man will usually respond gently, affectionately, appreciatively and admiringly toward a consistently faithful, soft, yielding woman. We've already talked about how this turns him on to her, which turns her on, which further turns him on, and so on. But a woman should not be motivated to make a decision to yield just because her husband has put her in a good mood, or because she finds herself in a romantic state of mind.

She earlier (prior to the altar) should have made the heart resolve — once, committed for all times — to be yielding. For her, it became, and still remains, her resolve. This resolve then governs her attitude, and her attitude governs her behavior. Her behavior, then, is sweet and willing . . . and thus her husband is turned on to her and wants to show his appreciation, affirming that he is knocked-out over her surrendered life with him.

To hear the experts tell it, sex begins in the kitchen. So whenever the husband wants sex, he begins early by being nice to his wife in the morning. Then he calls her at noon, and picks back up that evening in the kitchen where he left off. Yes, that's a nice way to romance his wife, but it's so manufactured, so Pavlov-like, and so inadequate in and of itself.

The forms of harmony between husband and wife actually begin with where his heart is, and whether she is first in his life (after God), or if he puts his work or golf or hobbies ahead of her. It begins with his actions being sweet, loving, patient, supportive, attentive and appreciative of her, and most of all, real.

Further, it requires her open willingness to give herself to him in all ways, in little things and big, in the kitchen and in the bedroom. Her actions cannot be half-hearted, either.

These heart issues are far, far deeper than the talked-about "mood" and are critical to creating and sustaining the mutual desire for ever-increasing intimacy. So I say that the responsibility for a harmonious marriage rests equally with the husband and the wife.

Tonight, as we finished talking, the tones of your voice sounded very much like you had snuggled back into that "palm" of safe haven, and were as content as a purring kitten. You, being there, made me feel very happy and light-hearted. It was as if I hadn't a burden in the world to be concerned about. I knew my babygirl, my responsibility, was back safe where she belonged, where I knew I could keep her safe. I felt very good about that, and very happy that you were feeling so contented. And then I began to feel very impassioned about the thought of what you had done to put yourself back in that palm, and that made me feel incredibly proud.

Yes, I'd like to think I had a little to do with it since I helped lead you back there. And yes, I will continue my role and responsibility to you, to maintain an environment for you to cause you to want to continue evermore resting there in your safe haven.

But what I really would like to see happen is for you to stay in that haven, to stop jumping over the side without me there to watch over you. Every time you do, it puts you in danger and we both know it.

It also means I have to put aside those things I'm doing that are to make you the happiest. Instead, I find myself running helter skelter after a little lamb darting first this way and then that, making it almost impossible for me to catch, not to mention gently returning her to her place of solace. (A good husband would ask God to send in the "spiritual sheepdogs" to help, because little lambs can run fast!)

86 You asked me tonight if I loved you

You asked me tonight if I loved you, so let me say it again . . . and as often as you want to hear it. *I love you very much!* I want and need you with me.

Apparently something from another part of your day was troubling you, something that left you feeling insecure, very tired, and drained emotionally. As a result, you needed to feel safe again; you needed to be reassured that all was well.

You make it so easy to understand you, and to value and love you, because you tell me what you need by the questions you ask, like, "Do you love me?"

As long as I know how to interpret what you need, I'm hopefully going to know how to provide it. That's the beauty of what we already have going together, and we haven't even entered our Garden yet. Yes, precious girl, I love you. I love you very much indeed.

You bring pleasure to my life. You bring happiness to my heart. With you, life has been the best I've ever experienced. As the song says, *"You light up my life."*

Just now I was looking at some of your pictures. One of them is where your sweet little head is poking out from under a snow coat, with the rest of you snuggled up tight, buried under there somewhere. It's just one of the many joys I remember whenever I think of you.

Many times I look at your pictures (and yes, look you over), studying your beauty, memorizing your facial expressions and thinking of the sound of your voice. You're lots of fun, and a pleasure to know. The more I know about you, the more I like about you. Definitely, you can be a male trap: captivating, alluring and fetching.

Tonight you were really good for me. Actually, you mesmerized me with what you said. It was as if it was coming from the mouth of a romantic poet, a woman of softness and a rare depth of understanding, of love that seemed to reach far beyond most women. Thank you for sharing yourself with me, so openly and with the vulnerability you did.

You inspired me.

Tonight you made my heart sing.
You spoke your feelings and other good things.
You made me happy just hearing you talk
of journeys and paths but especially your walk
to the Garden that awaits the price of admission:
a wife who lives her life in submission.

87 I like the way things are going

No longer will we be our own persons. You will belong to me; I will belong to you. We are equals, even having a similar job title: *Servant.* I will serve you through my love and leadership. You can serve me through your cooperation with that leadership.

When we first met online, I looked, then liked, then loved what I saw in you. And what I saw was an exotic, desirable fruit, ripe for the plucking.

Still, I had to know more than whether you and I shared the same value system. I had to know whether you could grow and thrive in the unique lovestyle I would provide you — a lovestyle so rich and deep that I suppose not many women ever get an opportunity to experience it.

And so I stood on the path that led to the Garden and described to you the adventure on which I would take you if you chose to follow. I invited you to join me if you liked what you saw, and held out my hand to you. Throwing caution aside, you took my hand by faith and stepped onto the path. Skeptical at first, you joined me at my side — as my equal and as my necessary partner.

I don't take your trust lightly. I intend with all the power within me, and within my reach, to give you fulfillment and satisfaction as I complete you. I intend, with all the strength I can muster, to exercise my greatest protection and care of you. I intend to use all the gifts and skills I have been able to develop for such a special woman as you, some to resolve your worrisome needs, and others to fill your heart with delights.

I could not be more proud or more pleased to have you as my beloved than I am right now. You are so very precious to me, more even than your feelings yet tell you. But that is only because of the miles between us – you have not yet felt enough of my arms securely around you and my lips caressing yours, nor did the brevity of my visit provide much time for us to hug tightly while our cheeks touched lightly. If there had been more time, I would have kissed you a thousand times more, and in a way that your lips would surely know how preciously I hold you in my heart. For you have caused my heart to grow very soft and very large, for the only woman capable of growing into it.

All of this, our *Us*, is turning out to be real. You and I can both have what we are mutually working toward. We can each get from the relationship the sum total of what both are putting in.

I have been giving you my all, every ounce. I have been encouraging you to do the same. I like the way things are going. I like the way my feelings for you are growing. And though your wonderfully intriguing personality is still very much a handful for me in this phase of my learning curve about you (and probably always will be), I know that I am not feeling overly challenged or inadequate for the job.

88 I love the way you are

I love you, babygirl. I love the way you wear my love so eloquently, allowing it to flow over you and caress you. I love the way you wear the knowledge and the feeling that you're becoming that most beautiful, most alluring essence of femininity, yet not allowing it to destroy your humble attitude with any false pride.

I love the way you're able to carry your presence, your new aura, into a gathering where men and women are present, and attract their favorable attention. (Or not so favorable, perhaps, if it's coming from a jealous-type woman — nevertheless, she is her own problem).

I love that you're becoming a woman of women because, more than that, you're gaining all the benefits that go with that status for which other women can only wish. That turns me on so much!

I'm going to take such good care of you. You're going to be in awe! I love that I can keep anointing you with the truth of my love and my affections, but you don't allow these to cause you to become (too) puffed up around other females.

You're the only woman who has ever gone the extra mile necessary to try to be my life's pleasure. Indeed, you're the only female I have ever known who has taken her training seriously enough to reap its rewards. By paying close attention to my teaching, your understanding has reached that certain level that my lovestyle requires of a woman. Because only from there can she actually *become* all those things — and all the other things that a man like me must be given to keep his attention vested in his woman.

It pleases me very much that you want to keep growing for me, and equally important, that you have had from birth the ingredients necessary for that growth. You're my hot chili pepper, and here are my thoughts on that.

> *Pepper (1)*: A powder made from a green pepper plant that makes one sneeze. Or sets one's tongue on fire. Or turns one's forehead red. But when cooked and served in the proper amount, it provides that indispensable, "just right" improvement to one's food.

> *Pepper (2):* A hot woman full of excitement and spice, a little crazy (in a lovable way), who thinks of herself as a gorgeous wild filly, running and kicking up her heels in frivolity, but also as a seductive woman capable of confusing her victims and keeping them off balance — thus her well-earned nickname, Mixie the Pixie.

I love my babygirl, my seductress.

89 You're even more exciting

I am enamored with you; the mere thought of you supercharges me. It's really true, you know.

You inspire me. It's not ridiculous to think of a woman inspiring a man, but it is strange, I think, when I realize that you are the first woman to ever inspire this man . . . continuously.

You are interesting, spiritual, intelligent, pretty, yielded (of course) and challenging. In fact, I want to tell you something. You are the most challenging woman I've ever known.

But miraculously, I feel more competent in being the right man to complete you than I've ever felt with any other woman I've known. There's just something that goes on inside me that seems to know what to do with you, and how, and when. Of course that voice inside me is not always right. But from what I'm hearing you tell me, my inner voice is right often enough to be getting the things done for you that you need.

Do you remember feeling like the worn-out, wilted flower, planted in sun-parched soil when we first met? Just think about how much you've changed, revitalized, how much you've already blossomed! What an honor it has been for me to be a part of you, to provide some moisture and sunshine so I could see God give the increase and effect that beautiful change.

But wouldn't you want to know what is really exciting about you? It's this: You're even more exciting to me now than ever. It's like, the more I know you, the more I want to know, and so on. By this time, even the most interesting women I've crossed paths with over the years would have turned boring. But not you! You've got layers I haven't even glimpsed before. Boy, do I ever enjoy loving you . . . and will love loving on you.

Back when you were playing cat and mouse with me, acting like you weren't interested, little did I know that you were "measuring" me with many other suitors, while deciding which one thought you valuable enough to pursue "to the end of the earth." I'm glad I was the only one to score a "100" on your test.

Meanwhile, I didn't know what you were thinking or doing (which shows I need to continue my study of women). Frankly, I wondered if you would be like "all the rest" that couldn't live up to what I needed in a woman. But I decided to just go ahead and "waste my time" on you anyway.

Well, you didn't just live up to my needs. You rose above them. Baby, you soar!

Thank you for who you are, and for what you want to do for me. I love you so much.

90 The perfect vision of a marriage

What would you consider to be the perfect vision of a marriage? In other words, what would you say is that certain ambitious goal that a married couple can have and work toward daily?

I know this is wishful thinking, but I believe the perfect vision for a married couple (were it even possible) would be to love one another, always and unconditionally, with the view of achieving peace and intimacy of oneness with each other and with God – in our minds, in our wills, in our emotions, and in our spirits.

Toward this end, I believe married couples are provided two very intimate ways in addition to following the Bible daily. One is to have honest and vulnerable talks of a deeply personal nature after the noises of the day have gone away. The other is through sexual expression, to suggest the glory that is to come.

In his book, *"Mere Christianity,"* the intellectual and world-acclaimed Bible scholar and author, C. S. Lewis, wrote:

> *"Creatures are not born with desires unless satisfaction for those desires exists. A baby feels hunger: well, there is such a thing as food. A duckling wants to swim: well, there is such a thing as water. Men feel sexual desire: well, there is such a thing as sex. If I find in myself a desire that no experience in this world can satisfy, the most probable explanation is that I was made for another world. If none of my earthly pleasures satisfy it, that does not prove that the universe is a fraud. Probably earthly treasures were never meant to satisfy it, but only to arouse it, to suggest the real thing."*

Neither C.S. Lewis nor I am talking about satisfying earthly pleasures by filling our days and nights in unending hedonistic delight and epicurean pleasures. Such a consumed lifestyle wastes away in decadent self-indulgence and moral decay. But I do believe that to approach the intimacy of oneness in our marriage, we will need to press the limit while also keeping those pleasurable desires in balance.

I believe by our taking the same route of celibacy as Solomon and his bride-to-be in their courtship, yet being just as open and frank, we have allowed ourselves to be freer, non- intimidated, and relaxed in our relationship. I believe that my stimulating your thinking about new kinds of intimacies to come has enabled you to be openly vulnerable to me, and to invite me to be the same with you.

Keeping our relationship honest and without the little fears ordinarily associated with courtship gets rid of stigmas. Otherwise, whenever stigmas are allowed to remain, they still have to be dealt with . . . only later, when marriage begins, which is the worst possible time to have to deal with stigmas.

You are a spectacular female, an incredible woman, and it seems I fall in love with you more each day.

91 I followed my heart. . . and it led me to you

I followed my eyes and they led me to you.

I followed my dreams and they led me to you.

I followed my thoughts and they led me to you.

I followed my fantasies and they led me to you.

Never could I imagine it being any other way than to be with you . . .

wanting you,

loving you,

needing you.

All because I followed my heart . . .

and it led me to you.

92 Chemistry in force

Babydoll, thank you for taking seriously the need to be acquiescent. I've not stopped needing and wanting you all day because of what your surrendered attitude does to me. You have no idea how desirable you become when you're in that frame of mind, and how masculine I feel when you are. It causes me to feel so enabled and ready to make love.

Thank you, also, for telling me that you think I look sexy from head to toe . . . the way I stand, hold myself, walk, etc. Although we both have God to thank for the way He made us, your affirmation nevertheless makes me feel good.

Yet mostly what I'm glad of is that the woman with the body I'm attracted to, is also attracted to mine. I'll have to admit, while I was there I didn't attempt to conceal from others that I was enjoying the sight of you very much — top to bottom and front to back — when we would be standing together; while you were talking to someone; while you were walking in front of me; while you were talking on the phone, and all the times in between. Nor did I feel the least twinge of conviction to stop. Maybe that's because my motives were pure?

They say one can tell the quality of a person by the quality of the friends around them. Since meeting even more of your family and friends during this last visit, and being treated as a royal guest in Robert and Sue Ann's home for the week, I would certainly have to say this holds true in your case. You are definitely surrounded by people of quality.

93 Powerful imagery

We would have to be blind and numb not to know that one of the main reasons we're deeply drawn to one another is our chemistry. This is as it should be, since sexual attraction is a major force that keeps couples bonded together.

So let's look at an excerpt from *The Intimate Marriage* by Dr. R.C. Sproul to see how that force fits into God's overall strategy for married couples.

> *"Some of the most powerful imagery used in Scripture to describe the relationship between God and his people is that of husband and wife. Because much of that imagery is sexual in nature and content, it's just one of many ways we know that God is as much interested in our fully pursuing His gifts to us of sexual enterprises as He is in the effort we put forth in any of our other worthwhile pursuits."*
>
> *"As has been previously said, God does not reward the wasteful. It can also be said that since God is in the details, and is the Creator of sex, that He enjoys seeing husbands and wives utilize fully and enjoy that relational avenue well and often. 'Therefore . . . whatsoever you do, do to the glory of God.' "*

One might never guess that R.C. Sproul is the senior pastor at Saint Andrew's Chapel in Sanford, Florida, because most people never hear a preacher talk about sex. Isn't it regrettable that most people don't know things like this are in the Bible?

And not just about God's attitude toward sex. Most people, if they would read it, would be shocked to know that God's intent is for people to be happy and without burdens, that He is not our enemy, and that He is not out to "get us." That instead, He is our loving Father who wants to protect His children and see them live joyfully.

But unfortunately, most people don't know that, because they rely on other people to tell them what to think and how to think, not knowing that some of these people (even from the pulpits) are twisting the Bible's truths like pretzels. Regrettably, like lambs led to the slaughter, they're putting their very lives in the hands of others without so much as testing even one single thing they are told to believe. It would be so easy for them to simply ask a person claiming to speak for God, "Please show me in the Bible where that is talked about, because I would like to know more." Any credible person would be happy to let the Bible validate what they are teaching others. This is because any legitimate person would be pleased to see the inquiring person taking an interest.

For example, to support what he writes in the above book, Dr. Sproul includes in the last paragraph a direct quote from I Corinthians 10:31. *"Therefore, whether you eat or drink, or whatsoever you do, do to the glory of God"* . . . *Can* you imagine how many people would be shocked to learn that God includes the joy of sex in the list of *whatsoever you do* things He wants spouses to enjoy to the fullest . . . so He will be glorified?

And why would it glorify God? Because He created it for the enjoyment and bonding of his children under the covenant of marriage. And when God sees his children enjoying to the ultimate that which He invented for them to enjoy, He is glorified. It's like a parent giving a very special gift to his child, and seeing the delight on the child's face as he jumps right in and gets involved with the gift. Now that's a glorified parent!

We've talked on the phone about God's take on sex, that whatever a married couple can think up to do to each other is plenty alright with God. And of course we know that this is good providing both spouses are okay with it. This is explained by the verse at Hebrews 13:4:

"Marriage is honorable in all,
and the bed undefiled."

Please allow me to translate that liberally:

> **"Marriage is *honorable*"** – The sexual intimacy between wife and husband should be honored, guarded or considered sacred,
>
> **". . . and the bed *undefiled*"**– Any and every variety of sexual activity that an agreed married couple wants to engage in is acceptable and pure (undefiled) in God's eyes.

In other words, God sanctions whatever a husband and wife want to do together sexually, because whatever they choose to do will be undefiled (pure, kosher, unsullied and uncorrupted).

You and I share a unique love. We are acting and reacting toward one another with the kind of love that only a man committed to that woman, and a woman committed to that man, can share. Ours is a love shared exclusively by those couples who have discovered and faithfully live out the perfect (and therefore) successful marriage formula, because it is the only formula that is *certain* to bind a husband and wife together in love, respect, peace, harmony, and passion . . . for a lifetime.

It's unfortunate that so many couples overlook such a simple formula. It's certainly not hard to learn — it's even in the Bible (*Ephesians* 5:22-33): A husband is to love and cherish his wife, so much so that he would be willing to die for her, if necessary; whereas a wife is to honor and yield to her husband's headship.

So what does this say to us? It says to me that every couple should faithfully apply this formula to their marriage. Only then will they truly understand its power, because only then will they *experience* its power. And what is that experience? It is to enjoy an ongoing peace, intimacy and passion in their marriage.

We have a mutual respect, you and I, knowing that each is unselfishly fulfilling a role at a personal cost for the benefit of the other. Certainly this is stimulating our love, our respect and desire for one another. As long as each of us is obedient regarding this calling, this duty to one another, our love will grow stronger and our happiness brighter. To me, that is the best way to protect love.

94 For the woman I cannot do without

I may

. . . write the words, but you are the song that is sung;

. . . conduct the symphony, but you are the instrument that creates the music;

. . . have passion, but you are the one who gives it expression;

. . . have poetry in my soul, but you are the one who releases it.

I have

. . . fire in my body, but you are the one who starts it.

. . . desire in my heart, but you are the one who completes it.

. . . dreams in my mind, but you are the one who inspires them.

I feel

. . . the deepest kind of need and love for you,

. . . but you are the one who can satisfy it.

95 Music to my heart

Something exciting happened last night! I'm talking about when I was asking you to do something and your automatic response was "No." But then immediately you switched back into the role you've been working on, acquiesced, and reversed your answer.

Even though my request was simple and easy to fulfill, it was as if, for the first time, all our work together in preparation for marriage had come together and was paying off. It seemed like an automatic trigger had prompted the reversal in your mind and will, and I couldn't have been more delighted than I was at that very moment.

Then you said something astonishing! You said you could actually be even more yielded, and are going to be. You have no idea how much music that played to my heart.

The things you've learned and been able to do just by becoming receptive . . . being open to me, showing me honor, being faithful to the role, etc.; you cannot imagine how aroused with passion these things can make a man become. My automatic reaction to your behavior last night caused me to feel unusually romantic and loving toward you, to the point that I'm still feeling it today.

You're making me so appreciative of your "weaker vessel" attributes. They make me want to be all the more gentle with you, with enhanced understanding of your side of the picture. Frankly, your deference is enabling you to push the envelope on your femininity. You're expanding it, becoming even more feminine, more sensuous, and that makes me desire you all the more.

We talked about this a while back, where in the Bible (in I *Peter* 3) the apostle Peter is writing a section to women in which he "gives away the secret" of how a woman can become a magnet to her husband. He tells these women that there is a certain kind of woman who will become very attractive to her husband, much more so than those women who merely dress up. And what is this certain kind of woman? Peter says it is that woman who surrenders to her husband in the attitude of her mind and heart.

Isn't that amazing? It's the woman who yields who is the powerful woman. But that's not how we humans reason things out, is it?

Yet that's exactly what you've done, and are doing to me now through your gentle, respectful and meek attitude. You've made yourself a very powerful magnet that overtakes all else within me, causing me to want to lay blessing upon blessing upon you.

It continues to amaze me as we follow God's natural laws, just how very much harmony and balance there is, and controls on both sides of the seesaw. If ever there was anything that worked together so perfectly, this is it!

96 Your raspberry lips

Tonight you told me you were wearing a raspberry colored lipstick. Well, after we hung up, I began putting together this poem.

Your raspberry lips,
so soft and tasty.
Your curvaceous hips...
but lest we get hasty.

Vineyard Reserve is best savored
reclining by firelight.
Your vintage, most favored,
will surely delight.

Your wine, still not served...
Oh cork, stay in place!
Rare contents reserved
in soignée black lace.

Into resplendent glass, *Post-haste!*
your wine I now pour.
Naked you've been placed,
as I taste your *du jour*.

97 Because your attitude is now one of cooperation

I am amazed! Yes, amazed! Never in my life have I ever experienced such a relationship as I have with you! It's just *wonderful!*

Sure, I've read the books (at least most of the better ones) on good, healthy courtships and marriages and the like. I've also read books and attended classes on conflict resolution to resolve husband–wife issues, and so on. I came to believe that with hard work, plus meeting the right person, I could eventually expect to actually *be* in a relationship where everything worked the way it was supposed to.

But never did I really expect everything to fit so beautifully as it does with us. Everything is working so smoothly together (including our telephone love fights) . . . all because your overriding attitude is now one of respect, a willingness to learn, and to cooperate, and I truly value, respect and love you immensely.

I'm coming to realize that you are the most valuable asset I could ever possibly have. There have been times that although we live thousands of miles apart, you have seemed more tangible and necessary to me than even the food I eat. Something wonderful is happening to me, something almost magical, and it's all because of you. I know this: I'm a better man now than I was, and because of you, a much happier one, too.

You know, it was only a little over a year ago (it seems like only yesterday) that I began telling you all I wanted was a stress-free life, like the one I was already enjoying. I didn't want to give that up or place it at risk for anything or anyone. Well, babygirl . . . *bring on the stress.* Lay it on me thick and heavy. Just make sure that it's a Mixie the Pixie kind of stress, blended with cute filly, hot chili pepper, sensuous babydoll and all the rest. I'm hooked on you, and I mean *really* hooked — I've got the Mixie habit in a big way and I need a fix!

So now that you've got me addicted to you, I need to be drugged with your essence regularly. Does this mean I've fallen so deeply in love with you that I can no longer do without you? Well, if it does, it's only because it's your entire fault; you're to blame. You make me drunk with you!

Your hopelessly hooked addict.

98 I'm so happy!

Baby*doll* — Yes, with all the connotations the word *"doll"* implies, because it's a part of your nature, and because you *sooo* enjoy wanting to be a babydoll for me.

I am so happy! Happy about you, about us, about our future together; I so want to be able to look forward to completing you as my wife, in all the ways that a husband can, and as you crave to be completed. Yes, you will experience the safety and comfort of being able to curl up in the warmth of your husband's palm. I will see to it that you can . . . spiritually, physically, financially, emotionally, with all that is within my power.

As your husband, I am responsible for you, and the further and deeper you trust me to fulfill that which the entire role implies, the freer and safer you will feel. Because I love you unconditionally, and your soft, yielding spirit motives me to new heights, I will adorn you in as many of life's exciting facets as I am able.

We have walked the path to the Garden; you have followed (often in lockstep) close beside me. Now the Garden is near, and soon I will carry you through the gate to take possession. Once inside, you will be transported in delight, and indulged in intimacy beyond your dreams, intimacy of growing proportions to gratify your every fantasy. Yes, each will be done for your pleasure, to enchant and enrapture you, for you to experience a life blessed with the same happiness with which you have blessed me.

99 A secret place

My precious hot chili pepper,

Let's do something different. I want to give you a visualization of what is to come, the 'fruition of the promise.' So as you read this tonight, let's imagine that I'm right there with you. Imagine we're seated comfortably, face-to-face. Our chairs are drawn closely together; so close, our knees are touching.

As you stare into my eyes, you see them softening, seeking intimacy with you. Your seductive eyes respond.

Then, in our fantasy, I lean forward and take your hands in mine. Softly, gently, I begin caressing them. Then we kiss — at first innocently, tenderly, meaningfully. But then . . . passionately.

My eyes are captured, drawn deeper into yours by your message of alluring love. You're savoring with delight the effect you're having on me, aren't you? As you watch me gaze upon your loveliness, you have me incapable of averting my eyes from you as they flash with excitement, feasting on your womanly features.

You hear my voice; my words touch a chord in your imagination. They're describing romantic states I'm going to place you in. They're picturing scenes I'm going to perform on you, to seduce you into a love of intimate depth that is nurturing and delighting your spiritual and physical senses.

You're aware of my taking you into some inner place, a secret place. Your entire body is feeling a presence, an energy. Somehow, as we enter, you know it is here that I will take you to the very edge of the physical realm.

You make no effort to resist; you know it's too late. You're richly and deeply involved now in a love scene far more intimate and exciting than you have ever before experienced — two souls sharing one body, and in that body two entwining spirits.

Now we're going deeper, even to the brink of the cliff, to the very edge — further than you've ever been taken. You're afraid of falling, but even more afraid of losing this moment. Your body and soul beg to be taken, further, deeper into erotica . . .

Suddenly, as one flesh, we step over the edge.

But unexpectedly, you realize we're not falling ...

we're soaring.

Is there not a word in the English language to describe a couple so intimate, so giving — each to the other in such oneness of spirit, body and emotions — that with each breath drawn these two lovers become almost indistinguishable, one from the other in the love they share? If there is a word that can express such joy, such intimacy that transcends all else, then I don't know of it. Yet it is there, I know it must be there. It's waiting for us . . . our world to share.

100 You are so very important to me

You are so very important to me are words we all want to hear. I suppose no one can hear them too often. You've heard me say them to you many times and in many ways, yet I know you're a soul who can't hear them enough, so gladly I'll tell you again . . .

My life is devoted to you. It was devoted to you yesterday, it is devoted to you today, and it shall be devoted to you tomorrow . . . and forever. My life is yours, for your sake, for your happiness, and for your benefit.

When you forsook your path in favor of following mine, you finally turned the corner. You chose to replace an independent, controlling spirit with a cooperative one. You stepped out of the vicious, downward-sucking whirlpool created by misinformation and the erroneous thinking of unhappy women. At that very moment, with a heart filled with trust in me, you left behind the scraps — the ordinary, the argumentative environment, the complacent lifestyle of bored women living with their meager returns and leftovers of happiness.

Instead, you chose the noblest way of all; you chose to follow "whithersoever I lead," and to go "whithersoever I go." Again, at that very moment, you laid down your life of rebellion to become the beautiful and triumphant person you were ordained to be. Lovingly, you laid your heart in my hands. Courageously, you placed yourself under my leadership. Trustingly, you placed your future in my care.

You earned my respect. You won yourself a husband, a protector, a watchman, a caretaker, and a devoted lover. What I'm trying to say is that you are so important to me that you've won my lifelong commitment to take care of you . . . always. I love you in ways so deep and so mysterious that only God understands.

And so, I want your body, I want your mind, I want your will. I want your obedience, I want your warts, and I want your problems. I want your fears and I want your doubts. Most of all I want you, the little girl that wants so much to come out and play. And I want that little girl's mommy, too. But I want mommy to just simply rest, forever, in my care. It's time now for that little babygirl inside you to get to happily live her life, with my life, for the rest of our lives.

You are mine, little girl, and I'm coming to get you . . . all of you. I will make my possession of you very real, very certain, and very powerful. We are well past the "will she, will he like me" stage, and well past the no-turning-back stage. For if you run, I will catch you. If you hide, I will find you. Soon you will belong to me, to have, to love, to honor, to cherish, and most of all, to keep . . . because you are *my* babygirl.

Mixie (or as I otherwise call her, *my hot chili pepper*) "discovered" my proposal of marriage rolled up as a parchment scroll. Earlier, I had slipped it into an empty wine bottle, then replaced the cork and "planted" it in the very front of the wine cooler. Later I asked if she would pour the wine. The rest is history . . . .

My proposal of marriage

How can the object of one's search for love be described?

First, I imagined a girl: a blessed one-of-a kind, uncommonly feminine girl . . . vivacious, full of the love for life, a drop-dead gorgeous personality, sexy, vibrant, and mischievously seductive.

Then I dreamt of her.

Then I made a written list of everything I needed in her.

Then I added a second list of all I would like to have in her.

Then I added a third list of things that were totally, outrageously, unreasonably beyond my hope of ever finding in her.

Then God took over . . .

He read those lists, then abundantly added more to them, even providing the name for her — the "Fountain of Femininity." The result was you, babygirl, for you *are* that Fountain of Femininity.

I have written reams of pages to you, telling you of my feelings for you and how very special you are to me. Never have I desired, and wanted, and longed for anyone like I desire and want and long for you. Never will I want to change you. Always will I love you. Always will I try to lead you to the places God wants you. Along the way, we'll visit the places and do the things that will bring you happiness, where you can enjoy and savor life on the fullest and highest plane, as God intends.

To you and to this cause I am bound — to have you, to possess you, to care for your needs and wants, to love you intimately, and to fulfill you. For me to be complete, and to complete you, I must be your husband and you must be my wife.

If only you knew
how my heart overflows
with love for you.

If only you could see
the way you fill my hopes and dreams.
Though I am to lead and protect you,
you are the owner of my heart.

Even in the dark of night,
I've only to think about you here with me,
to feel your presence and influence on me.
Before you came, I was adrift in this world,
feeling as if God had no further purpose for me.

If only you knew
how I imagine you at my side.
When others approach,
it's always you my soul seeks.

If only you knew
how your presence heals
all the past wounds inside me.
You've made me forget
the pain of yesterday,
and you've taught me that the past
can no longer prevent
what I want to achieve...

If only you knew.

If only you knew
the way you've shown me
how much more of a man I can be,
but only for you.

If only you knew
how I am never so much more
as when I am yours,
or so much lost
until I find myself in you.
Or how, when I find myself in you,
I find I am home.

Whatever I do,
I do for your sake.
Whatever I desire,
I desire for your happiness.
But oh how I yearn
for you...

If only you knew.

Will you marry me, darling girl? Will you be the wife I so desire, long for, want and need?

Will you be the object of my love . . . so I can protect, cherish, and take care of you, up close and personal?

~ *Your loving Adam*

~~~~~~~~~~~~~~~~~~~~~~~~~~~~
~~~~~~~~~~~~~~~~~~~~~~~~~~~~

Please, pretty please, with sugar on top,

If you liked this book,
please leave a REVIEW on Amazon.com

Reviews are gold for authors!

Thank you!

www.ingramcontent.com/pod-product-compliance
Lightning Source LLC
LaVergne TN
LVHW051252080426
835509LV00020B/2931

* 9 7 8 0 6 9 2 7 6 5 5 0 0 *